The Failure of Philosophical Knowledge

Also available from Bloomsbury:

A Philosophy for Future Generations, by Tiziana Andina
Four Views on the Axiology of Theism, edited by Kirk Lougheed
Knowledge, Number and Reality, edited by Nils Kürbis, Bahram Assadian, and Jonathan Nassim
Philosophy, Literature and Understanding, by Jukka Mikkonen

The Failure of Philosophical Knowledge

Why Philosophers are not Entitled to their Beliefs

János Tőzsér

BLOOMSBURY ACADEMIC
LONDON • NEW YORK • OXFORD • NEW DELHI • SYDNEY

BLOOMSBURY ACADEMIC
Bloomsbury Publishing Plc
50 Bedford Square, London, WC1B 3DP, UK
1385 Broadway, New York, NY 10018, USA
29 Earlsfort Terrace, Dublin 2, Ireland

BLOOMSBURY, BLOOMSBURY ACADEMIC and the Diana logo
are trademarks of Bloomsbury Publishing Plc

First published in Great Britain 2023
This paperback edition published 2024

Copyright © János Tőzsér, 2023

János Tőzsér has asserted his right under the Copyright, Designs and
Patents Act, 1988, to be identified as Author of this work.

For legal purposes the Acknowledgements on p. vi constitute
an extension of this copyright page.

Cover image © Cargo/Getty Images

This work is published open access subject to a Creative Commons Attribution-
NonCommercial-NoDerivatives 4.0 International licence (CC BY-NC-ND 4.0, https://
creativecommons.org/licenses/by-nc-nd/4.0/). You may re-use, distribute, and reproduce
this work in any medium for non-commercial purposes, provided you give attribution to the
copyright holder and the publisher and provide a link to the Creative Commons licence.

Bloomsbury Publishing Plc does not have any control over, or responsibility for,
any third-party websites referred to or in this book. All internet addresses given
in this book were correct at the time of going to press. The author and publisher
regret any inconvenience caused if addresses have changed or sites have ceased
to exist, but can accept no responsibility for any such changes.

A catalogue record for this book is available from the British Library.

A catalog record for this book is available from the Library of Congress.
Library of Congress Control Number: 2023939459.

ISBN:	HB:	978-1-3503-4004-6
	PB:	978-1-3503-4008-4
	ePDF:	978-1-3503-4005-3
	eBook:	978-1-3503-4006-0

Typeset by Integra Software Services Pvt. Ltd.

To find out more about our authors and books visit www.bloomsbury.com
and sign up for our newsletters.

Contents

Acknowledgements — vi

Introduction — 1

Part 1

1. Philosophy as an Epistemic Enterprise — 11
2. Philosophy as a Failed Epistemic Enterprise — 43

Part 2

3. Therapy for Philosophers — 81
4. Philosophy With (Intended-To-Be) Compelling Justification — 99
5. Philosophy Without Compelling Justification — 119
6. Meta-skepticism — 159

Part 3

7. Breakdown — 209

Bibliography — 219
Index — 227

Acknowledgements

Over the past few years, I have had conversations and discussions with many philosophers on the main topics of this book, both in person and in writing. For all the above, I'd like to express my thanks to Tibor Bárány, Tim Crane, Tamás Demeter, Márton Dornbach, Gábor Forrai, Ákos Gyarmathy, Gábor Hofer-Szabó, Ágnes Katona, Daniel Kodaj, Andrea Komlósi, David Mark Kovacs, Péter Lautner, Bence Nanay, László Nemes, Tamás Paár, Michele Palmira, Jenő Pöntör, Daniel Schmal, Tibor Sutyák, Peter van Inwagen, Péter Varga, and Zsófia Zvolenszky.

My special thanks go to László Bernáth, Boldizsár Eszes, Kati Farkas, Judit Gébert, George Kampis, László Kocsis, Miklós Márton, and the anonymous referees of Bloomsbury Publishers for their thorough and detailed comments on earlier versions of the manuscript of my essay, in which they pointed out several errors, inaccuracies, and other mistakes.

Finally, I'd like to express my gratitude to Zsuzsanna Balogh and especially to Boldizsár Eszes for their invaluable help with preparing the English text, and to the editors at Bloomsbury, Liza Thompson, Colleen Coalter, and Suzie Nash, and to my copyeditor, Dawn Cunneen, for lots of patience and help.

The research leading to this essay was supported by NKFI/OTKA (Hungarian Scientific Research Fund of the National Research Development and Innovation Office) grant No. K123839, K132911 and MTA Lendület "Moral and Science."

Introduction

All areas of philosophy are characterized by dissent. Philosophers disagree among themselves in innumerable ways, and this pervasive and permanent dissensus is a sign of their inability to solve philosophical problems and present well-established philosophical truths. Every philosopher who has not buried his head in the sand knows or at least suspects this.

The saddest aspect of this failure is that philosophers have been unable to solve philosophical problems which deeply affect all of us existentially—problems whose stakes were the highest out of all theoretical problems. What I have in mind are questions like "Is there a God?"; "What is the relationship between mind and body?"; "Do we have free will and moral responsibility?" Philosophers have also been unable to solve those big philosophical problems whose existential weight cannot be compared to the above three, but whose theoretical significance is unquestionable. These include, for example, questions such as "What is the distinguishing mark of mental phenomena?"; "Do we have direct access to a mind-independent reality in veridical perception?"; "Do physical objects have spatiotemporal parts?" And philosophers have not managed to solve those philosophical problems that have no particular existential weight or even theoretical significance, either. Some examples are questions (concocted in philosophical laboratories, so to speak) such as "What kind of entities are holes?"; "Are disjunctive properties genuine properties?"; "Can one unintentionally produce abstract artifacts?"

I'm not claiming that the community of philosophers has no philosophical knowledge at all. All I'm saying is this: if we collected all consensually (or at least near-consensually) accepted philosophical truths, the result would be painfully modest—especially in light of the big questions that have been left unanswered.

For what would this collection include? On the one hand, it would have trifles like "Nobody can know false propositions"; "Our dream experiences fail to provide adequate justification of our beliefs about the external world." On the other hand, it would include some "If ..., then ..." type statements such as "If the intentional properties of our mental states supervene on the phenomenal properties of those states, then intentional contents cannot be Russellian propositions"; "If proper names are rigid designators, then there is a posteriori necessity." Moreover, it would include some assertions about the virtues and difficulties of various philosophical theories, such as "Presentism has the virtue of being consistent with the phenomenology of time, but has a hard time finding adequate truth-makers for true propositions about the past"; "Class nominalism has the virtue of not being committed to the existence of multilocal entities, but has a hard time reducing necessarily coextensive properties." Apart from these, the collection would include some conceptual distinctions like "*De dicto* modalities must be distinguished from *de re* ones," or "Determinism must be distinguished from fatalism." Finally, it might include negative substantive truths such as "The Leibnizian thesis that 'All true propositions are analytic' is false"; "The thesis that 'all mental states are behavioral dispositions' is false." And that's all—I believe I have just listed all kinds of consensually accepted philosophical truths.

Now, if you reflect on the facts that: (1) during the 2,500-year-old history of philosophy, philosophers most certainly did not want to come up with merely these kinds of truths, as they had "a somewhat" more ambitious dream, namely to come up with *substantive* and *positive* truths, and that (2) pervasive and permanent dissensus about philosophical problems is a clear sign of the philosophers' failed attempts in this regard, and their failure to fulfil their commitments no matter how hard they try—then you will be hard pressed to conclude that philosophy is a *failed epistemic enterprise*. If that is the case, then we, philosophers, are members of a failed epistemic enterprise, and our philosophical beliefs are beliefs held by the participants of a failed epistemic enterprise.

This is not a heartwarming thought, so much so that in my opinion, we are epistemically and morally obliged to face philosophy's epistemic failure, to react to the fact that the community of philosophers (to which we belong) does not know substantive and positive philosophical truths, and to try to account for the epistemic status of our own substantive and positive philosophical beliefs in light of the foregoing. Thus, we have to ask ourselves "What should we do with our substantive and positive philosophical beliefs in the face of the epistemic failure of philosophy?"

It is wrong for us to act as if everything were in perfect order. It is wrong for us to deny philosophy's epistemic failure (for example, by saying that "Doing philosophy has nothing on earth to do with seeking truths—philosophers misinterpret their own intentions when they think they are making attempts to solve philosophical problems"). And it is wrong for us to play down philosophy's epistemic failure (for example, by saying that "There is nothing bad in philosophy's not having the final answers—our life would be bleak indeed if we could announce winners in philosophy and thereby make all philosophers regurgitate these winners' theses all the time"). These, I believe, are unworthy and unscrupulous reactions.

* * *

Apart from unworthy and unscrupulous reactions, in light of philosophy's epistemic failure, there are four ways for philosophers to react to the epistemic failure of philosophy and think about the epistemic status of their substantive philosophical beliefs.

Some philosophers think that they have succeeded in supporting their substantive philosophical beliefs with compelling arguments and urge others to formulate such knock-down arguments. They think that the only way for us to rationally stick to our substantive philosophical beliefs in light of the pervasive and permanent dissensus in philosophy is to be able to compellingly justify them. For if we have compelling arguments for p, then it is irrelevant that others think that p is false.

I cannot identify with this proposal. For one thing, I cannot entertain the idea of being so lucky that I am the one (and not anyone else) who has managed to formulate knock-down philosophical arguments for my substantive philosophical beliefs. For another thing, the philosophers who are absolutely convinced that they have knock-down arguments thereby vindicate an epistemically privileged position to themselves, but they cannot appropriately (non-circularly) justify this privilege or superiority in any way. On top of that, they must consider their interlocutors to be their epistemic inferiors, as they are unable to see the compelling nature of their arguments. Now, I feel that this is not the right attitude—to me, it is not an example to be followed.

Other philosophers think that the pervasive and permanent dissensus in philosophy is a clear proof of the inadequacy and unsuitability of philosophy's truth-seeking and justificatory tools for establishing substantive philosophical truths, so our philosophical beliefs are inappropriately justified. But if they are inappropriately justified, then we cannot rationally stick to them and have to suspend all of them, however difficult and painful this may be.

I cannot identify with this reaction, either. I have several reasons, but for now I will mention just the three most evident ones. First, I don't think that anyone could argue for this skeptical (or rather, *meta*-skeptical) view in a non-self-defeating way. Second, I think that the only way for me to actually suspend all of my substantive and positive philosophical beliefs is to sink into intellectual apathy, and I would not like that to happen. Third, concerning our moral beliefs, I feel that I would be wrong to try to suspend them because if I did so, then I would have to toss a coin (or choose something similar) to decide what to do in difficult situations.

Yet other philosophers think that we can rationally stick to our beliefs even if we are unable to justify them compellingly. We do the right thing if we develop a philosophical theory that is in harmony or equilibrium with our fundamental pre-philosophical convictions and defend it from possible objections by showing that none of those are compelling. Once we have successfully accomplished these two tasks, we can rationally believe in our substantive philosophical theses—independently of whether others hold them to be false.

I can't identify with this approach, either. It says that my fundamental pre-philosophical convictions are epistemically unjustified, so they are not based on anything that would indicate what the truth is. Thus, this approach boils down to the following: "I can rationally believe that p is true because (1) I can show that no compelling argument can be made against p and (2) p is in harmony or equilibrium with my fundamental pre-philosophical convictions that I cannot suspend without damaging my personal integrity and my cognitive household." Now, I think that this kind of justification for p doesn't entitle me to seriously and sincerely believe that p is *true*—to believe that p really describes things as they are. It merely entitles me to say "It *seems* to me that p is true in the light of my pre-philosophical convictions"—and this is clearly not enough for my taking epistemic responsibility for the truth of p.

Finally, some philosophers think that all philosophical problems are meaningless, and so are all of our philosophical beliefs, consequently we cannot rationally stick to any of them. The only meaningful task of doing philosophy is to debunk the appearance-creating mechanism responsible for the genesis of philosophical problems and to work out an effective therapy which cures all persons infected with philosophy of unnecessarily troubling themselves with trying to solve philosophical problems.

I can't identify with this standpoint, either. For one thing, I think that all arguments are bad (and may be self-defeating) whose intended conclusion is that some appearance-creating mechanism is responsible for the existence of each philosophical problem—that the surface grammar and the pictoriality of language systematically mislead me. For another thing, I think that all therapeutic exercises are ineffective insofar as they are aimed at curing me of my engagement with philosophical questions so they stop troubling me unnecessarily.

So where does all this lead? As far as I can see, these four reactions (or metaphilosophical visions outlined in a nutshell) exhaust the scope of possible responses, *and yet* I cannot commit myself to any of them with a clear intellectual and moral conscience. Unfortunately, this means that I cannot reassuringly account for the epistemic status of my philosophical beliefs. I can't stick to them in cognitive peace, with epistemic responsibility and without self-deception, and I can't abandon them in cognitive peace, either, with epistemic responsibility and without self-deception.

You may say these four reactions don't exhaust the scope of possible responses. You may think that the community of philosophers will acquire new and reliable truth-seeking method(s) (whatever they are, e.g., experimental philosophy, conceptual engineering, etc.) with which it can find—or has already found some hitherto unrecognized—compellingly justified substantive philosophical theses.

You're right—I could hope for that. In what follows, I will discuss how much this hope is reasonable (not much, I guess); still, reasonable or not, it isn't helpful at all when I want to account for the epistemic status of my substantive philosophical beliefs. For the truth-seeking method(s) (however good they be) that community of philosophers will acquire *in the future* can neither justify nor refute my *present* substantive philosophical beliefs.

You may also say that I am the only one to blame for my "writhing" and "impotence," as I want to account for the epistemic status of my philosophical *beliefs*. Of course, if I were able to do philosophy in the spirit of "I don't believe that p (I don't hold p to be true), I only *accept p* as a working hypothesis"—that is to say, if my commitment to p were of no significance and consequence to me—, then everything would be in perfect order. In this case, I'd really be able to do philosophy without any cognitive uncertainties, because I could remain personally uncommitted while arguing for or against any philosophical theory.

I'm ambivalent about this strategy. On the one hand, I'm a little bit envious of those philosophers who don't have any definite philosophical beliefs (or have no philosophical beliefs at all), and so, after all, it makes no difference to them which philosophical theory they develop. Thus, they are able to serve philosophy's "great" and "noble" goal of populating the logical space more and more densely with well-constructed and consistent philosophical theories with a clear conscience. On the other hand, this is not an option for me, because I *do have* some substantive philosophical beliefs, and they are not arbitrary. For example, I don't merely accept the philosophical thesis that we are morally responsible for certain acts of ours, and the falsity of physicalism is not a mere working hypothesis to me, because I *believe* that we can be held to be morally accountable for certain acts of ours and I also *believe* that not everything is ultimately physical—and these beliefs are significant to me, as I have a personal stake in them.

To make a long story short, I do have some substantive philosophical beliefs, so I cannot ignore these while doing philosophy. At the same time, it seems to me that there is no such metaphilosophical vision that I could commit myself to in order to reassuringly account for my substantive philosophical beliefs with a clear conscience. Since, in my opinion, most philosophers resemble me in that they, too, have some substantive philosophical beliefs, and since—I suppose—my misgivings about the above four metaphilosophical visions are not entirely groundless and idiosyncratic, it may seem to others as well that we come up against an *aporia* in trying to account for the epistemic status of our substantive philosophical beliefs. In short, we find ourselves in a situation with seemingly no way out.

* * *

I will try to raise the issue differently, with the emphasis laid elsewhere. I assume that you already have some substantive philosophical beliefs—that you hold certain substantive philosophical theses to be true. I also assume that you have philosophical justification for your beliefs—you can underpin their truth with philosophical arguments. And I also assume that you are able to respond to objections to your philosophical beliefs—you can put your finger on some or other weak spots in them. In short, I assume that you have done your best to be able to assert your philosophical views in a form which is as strong and immune to objections as possible.

Nevertheless, even if all the above is correct, you may be faced with three quite nagging questions:

(1) Can you seriously and sincerely believe in the truth of your philosophical theses, and take epistemic responsibility for the truth of your philosophical beliefs in light of the fact that there probably are some philosophers whom you consider your epistemic peers and who, holding opposing philosophical

views, do not share your philosophical beliefs? This question is nagging because the fact that your epistemic peers do not share your philosophical beliefs may seem to you to be just as strong evidence for thinking that your philosophical beliefs can easily be false after all as the evidence based on which you have committed yourself to their truth.

(2) Can you seriously and sincerely believe in the truth of your philosophical theses, and take epistemic responsibility for the truth of your philosophical beliefs in light of the fact that you have good reason to think that they are shaped and determined by factors (upbringing, socialization, personality traits, epistemic character, etc.) which are not under your control and have nothing to do with their truth or falsity? This question is nagging because if your philosophical beliefs are really determined by such factors (for example, you believe that *p* is true because you wish that *p* be true, or you believe that *p* is true because you were socialized to hold *p* true), then it may seem to you that your philosophical beliefs are biased.

(3) Can you seriously and sincerely believe in the truth of your philosophical theses, and take epistemic responsibility for the truth of your philosophical beliefs in light of the fact that philosophy as an epistemic enterprise has failed—philosophers have been unable to solve philosophical problems and come up with compellingly justified substantive philosophical theses? This question is nagging because it may seem to you that the best explanation of philosophy's epistemic failure is that its truth-seeking and justificatory tools are inadequate and unsuitable for establishing substantive philosophical truths—and if this is the case, then your substantive philosophical beliefs are inappropriately justified, and consequently you cannot trust in their truth anymore.

What is common to these questions or challenges is that none of them concerns the content of your philosophical beliefs—they do not bring out the special internal difficulties of your philosophical views. Neither do they concern whether you were maximally circumspect when making sure that you have true rather than false beliefs. Each of these challenges arises "beyond" the point where you have already carefully underpinned your philosophical views with arguments.

And *yet*, you cannot wave them aside. *You would not be right* to say: "As I've done my best to underpin my philosophical beliefs with the strongest arguments possible, I don't have to address these challenges—I can safely dismiss them." In short, you have an epistemic and at once moral duty to face these *further* (meta-level) *challenges, too, regardless* of *what* philosophical beliefs you have and *how* good your arguments underpinning these are.

Of course, these questions or challenges can be given stock answers aimed at reassuring you. For example, you may reply to question (1) that "It is indeed reasonable that I give more weight to my own view concerning philosophical issues, because the evidence based on which I committed myself to the truth of *p* has more weight than the fact that others think *p* to be false." A possible reply to question (2) could be that "Doxastic determinism is false, I freely decide to believe in the truth of such and such philosophical theses; moreover, even if doxastic determinism were true, it would still not follow that my philosophical beliefs cannot track the truth." You may address question (3) by saying either that "Philosophy's epistemic failure is not a challenge for me, because I have compelling arguments for my philosophical beliefs," or that "I don't need any compelling arguments to be able, in good conscience, to stick to my philosophical views that elaborate my fundamental pre-philosophical convictions, as I can show that no objection of compelling force could be made against them."

In this book, I deal with the third of these challenges—I only discuss the first and the second where they have special importance for one or another reason. The reason I focus on the third one is that in my opinion, out of the three, this challenge is the greatest that we as philosophers must face. I also focus on it because facing this challenge offers me the most convenient conceptual framework to show that, however we want to, we cannot reassuringly account for the epistemic status of our substantive philosophical beliefs—we cannot take epistemic responsibility for their truth.

To sum up, I don't argue for meta-skepticism, according to which we must suspend our substantive philosophical beliefs. If I were to name the view I side with, I would call it "*meta*-meta-skepticism" for lack of a better name, immediately adding that instead of attempting to develop a stable metaphilosophical conception, I offer a *dialectical path*, which—inevitably, I think—leads to intellectual breakdown.

Part One

1

Philosophy as an Epistemic Enterprise

Philosophy is a heterogeneous formation, which involves quite a wide variety of activities. That is why I'm not even trying to define it. But despite its heterogeneity, there is a (more or less uniform) philosophical tradition, whereby the main purpose of doing philosophy is to assert *substantive truths* about the nature of reality, knowledge, the right action, and to justify the asserted propositions with a claim to truth *compellingly*. In other words, to provide correct answers to a variety of metaphysical, epistemological, and ethical questions—to solve philosophical problems. I will refer to this tradition as the *epistemic or truth-seeking tradition of philosophy*.

The philosophers of this tradition do not set themselves the less modest goal of exploring logically possible (i.e., consistent) stances on philosophical problems. They do not consider making types of propositions such as "If mental content is broadly individualized, you must deny *a priori* self-knowledge" or "If meanings are in the head, you must deny that meaning determines reference." The epistemic tradition of philosophy is not content with such non-substantive truths. It does not seek to show which propositions *can be true at the same time*, but to show which propositions *are true simpliciter*. Seen from the epistemic tradition of philosophy, this more modest goal is at most preparatory work, since the main purpose of philosophy is to establish the truth—to choose the true set of propositions from the various consistent sets of propositions.

I don't claim that all great dead philosophers belonged to the epistemic tradition of philosophy. But I do claim that *most* great dead philosophers were followers of this tradition. They pursued philosophy in the spirit of this tradition and interpreted their own activities in the same spirit. Anyone who denies that most of the great dead philosophers intended to assert compellingly justified substantive truths doesn't have acquaintance of the history of philosophy. Nor do I claim that the trust in the success of philosophy as an epistemic enterprise today is as unbroken as, say, at the dawn of the modern era. But I do claim that this tradition *is alive today*. Anyone who considers this tradition to be a thing of the past doesn't have acquaintance of contemporary philosophy. And anyone who simply denies the existence of this philosophical tradition doesn't have acquaintance of philosophy itself, or (worse but more likely) misinterprets the intention of most philosophers, either deliberately or due to some prejudice.

Of course, one could argue whether or not a philosopher is a follower of the epistemic tradition. Obviously, there are clear and less evident cases. Parmenides, Plato, Aristotle, Augustine, Thomas Aquinas, Descartes, Malebranche, Spinoza, Leibniz, Locke, Berkeley, Hume, Kant, Fichte, Schelling, Hegel, Marx, and Husserl certainly pursued philosophy in the spirit of this tradition; Jacques Derrida, Pierre Hadot, and Richard Rorty certainly didn't, and although I would classify Nietzsche, Kierkegaard, and Heidegger, for example, as followers of the epistemic tradition, the jury is still out on them. In short, all I am saying is that there was and still exists a truth-seeking philosophical tradition, not as a small minority, but—at least until the twentieth century—as a prevailing trend, and it is not on display in the wax museum of the history of ideas but is a living tradition.

In this chapter I characterize the epistemic tradition of philosophy by outlining its defining features. I just want to say some platitudes or commonplaces about it. Of course, this is not an easy task. The epistemic tradition itself is also a heterogeneous and very old (2,500 years) formation, so my characterization will inevitably be simplistic and sketchy, and will surely contain minor or major distortions and anachronistic wording. In brief, everything is much more complex, complicated, and colorful than I will describe it—my characterization would require deeper analysis and further refinement at every point.

If the main aim of doing philosophy is the assertion of substantive truths (compellingly justified true propositions)—as the members of epistemic tradition of philosophy claim it to be—, then *the only* epistemic value of philosophy in its *own right* is *knowledge*. So, in characterizing this tradition, I need to clarify two key concepts. On the one hand, the concept of *truth* or true propositions, since the followers of this tradition want to assert truths. On the other hand, the notion of philosophical *justification*, because the members in this tradition try to justify (moreover, compellingly justify) their philosophical beliefs. Make no mistakes: by doing so I don't commit myself to the *JTB* theory of knowledge *in general*. All I claim is this: no matter what we think about the general definition of the concept of knowledge, the epistemic tradition takes philosophical knowledge to be compellingly justified true belief.

1 Truth

Many truisms have been mentioned about the concept of truth (see Lynch 2009: 7–13; Wright 1998: 60). Now, I will only pick out the three most innocent of them to characterize those truths that philosophers intend to assert. In what follows, I will use the term "proposition" to refer to truth-bearers—in my intention, in a neutral sense, without any metaphysical commitment. Here they are:

(1) A proposition is true if and only if things are as it says they are.
(2) Two contradictory propositions cannot both be true.
(3) Truth does not admit of degrees.

Truism (1) tells us just that: the truth of a proposition depends on how things are (whatever they may be and however they may be), and not on how we would like them to be. It says what Aristotle did: "[T]o say of what is that it is, and of what is not that it is not, is true" (*Metaphysics* 1011b25).

In my opinion, (1) is indeed an innocent truism, without any substantive commitment to the nature of truth. By asserting (1) I do not commit myself to the correspondence theory of truth, according to which a proposition p has the property of being true if and only if p is in the appropriate correspondence relation to the world that exists independently of p. (1) says nothing about correspondence relations or the mind-, language-, or proposition-independent world—it says nothing about what kind of special relationship there is between the truth-bearer and the world described and represented by it, or about what kind of entities (facts, events, objects, properties, etc.) the world must contain in order for the truth-bearers to be in the appropriate correspondence relation to the world.

What truism (1) says is this: when we claim about a proposition that it is true (e.g., it is a true proposition that "All ravens are black"), what we claim is that things *are in a certain way*—things are (the world is) in a way that all ravens are black. We can have a more formal expression of this by using the so-called (T)-schema:

(T) The proposition that p is true if and only if p.

Whatever meaningful sentence we replace "p" with, we will get a true biconditional, and every appropriately replaced instance of (T) is necessarily true and can be known *a priori*. Thus (T), says the same as (1), which everyone accepts, independently of the ways in which they attempt to define truth more accurately or informatively. Debates about theories of truth among correspondists, coherentists, pragmaticists, verificationists, pluralists, primitivists, and deflationists are almost exclusively about the epistemic status of (T)-biconditionals. In other words, they are about whether the (T)-biconditional is sufficient in itself to clarify the concept of truth, or if it is not, how it should be amended in a way that complies with the next schema, i.e., what we should put in the place of "F" in the formula (T+) below.

(T+) The proposition that p is true if and only if p is F.

(T+) actually says more than (1) and there is no agreement among theorists of truth about what "F" should be replaced with in it. I, however, don't have to deal with this problem, as my asserting (1) commits me only to (T), but not to (T+).

Truism (2) is the principle of non-contradiction, according to which either p is true or not-p is true, but they cannot both be true. No one thinks that the propositions "There are immortal souls" and "There are no immortal souls" are both true. No one thinks that the propositions "Every event has a cause" and "Not every event has a cause" are both true. No one thinks that the propositions "All of our ideas are innate" and "Not all of our ideas are innate" are both true.

There are kinds of logic that reject the principle of non-contradiction (see e.g., Priest, Beall, and Armour-Garb 2004). This is undoubtedly an interesting thing, but I do not have to deal with it now. For philosophers of the epistemic tradition certainly do not want to commit themselves to inconsistent propositions, whatever they think about paraconsistent logic. I suppose, even paraconsistent logicians wouldn't be happy to see that their paraconsistent logical theory is paraconsistent itself.

Truism (3) says that if a proposition is true, then it is not a little bit, somewhat, or very but *completely* true. (If you think this claim is false because there are "half-truths," complex propositions that can be part true and part false, e.g., "Napoleon was born in Corsica and died in Paris," consider a simple subject-predicate proposition.) As opposed to the justification of our beliefs which can have degrees, truth or falsehood cannot. As Frege puts it: "Truth cannot tolerate a more or less" (1918/1956: 291). Just think about it. If there was a truth which was only partially true, then that would mean that it would be partially false. Or, if there was a falsehood which was only partially false, then that would mean it is partially true. To be honest, I don't think anyone could take the dispute of Theists and Atheists seriously if they concluded that the proposition "There is a God" is very true, but a little bit false, and the proposition "There is no God" is very false but is a little bit true.

Some philosophers dispute (3). In their view, truths have degrees indeed (see e.g., Sainsbury 2009: 56–63). But I don't have to deal with this possibility now, because the members of the epistemic tradition certainly do not want to assert half or so-so true, but only completely true propositions.

In the light of these three (I think genuinely innocent) truisms, I claim the following platitude or commonplace. The followers of the epistemic tradition want to assert truths, not falsehoods. They want to assert propositions that describe things as they really are; in doing so, they do not want to describe things as they rather are, but completely as they are; and they try to be consistent when developing their philosophical theories, that is, they are careful not to endorse contradictory propositions as both true. For example, when Berkeley argues that there is no mind-independent existence, he tries to assert something true and not false. When he says *esse est percipi*, he asserts that things are the way the proposition "*esse est percipi*" describes them. He does not claim that idealism is rather the truth than materialism, or that materialism is less true than idealism, but that idealism is completely true and materialism is completely false. And he does everything so that his view can be consistent—for example, he denies that it is meaningful to distinguish primary and secondary qualities.

But there is something else here that is perhaps worth clarifying—beyond the truisms about the concept of truth. Some may think that I can only claim that the epistemic tradition of philosophy is aimed at asserting substantive truths if I also commit myself to metaphysical realism—the thesis that reality (at least its non-mental and non-linguistic part) is mind- and language-independent, which means that the entities whose existence we posit are what they are, independently of any kind of representation, i.e., the way we get to know them does not affect their nature in any way. And some may also think, in connection with this, that I can say that the epistemic tradition of philosophy is aimed at asserting substantive truths only if I hold the task of philosophy (or at least metaphysics) to consist in revealing reality's fundamental structure. That is, if it should carve, using Plato's phrase, "nature at its joints" (*Phaedrus* 265e), to find "perfectly natural properties" (Lewis 1986: 61), since "only an elite minority are carved at the joints, so that their boundaries are established by objective sameness and difference in nature" (Lewis 1984: 227).

All this is false. It is false because from the fact that someone rejects metaphysical realism and advocates anti-realism (also known as deflational metametaphysics) it follows that they are still doing metaphysics. As Theodore Sider puts it: "There is no ametaphysical Archimedean point from which to advance deflationary metametaphysics, since any such metametaphysics is committed to at least this much substantive metaphysics: reality lacks a certain sort of structure" (2011: vii). If anti-realists commit themselves to the image of reality as an "amorphous lump" (Dummett 1981: 577), in which, to use Putnam's metaphor, we need to use a "cookie-cutter" (1987: 35) to experience the world in order, then they hold a substantive metaphysical view. And since they do, the question of truth or falsehood obviously arises about their thesis. Let's take this well-known passage:

> Now as we thus make constellations by picking out and putting together certain stars rather than others, so we make stars by drawing certain boundaries rather than others. Nothing dictates whether the sky shall be market off into constellations or other objects. We have to make what we find, be it the Great Dipper, Sirius, food, fuel or a stereo system.
>
> (Goodman 1984: 158)

It is evident that Goodman wants to assert a substantive philosophical truth with the above, namely that in contrast to metaphysical realism, things are in a certain way *only for us*, and they are not in any way in themselves. If someone thinks that Goodman's statement doesn't have a claim to truth and so cannot be true or false, then I wonder what they mean by "true" and "false."

2 Justification

The members of the epistemic tradition of philosophy do not merely wish to declare their philosophical theses, nor do they only hope that they are the lucky ones whose theses are true, but also try to justify the truth of their theses in a compelling manner.

Candidates for compelling philosophical justifications almost always take the form of some philosophical *argument*—the majority of the followers of this tradition want to make compelling argument(s) in support of their theses. That is to say:

> [A]rguments [...] are the best when they are *knockdown*, the arguments *force* you to a conclusion, if you believe the premises you *have* or *must* believe the conclusion, some arguments don't carry much *punch*, and so forth.

A philosophical argument is an attempt to get someone to believe something, whether he wants to believe it or not. A successful philosophical argument, a strong argument, *forces* someone to a belief.
> (Nozick 1981: 4, italics in original [What Nozick claims here is some other philosophers' view, not his own; he himself doesn't believe in the possibility of knock-down philosophical arguments.])

Some philosophers (typically phenomenologists), however, do not attempt to use arguments in support of the truth of their philosophical theses—*they want to point to* certain truths *directly*. They suggest a procedure in which certain truths are "revealed" or "uncovered" to us—these truths "step out from hiding into the open."

2.1 Compelling justification—knock-down philosophical arguments

A compelling argument can only be one that has (or can be transformed into) a deductive form. The conclusion of a deductive argument necessarily (apodictically) follows from the premise(s). It is such an argument that *if* its conclusions follow from its premises and *if* its premises are true, *then* it is impossible for its conclusion to be false. (For a stripped down, deductive-formal formulation of famous philosophical arguments, see Bruce and Barbone 2011.)

The usual definition of a compelling argument is as follows:

> *Argument A* (deductive form) is compelling if and only if (1) a person who sufficiently understands *A*'s premises and the epistemic reasons for them can only irrationally deny the truth of the premises, and (2) a person who recognizes that *A*'s conclusion follows by the laws of logic from *A*'s premises can only irrationally deny *A*'s conclusion.

Because the term "irrational" has many uses, it is worthwhile to make it clear in which sense it is used in the above definition. It doesn't say that one cannot deny in a coherent way all the premises and the conclusion—in a coherentist sense, even mad theories can be rational. It doesn't deny either that the denial of the premises and the conclusion can be rather useful—in a pragmatic sense, even madness can be rational if it plays out well. Rather, it says that one cannot have the epistemic right to deny the premises and conclusion of a knock-down argument because one cannot have good epistemic reasons to regard them as uncertain or false.

In philosophy, there are three kinds of arguments intended-to-be compelling. I briefly introduce them below.

2.1.1 Infallible arguments

According to a great number of philosophers belonging to the epistemic tradition, a logically valid deductive argument is a compelling one if and only if its premises are *infallibly* justified, and consequently the justification of the premises *guarantees* their truth and, indirectly, the truth of the argument's conclusion.

It is easy to see why these philosophers try to find arguments with infallibly justified premises. The reason is that if their arguments are good, then their conclusions cannot under any circumstances be false—they are necessarily true. Thus, these philosophers will not have to worry about someone refuting their arguments in the future.

Candidates for compelling infallible arguments must contain premises that are justified *directly*, that is, *non-inferentially*—otherwise there will be either infinite regress or circular reasoning. As far as I can see, *three* different types of propositions have been proposed as non-inferred and infallibly justifiable.

The first type includes propositions beginning with the words "It seems to me …" For example, "It seems to me that there is a red spot with a visual depth before me." This proposition is infallibly justified because I experience it so, and the way I experience something (how it seems to me) cannot be mistaken. So, the first type of infallibly justified propositions is made up of certain subjective truths justified by our phenomenological-introspective insights.

The second kind involves necessary conceptual truths. According to some philosophers, for example, it is a necessary conceptual truth that "God is an infinitely perfect being"; "Where there is a mistake, there must also be truth"; "If F is not an essential property of x, then x can exist without F." In their view, these propositions are infallibly justified because if we understand the concepts contained in these propositions, we will see with a single intuitive "glimpse" that these propositions are necessarily true.

The third kind includes such propositions as "Every event has a cause"; "There are entities that are self-caused"; "There are indivisible entities (atoms)"; "Physical space is Euclidean"; "Physical objects have essential properties"; "There are things that exist in themselves and there are things that need something else to exist"; "What has happened cannot be undone or changed." These propositions are not mere conceptual truths. Each one "goes beyond" our concepts and is *about reality* itself. Many in the epistemic tradition think that there may be some infallibly justified propositions about reality itself—we are able to "glimpse" into the necessary structure of reality.

I'm not sure if the reason for introducing this third category is clear to everyone, but I have to introduce it to avoid painting a misleading picture of the epistemic tradition by merely saying that in this tradition the set of infallibly justified propositions includes only credible phenomenological-introspective accounts and analytical truths in the Humean sense. It seems to me that philosophers before Hume did not make a sharp distinction between necessary conceptual truths (i.e., analytical truths) and necessary truths that go *beyond* our concepts (i.e., non-analytical necessities)—in my division the second and third kinds of infallibly justified propositions, which correspond to *a priori* analytic and *a priori* synthetic true propositions in Kant's division. It was Hume who narrowed down the range of necessary truths to analytic truths, and now, I will introduce this third category to indicate that the philosophers of the epistemic tradition have also considered many propositions as infallibly justified necessary truths that are neither describe some phenomenological fact nor are merely true by virtue of the meaning of the terms they contain.

This is what I refer to with the metaphor of "intuitive glimpse into the necessary structure of reality." Because of the possibility of this "glimpse," many have long believed that, for example, not only the analytical proposition that "Every effect has a cause" but also the non-analytical proposition that "Every event has a cause" is infallibly justified.

Let me show two well-known candidates for compelling arguments that contain infallibly justified premises. One is the Cartesian argument for the real distinction between body and soul. Here is a possible reconstruction of it, brought to a deductive form:

(1) I can conceive clearly and distinctly that I can exist only with the property of thinking and without the property of extension, and I can conceive clearly and distinctly that my body can exist only with the property of extension and without the property of thinking.

(2) If I can conceive clearly and distinctly that thing x can exist only with property F and without property G (where F is not identical with G), and I can conceive clearly and distinctly that thing y can exist only with property G and without property F (where G is not identical with F), then x can exist without y and y can exist without x.

(3) If x can exist without property G, then G is not an essential property of x and if y can exist without property F, then F is not an essential property of y.

Therefore:

(C1) It is not my essential property that I have a body.

Furthermore:

(4) If it is not my essential property that I have a body, then I really differ from my body.

Therefore [from (C1) and (4)]:

(C2) I really differ from my body.

Why do some people think that the premises are infallibly justified? Concerning (1), they think so because propositions beginning with "I conceive clearly and distinctly that …" function like those that begin with "It seems to me …" and as such are justified by the fact that the truth in question "shines" with a specific phenomenology. (3) and (4) express necessary conceptual relations the truth of which is directly seen. I'm uncertain about (2). You may think of (2) that its truth is directly apparent from the concept of property and the meaning of modal terms. In this case, (2), like (3) and (4), is a necessary conceptual truth. But you may also think that (2), as opposed to (3) and (4), is not a mere conceptual truth but rather the result of an intuitive "glimpse" into the necessary structure of reality.

Let me present another well-known contemporary philosophical argument which, if compelling, has premises and conclusions that are infallibly justified. Here is a received reconstruction of David Chalmers' conceivability argument:

(1) Zombies (creatures that are identical with us in physical, functional, and intentional properties, but lacking phenomenal ones) are consistently conceivable.
(2) Everything that is consistently conceivable is metaphysically possible.

Therefore:

(C1) Zombies are metaphysically possible.

Furthermore:

(3) If zombies are metaphysically possible, then physicalism is false.

Therefore [from (C1) and (3)]:

(C2) Physicalism is false.

Why do some people think that the premises are infallibly justified? The case of premise (1) and (3) is relatively clear. In the case of (1), we intuitively see that the concept of "a being with such and such physical, functional, and intentional properties" does not include the concept of phenomenal property. Premise (3) is a conceptual truth derived from the definition of physicalism and that of zombies. Here is the conceptual relation: according to physicalism, physical properties necessarily determine mental properties. If, however, zombies are metaphysically possible, then it is not true that all mental properties necessarily supervene on physical properties, therefore the latter ones do not determine the former ones—for zombies are beings that have exactly the same physical properties as us, yet do not possess phenomenal properties. There is disagreement about the status of premise (2). I tend to think that those who hold (2) true, consider (2) to be a necessary conceptual truth—even if some "training" or "support" is needed to recognize this conceptual truth, such as the introduction of two-dimensional semantics which "performs" the necessary conceptual clarifications (see Chalmers 2002, 2004).

Many philosophers of the epistemic tradition deny that infallible philosophical arguments are possible or, if they don't deny that, then they think that there can be compelling philosophical arguments *other* than infallible ones. They think that the fact that a philosophical argument contains a fallibly justified premise does not entail that it cannot be compelling. Thus, these philosophers allow in their arguments intended-to-be compelling some premises that are not infallibly justified—which in principle may turn out to be false. At the same time, they think that the truth of these premises can only be irrationally denied by anyone who sufficiently understands them and the epistemic reasons behind them.

There are two kinds of philosophical arguments intended-to-be compelling with fallibly justified premises. One category includes so-called modest transcendental arguments. The other includes arguments that contain an empirically justified premise.

2.1.2 Modest transcendental arguments

Modest transcendental arguments must be distinguished from strong transcendental arguments. The latter are intended-to-be *infallible* arguments—their structure looks like this:

(1) p.
(2) If p, then q. (Since q is a condition of possibility of p.)

Therefore:

(C) *q*.

For example:

(1) I think.
(2) If I think, (then) I exist.

Therefore:

(C) I exist.

Contrary to strong transcendental arguments, modest transcendental arguments are *fallible*. They contain a proposition *p* (premise *p*) that can be false. At the same time—and this is crucial!—even if *p* *is* false, we cannot rationally reject *p*. That is, we cannot have appropriate epistemic reasons to reject *p* even if we are not able to infallibly justify that *p* is true, or even if *p* is de facto false. The structure of modest transcendental arguments looks like this:

(1) *p*. (Meaning that even if we cannot infallibly justify that *p*, we cannot rationally reject *p*.)
(2) If *p*, then *q*.

Therefore:

(C) *q*. (Meaning that even if we cannot infallibly justify that *q*, we cannot rationally reject *q*.)

What is interesting to us now is premise (1) of this argument, which the proponent of the argument always supports in this way: we could only rationally reject *p* if *p* were true, and so we cannot rationally reject *p* under any circumstances. At first glance, this type of justification may seem strange—let me explain. Let's look at the following modest transcendental argument, which I borrow from Robert Lockie (2018), who takes it from Epicurus:

(1) We have epistemic duties. (Meaning that even if we cannot infallibly justify that we have epistemic duties, we cannot rationally deny the existence of our epistemic duties.)
(2) If we have epistemic duties, then determinism is false.

Therefore:

(C) Determinism is false. (Meaning that even if we cannot infallibly justify that determinism is false, we cannot rationally reject that determinism is false.)

Here's the thing. Our epistemic duties (in the deontic sense) are about what to believe in certain situations. For example, if, after a thorough investigation, a detective sees that all evidence is in favor of X's guilt, then he has a duty to believe that X must be prosecuted. This would be so even if X happened to be the victim of a global and inscrutable conspiracy, whose members deliberately arranged the circumstances so that all available evidence pointed to X's guilt, for the detective—due to his epistemic limitations—cannot rationally think that X is a victim of a global and inscrutable conspiracy.

The situation is similar with the premise (1) of the above argument. According to this, we cannot get into an epistemic situation in which we must rationally conclude that we have to abandon our belief in our epistemic duties. The reason why we cannot is that even if all the evidence pointed to the non-existence of our epistemic duties, it still would not be rational to reject our belief in them. It would not be rational because, if we did not have any epistemic duties, then in light of the evidence, we *would not have to* endorse or reject *any* of our beliefs. Now, if we recognize all this, then we must also recognize that, even if we do not have any epistemic duties, it is not rational to reject our belief in them.

Turning to premise (2) and (C): if we also have good reasons to believe that we can have epistemic duties only if determinism is false (otherwise, our epistemic duties may require us to do things that we cannot do due to deterministic laws of nature), then we also have good reasons to believe the conclusion of the argument, which says that we cannot rationally reject that determinism is false. And if we cannot rationally reject the proposition that determinism is false, then we must hold it true that determinism is false.

Of course, this last step is debatable. The fact that we cannot rationally reject p does not logically entail that p. However, if we think we cannot rationally reject p, then it seems that we also must think that p.

Whatever the truth about this may be, one thing is certain: if modest transcendental arguments work, they compel us in a peculiar way. They compel us to consider p rationally irrefutable, and then show us that recognizing the rational irrefutability of p entails that we must hold p true, and thus we must indirectly hold the conclusion of the argument true, even though we have no proof (infallible justification) of *p*'s truth and so we cannot consider the conclusion of the argument to be infallibly justified.

Let me give another example borrowed from Guy Kahane (2017):

(1) There are differences in values between actions and beliefs. (Meaning that even if we cannot infallibly justify that there are differences in value between them, we cannot rationally deny the existence of differences in value between them.)
(2) If there are differences in values between actions and beliefs, then there are values.

Therefore:

(C) There are values. (Meaning that even if we cannot infallibly justify that there are values, we cannot rationally reject the existence of values.)

Premise (1) can be false: *in principle*, it is possible that nihilism is true and everything is equally worthless. In this case, however, *it would make no difference* what we do or believe, because one act or belief is no better than another. Thus, *it would also make no difference* whether we believe (in this case, correctly) that there are no values or we believe in something else. Thus, if nihilism were true, we could not rationally think that—from any point of view, even an epistemic one—it is good to believe in nihilism. But if, even from an epistemic point of view, it was not good for us to believe in nihilism (even if nihilism were true), then we would have no rational basis to believe in nihilism. This is because, from an epistemic point of view, it can only be good to believe in anything or reject any belief if nihilism is false and maintaining certain beliefs is epistemically better than maintaining other beliefs. Now, if we realize all of this, then we cannot rationally reject that nihilism is false and there are differences in value among actions, beliefs, and things.

Turning to premise (2) and (C): if there are differences in value, then there must be values. The modest transcendental argument above, at least according to its proponents, shows that we cannot rationally reject the existence of values. And if we cannot rationally reject that there are values, then we must commit ourselves to the existence of values.

To sum up, according to the proponents of modest transcendental arguments, there are fallible arguments which are nonetheless compelling and so their conclusions should be held true by all rational agents.

2.1.3 Compelling philosophical arguments with empirically justified premises

How can any philosophical argument intended-to-be compelling contain an empirically justified premise at all? Here is the thing. According to some philosophers, the natural sciences deliver some compellingly justified theses whose truth is rationally unquestionable for those who sufficiently understand these theses and the evidence adduced for them—even if they are not infallibly justified. Peter van Inwagen, for example, puts it this way: "[A]nyone who does not agree that continents are in motion either does not fully appreciate the data and argument a geologist could put forward in support of the thesis that continents are in motion, or else is intellectually perverse" (2009: 21). Now, if, like van Inwagen, a philosopher thinks that certain scientific theses are indeed compellingly justified (i.e., their truth can be denied only irrationally [or by perversion]), and she includes them as the premises of philosophical arguments, then she may hope that she will soon end up having many compelling philosophical arguments.

Nathan Ballantyne argues just this way (see 2014). He tries to show that if one thinks that there are compelling (knock-down) arguments in the natural sciences, then one must think that there are such arguments in philosophy as well. Here's one of his examples:

(1) It is an established (compellingly justified) astronomical thesis that the Earth is in motion.
(2) The proposition "The Earth is in motion" entails the proposition "There is motion."

Therefore:

(C) (Contrary to Zeno's teaching) There is motion.

Another example, in the spirit of Ballantyne, could be as follows:

(1) It is an established (compellingly justified) geological thesis that there are continents.
(2) The proposition that "There are continents" entails the proposition that "Existence monism is false."

Therefore:

(C) (Contrary to Spinoza's teaching) Existence monism is false.

According to Ballantyne, these arguments must be considered as compelling philosophical arguments by anyone who thinks that the scientific arguments in favor of the propositions "The Earth is in motion" and "There are continents" are compelling. This is because if certain scientific theses are compellingly justified, then their compellingly justified status is *transferred* to the corresponding philosophical theses. In other words, if p is a compellingly justified scientific thesis, and p implies q (where q is a philosophical thesis), then q will also be a compellingly justified thesis, i.e., a compellingly justified philosophical thesis. Simply put, q as a philosophical thesis *inherits* the compellingly justified status of p as a scientific thesis.

I'm quite sure that most figures in the epistemic tradition would not endorse the above two arguments as compelling. Let's take the scientific theses "The Earth is in motion" and "There are continents." To be able to consider them as compellingly justified, one must hold that the thesis "Perception is reliable" is compellingly justified, too—for the justification of the theses "The Earth is in motion" and "There are continents" certainly requires perceptual experiences. But, the thesis that "Perception is reliable" can only be justified *with philosophical arguments*.

Now, based on the above, one could argue in the following two ways for the claim that compelling philosophical arguments cannot contain empirical premises. One option is to say that the justification of the scientific hypotheses "The Earth is in motion" and "There are continents" *presupposes* the justification of the philosophical thesis "Perception is reliable"—one could compellingly justify the former only if the latter is already compellingly justified. This would mean that scientific theses cannot be compellingly justified without philosophical grounding, consequently the philosophical theses corresponding to them cannot inherit their allegedly "compellingly justified" feature. The other option (and this point is perhaps even more important) is to say that there can be no empirical premises in compelling philosophical arguments because *the standards* which determine what counts as a compelling argument in the natural sciences are *different* from the standards which determine what counts as a compelling argument in philosophy. Even if p counts as compellingly justified in the natural sciences, and even if p implies q, this kind of justification of q does not meet the standards of philosophical justification, for these are significantly stricter than the standards of scientific justification.

At the same time, we must also see that in the eyes of some philosophers of the epistemic tradition, the above two arguments are compelling. Here is the most important consideration in favor of it. We must start by assuming that science is the *only* truly successful epistemic enterprise of mankind. Now, if we assume that (i) the best scientific theories are the *best* theories *simpliciter*, (ii) scientific theories are literally about reality, and (iii) after careful consideration of all evidence available to us, it is irrational to deny the truth of the propositions "The Earth is in motion" and "There are continents," then the above two arguments are compelling indeed. Philosophical knowledge is far behind the natural sciences in terms of reliability, so it is downright *displeasing* for philosophers to appeal to higher standards of justification.

There is disagreement among philosophers concerning the validity of philosophical arguments containing empirically justified premises, and this disagreement brings out well an important and "chronic" *fault line* in the epistemic tradition. The question is: "What should the relationship be between the epistemic tradition of philosophy and the natural sciences?" The fronts are clear.

One may think this:

> The natural sciences are the *sole custodians* of the knowledge of reality. Consequently, we must give up (whether we like it or not) theses based on purely philosophical speculations that run counter to the theses of the natural sciences. Furthermore, since certain scientific theses can only be irrationally denied, those philosophical arguments whose premises include these scientific theses can also be compelling.

But one might also think this:

> Philosophy has stricter standards of justification than the natural sciences. There may be compelling scientific arguments for the claim that contemporary astronomy and contemporary geology are the best *scientific* theories, but there can be no compelling scientific arguments for the claim that astronomy and geology are the best theories *simpliciter*. This is because the latter question is par excellence a philosophical and not a scientific one. So, there can be no scientifically justified premises in compelling philosophical arguments.

All in all, the crucial question is this: "Is it true that scientific theories are the best theories *simpliciter* of reality?" A philosopher's answer to this question determines on which side of the fault line she stands. If she answers yes to it, then she thinks she can include scientific theses among the premises of compelling philosophical arguments. If he answers no to it, then she thinks she cannot include such theses.

2.1.4 Two more brief clarifying remarks

The first one: all philosophical arguments intended-to-be compelling are *a priori*. This assertion is relatively easy to misunderstand—I will try to make it clear.

By *a priori* justification we mean justification that does not rely on experience. But this does not mean that there is no need for experience in any sense to justify a proposition *a priori*. In order to *understand* proposition *p* that you want to justify, that is, to *master* the concepts included in *p*, you need experience. The justification of the proposition "Everything that is red is colored" is *a priori*, but understanding the concepts "red" and "colored" is impossible without perceptual experience. This means that the justification of proposition *p* is *a priori* because if you understand *p*, then you need *no further* experience in order to see the truth of *p*.

Let's move on. The assertion that all philosophical arguments intended-to-be compelling are *a priori* does not mean that all their premises are *a priori* justified. If this assertion were true, then those that contain empirically justified premises would be excluded *ab ovo* from among them. Rather, it means that once *you have already* regarded their premises as justified, you *no longer* need experience to see the truth of their conclusions. In other words, the *a priori* justification of philosophical arguments amounts to the following: by *already* regarding propositions p_1, p_2, p_3 as justified, you *combine* $p_1, p_2,$ and p_3 into a logically valid deductive argument. That is, *once* you have the (not necessarily *a priori*) justified premises at your disposal, you don't have to move out of your armchair; and the *a priori* work phase of making philosophical arguments is what you do in the armchair.

Some think that there are two philosophical arguments intended-to-be compelling which do not rely on experience at all. One is the ontological argument for the existence of God. According to this, the concept of God (as an infinitely perfect being) cannot be consistently conceived without considering God as existing, therefore there is a God. The other is that the concept of God (as an infinitely perfect being) cannot be conceived consistently, and therefore there is not God. Apart from these two, all philosophical arguments intended-to-be compelling require experience for their justification to a greater or lesser extent—but they are *a priori* arguments all the same.

The second clarifying remark: all philosophical arguments intended-to-be compelling are justified in an *internalist way*. I will explain this briefly as well.

According to justification internalism, our beliefs can be justified only by factors to which we have access in our first-person perspective, "from within."

One of the most convincing arguments in favor of internalism starts from the deontological concept of justification. It says that if our belief in the truth of proposition p is justified, then we must be able to say why we believe in the truth of p. If we cannot say why, then our belief is not rational, and so we cannot take *responsibility* for it. Now, we can only take responsibility for those beliefs whose justifying factors are accessible in our first-person perspective. In other words, we can only assert p *responsibly* if we are not only justified in believing that p is true, but we are also justified in believing that we are justified in believing that p is true.

Justification externalism claims that our belief p is justified if p is in a proper relationship with the truth at issue; if our belief p is caused, in an appropriate way, by a fact or state of affairs that makes p true; if our belief p is produced by a reliable (truth-conducive) belief-producing process. So, according to externalism, the justified status of our beliefs is partly dependent on factors that may be inaccessible to our subjective perspective and, in this sense, external to it. That is, our access to all justifying factors from a ("internal") first-person perspective is not a *necessary condition* of the justified status of our beliefs.

Why is it that internalist justification is the only game in town when it comes to philosophical arguments intended-to-be compelling? The reason is that we believe p to be justified *because of our philosophical arguments*, and so we obviously have access from a first-person perspective to the factors that justify p—the premises of our own arguments and our own inference. And this is true even if we happen to argue for justification or knowledge externalism. Even if the externalist grants that sound arguments track the truth quite reliably, she holds that we do not have access to why they have this feature. However, it is *not* good enough from the perspective of the epistemic tradition. To possess well-established philosophical truths, philosophers have to see *why* their arguments are reliable because without that, it would be inexplicable to others and themselves why anyone should rely on them (considerations about utility and similar factors don't count in this case). So, philosophers of the epistemic tradition need to have the ambition to justify their theses in an internalist way. As Alvin Goldman puts it: "I think my analysis shows that the question of whether someone knows a certain proposition is, in part, a causal question, although, *of course*, the question of what the correct analysis is of 'S knows that p' is *not* a causal question" (1967: 372, italics mine).

To put if differently, in order for S to be able to have good reason for believing that her justification for p is *compelling*, it is *not enough* that the cognitive process leading to p is reliable—*it is also needed* that S be able to transparently justify *why* the cognitive process leading to her belief p is reliable. This is because if S doesn't see from a first-person viewpoint *why* her philosophical arguments are reliable, then S cannot be certain to the required extent that they reliably lead to truth—and insofar as S cannot be certain to the required extent that her philosophical arguments reliably lead to truth, S does not have any good epistemic reason to think that she has compelling arguments for the truth of p.

Let me give an example. Let's suppose that God, as an infinitely perfect being, exists, and S believes in God's existence, although not based on philosophical considerations. Let's also suppose that just as S's belief in God's existence gradually deepens, so will certain philosophical arguments for the truth of p exert an *ever-increasing influence* on her, to the point that it definitely begins to *seem to S* that *these arguments show* the truth of p. (Let p be the proposition that only the present exists; and let the *chief argument* for p's truth be that while presentism is able to plausibly explain the main features of the experience of time, and thus, indirectly, phenomenal consciousness itself, the rival theories are unable to accomplish the same.) Now, if it is S's belief in God's existence and, eventually, (let's suppose) God himself that causes S to begin massively believing in the truth of p and the soundness of the chief argument for p, then the cognitive process leading to S's belief p is a *reliable* one. Moreover, it is the most reliable cognitive process of all, because God is all-knowing and (let's suppose) doesn't deceive His disciples. Thus, if the cognitive process leading to S's belief p is a reliable one (that is, the arguments based on which S believes that p track the truth, thanks to God), then (in the externalist sense of knowledge) S *knows* that p.

According to the followers of the epistemic tradition, S's knowledge is *not the kind* of philosophical knowledge that they intend to achieve. The reason for it is not that the proposition S knows (in the externalist sense) isn't a substantive philosophical thesis. Rather, it is that S's justification for the truth of p does *not* have compelling force. This is because *all* elements of a compelling justification must be transparent—but this condition is not met in the case at issue. Although, from a first-person perspective, S has access to her argument for presentism and against the rival theories, she does not have access to the critically important (and in a certain sense, the most important) factor which is *responsible for* the *reliability* (truth-tracking feature) of her argument—it *falls outside of S's subjective viewpoint*.

In other words, *if* God exists and *if* S's belief p is caused by S's belief in God's existence, and *if* God doesn't deceive S and *if* …, then S's belief p is the result of a reliable cognitive process indeed. However, the statements following this "if" are all *unjustified*—S merely *resigns herself to them*. Of course, S may attempt to justify the propositions coming after each and every "if," and insofar as she succeeds in "*cleaning*" the justification for the truth of *p* of all non-transparent elements, then her justification for the truth of *p* becomes an *internalist* one. And, in this case, her argument may even have compelling force.

In brief, the epistemic tradition of philosophy seeks to answer the question: "The truth of which propositions should we believe in?" It seems obvious that if we want to answer this question, we *need to* have access to the reasons for deciding what to believe—and externalism does not provide this access. Based on justification externalism, we can only say that *once we already* believe in the truth of *p*, and we have no perfectly transparent internalist justification of *p*, this does not in itself entail that *p* is not justified. However, if we have an ultimately externalist justification for *p*, we cannot know on the basis of it whether we should believe in the truth of *p* or not.

2.2 Compelling justification—without philosophical arguments

Most philosophers in the epistemic tradition seek to justify their theses with compelling philosophical arguments. However, there is another type of procedure designed to "force truth into the open," namely the phenomenological method.

In the eyes of certain philosophers, the phenomenological method is doomed to failure. David Bell, for example, says that "There is something dismal and dogmatic about a philosophy whose utility, cogency and plausibility depend essentially, not on objective arguments, rational analysis, or the critical consideration of evidence available to all, but rather on the individual philosopher's having undergone some esoteric experience" (1991: 162). In this section, I attempt to show how phenomenologists try to arrive at truths with the use of the phenomenological method, and how they try to provide compelling justifications for their theses.

To do this, I need to answer three questions. Firstly, what is the goal of phenomenology and what does the phenomenological method look like? Secondly, why do phenomenologists think that by using the phenomenological method they can arrive at compellingly justified philosophical truths? Thirdly, why do phenomenologists think that compelling phenomenological justification is not an argumentative activity that eliminates all inference? I try to base my answers to these questions on some of Husserl's well-known passages—as far as I can tell, he was the one who dealt with these questions with the most emphasis and methodological awareness in the phenomenological movement.

Ad one: The goal of phenomenology is to systematically analyze conscious experiences from the first-person perspective—to explore and plausibly and exhaustively describe how things seem *to* the subject, from the subject's *point of view*.

Phenomenology has strict methodological rules. One is that we have to take extra care not to let common sense and scientific convictions affect our investigation. They have to be bracketed, so to speak, during the course of our phenomenological investigations. This is the only way for us to focus on the *intrinsic* characteristics of the subject's conscious experiences—those characteristics which the subject's conscious experience has from his own perspective. This methodological principle is called the "phenomenological reduction." As Husserl puts it:

> [According to phenomenological reduction]: every transcendent (that which is not given to me immanently) is to be assigned the index of zero, that is, its existence, its validity is not to be assumed as such, except as at most the *phenomenon of a claim to validity*. I am to treat all sciences only as phenomena, hence not as systems of valid truths, not as premises, not even as hypotheses for me to reach truth with. This applies to the whole of psychology and the whole of the natural sciences.
>
> (1907/1990: 4, italics in original)

The other rule is that phenomenology should not describe particular experiences from a subjective point of view, but the nature of *types* of experience. This is what distinguishes phenomenology from pure introspection. For example, in describing visual experience, phenomenologists are not supposed to say that "This red mailbox appears to me in such and such a way and that yellow tram appears so and so," but they are to reveal the essential phenomenological characteristics of visual experience itself. They should undertake to describe those phenomenological characteristics that are *common* to all visual experience and which distinguish visual experience from all other types of experience. In a word, they are supposed to reveal the *inherent and distinctive* features of visual experience. This methodological principle is called "eidetic reduction." In Husserl's words:

> Phenomenological psychology in this manner undoubtedly must be established as an "eidetic phenomenology"; it is then exclusively directed toward the invariant essential forms. For instance, the phenomenology of perception of bodies will not be (simply) a report on the factually occurring perceptions or those to be expected; rather it will be the presentation of invariant structural systems

without which perception of a body and a synthetically concordant multiplicity of perceptions of one and the same body as such would be unthinkable.

(1927/1971: 81)

Let me quote Husserl again to recapitulate these two methodological principles of phenomenology:

> If the phenomenological reduction contrived a means of access to the phenomenon of real and also potential inner experience, the method founded in it of "eidetic reduction" provides the means of access to the invariant essential structures of the total sphere of pure psychical process.
>
> (1927/1971: 81)

Ad two: According to Husserl, the right application of the phenomenological method provides infallible (apodictic) justification. As he puts it:

> At every point this analysis is an analysis of essences and investigation of the general states of affairs which are to be built up in immediate intuition. Thus, the whole investigation is an *a priori* one, though, of course, it is not *a priori* in the sense of mathematical deductions. What distinguishes it from the "objectivizing" *a priori* sciences is its methods and its goal. *Phenomenology proceeds by "seeing", clarifying, and determining meaning, and by distinguishing meanings* [...] It does not theorize or carry out mathematical operations; that is to say, it carries through no explanations in the sense of deductive theory.
>
> (1907/1990: 46, italics in original)

Or:

> It is the spirit of [phenomenology] to count nothing as really scientific which cannot be fully justified by the evidence. In other words, [phenomenology] demands proof *by reference to the things and facts themselves, as these are given in actual experience and intuition*. Thus guided, we, the beginning philosophers, make it a rule to judge only by the evidence. Also, the evidence itself must be subject to critical verification, and that on the basis, of course, of further available evidence.
>
> (1929/1998: 6, italics in original)

And here's perhaps the most elucidating passage:

> Thus as little interpretation as possible, but as pure an intuition as possible [...] In fact, we will hark back to the speech of the mystics when they describe the intellectual seeing which is supposed not to be a discursive knowledge. And

the whole trick consists in this — to give free rein to the seeing eye and to bracket the references which go beyond the "seeing" and are entangled with seeing, along with the entities which are supposedly given and thought along with the "seeing", and, finally, to bracket what is read into them through the accompanying reflections. The crucial question is: Is the supposed object given in the proper sense? Is it, in the strictest sense, "seen" and grasped, or does the intention go beyond that?

(1907/1990: 50–1)

I will not leave Husserl alone with what he has just said—I will try to say more clearly what he claims. Phenomenology undertakes to describe conscious experiences from the first-person perspective. Now, the description and systematic categorization of conscious experience is, according to Husserl, apodictic (and thus compellingly justified) because the characteristics of our conscious experience are given to us directly, intuitively (*anschaulich*). And there can be no meaningful doubt about the proper phenomenological description of conscious experience because, in this case, the distinction between appearance and reality is meaningless. Doubts such as the following are meaningless: "For me, this and that conscious experience appears in this and that way, but is it not possible that it actually appears differently?" Or, "For me this and that conscious experience *appears as F*, but is it not possible that it actually appears *not as-F* but *as-G*?"

Ad three: Why does Husserl think he can manage without arguments? It is quite common for philosophical arguments to contain premises whose justification is based on some phenomenological insight. For example, arguments in favor of the sense-datum theory often have the premise that the objects of our perceptual experiences are given to us in a different way than, say, the objects of our thought acts or beliefs. However, Husserl does not treat these types of phenomenological insights as the premises of some arguments—in his view, we cannot leave the sphere or space of our conscious experience achieved through reductions. We have to stay *within* it. Thus, we do not rely on inferences to provide us with insights about more and more truths, but, as the passages quoted above say, we obtain these insights in such a way that each of them is accompanied by intuitive (*anschaulich*) evidence. Conversely, according to Husserl, a philosopher begins to argue and infer when he has already *fallen out of* the space of conscious experience. That is, for lack of a better method.

Husserl gives the example of Descartes. He sees it this way: Descartes reached a truly apodictic (phenomenological) evidence with the "ego cogito." And thus, says Husserl, for the first time in the history of philosophy, "[He] uncovered for us [...] through the apodictic *I am* a new kind and an endless sphere of being" (1929/1998: 11). But at the same time, he made a fatal mistake: "[He used] the *ego cogito* merely as an apodictic proposition and as an absolute primitive premise" (1929/1998: 11). He began to reason, argue, infer, speculate—instead of remaining in the space of conscious experience he had "opened" with the "ego cogito." Had he stayed in it, he would have been able to build all his philosophical insights on such an intuitive-apodictic evidence as the initial "ego cogito." Here is his critique:

> To make all this intelligible it is first necessary to do what was neglected by Descartes, namely, to describe the endless field of the ego's transcendental experience itself. His own experience, as it well known, and especially when he judged it to be apodictic, plays a role in the philosophy of Descartes. But he neglected to describe the ego in the full concretion of its transcendental being and life, nor did he regard it as an unlimited workproject to be pursued systematically.
>
> (1929/1998: 12)

Thus, Descartes has fallen out of the endless field of the ego's transcendental self-experience. But what do those who do not fall out do?

> To be a meditating philosopher who, through the meditations, has himself become a transcendental ego, and who constantly reflects about himself, means to enter upon of [...] [the] endless transcendental experience. It means to refuse to be satisfied with a vague *ego cogito* and instead pursue the steady flux of the *cogito* toward being and life. It means to see all that which is to be seen, to explain it and penetrate it, to encompass it descriptively by concepts and judgements. But these latter must only be terms which have been derived without alteration from their perceptual source.
>
> (1929/1998: 13–14, italics in original)

Or:

> [Contrary to Descartes] we remain true to radicalism in our self-examination and with it to the principle of pure intuition. We must regard nothing as veridical except the pure immediacy and givenness in the field of the *ego cogito* which the *epoche* has opened up to us. In other words, we must not make assertions about that which we do not ourselves *see*.
>
> (1929/1998: 9, italics in original)

Let me summarize. Phenomenology (at least the Husserl-initiated version) intends to assert exhaustive philosophical truths about the nature and phenomenological characteristics of conscious experience. It intends to justify these true propositions infallibly—it tries to trace them all back to an "intuitive fulfillment" (*anschauliche Erfüllung*). Since its justification is always based on intuitive fulfillment, phenomenological justification is inherently internalist. The phenomenologist does not seek to come up with deductive arguments, nor does she intend her phenomenological insights to be taken as premises of philosophical arguments. She tries to stay in the field of experience gained through the two reductions all along, and sees its systematic exploration as the job of his philosophy. Thus, phenomenology is that part of the epistemic tradition of philosophy which breaks with this tradition in that it abandons philosophical arguments, but does so in order to achieve the ultimate goal of this tradition of making philosophy a successful epistemic enterprise, in Husserl's words, "rigorous science."

3 Finishing touches

The epistemic tradition of philosophy cannot be characterized in a completely impartial manner. Obviously, my characterization also has some debatable elements—its focal points can be especially controversial. For example, you can easily think that I have unnecessarily discussed the phenomenological method in detail, because phenomenologists (even if they deny it) argue just as much as other philosophers do, except that they "rename" the consequence relation as intuitive fulfillment.

But there are two more things I need to talk about. One is that you can say that the epistemic value of philosophy as an epistemic enterprise is not only knowledge but also *understanding*. Not only do we want to know how things are, but we also want to understand them. The other thing is that you can also say that my characterization owes an explanation of *what secures the continuity* of the epistemic tradition. The question arises: what is it that determines the persistence of this tradition?

3.1 Philosophical understanding and knowledge

Apart from cases of linguistic understanding (viz. when we understand the meaning of a sentence or set of sentences), and also from the special hermeneutical conceptions of understanding (viz. Dilthey's "understanding as

Nacherleben" and the Heideggerian/Gadamerian "understanding as *Dasein's* mode of being"), we can talk about understanding in two different senses.

On the one hand, we can speak of understanding in the sense of "understanding *why*"—when we understand certain *particular* phenomena. I have in mind things like "*S* understands *why* the bridge collapsed" (because it exploded); "*S* understands *why* his neighbor's arm is plastered" (because he fell off the ladder); "*S* understands *why* his bike doesn't start" (because there's no chain on it). Such cases of understanding are also referred to as "atomistic understanding" (see Pritchard 2009).

On the other hand, we can talk about understanding in the sense of "understanding *how the pieces fit together*." Unlike the former, the latter is a conceptual grasp of some *complex* phenomenon or structure—an insight into how elements of a set of propositions are interrelated, how they are connected to each other. As Jonathan Kvanvig puts it: "to have understanding is to grasp explanatory and conceptual connections between various pieces of information involved in the subject matter in question" (2018: 699). I have in mind instances like these: "*S* understands the foreign policy of the Austro-Hungarian Monarchy" (because she *sees* what the purpose of each measure was and how they were interrelated); "*S* understands movement 4th of Mozart's Jupiter Symphony" (because she *sees* how the abstract musical structure is assembled from the large-scale imitative play of certain musical motifs); "*S* understands the great depression of 1929" (because she *sees* how different social processes led to the collapse of the economy). These cases of understanding are also referred to as "holistic understanding" (see Pritchard 2009).

Now, I see it as follows: if one wishes to, one can characterize the goal of the epistemic tradition in terms of "understanding," but in this case, one must make three basic stipulations.

Firstly, this kind of philosophical understanding *should not be limited* to the understanding of non-substantive philosophical truths. It shouldn't be limited to grasping true propositions of the type "*If* this is so and so, *then* this must be so and so," and to seeing the cost-benefit equations of philosophical theories competing for truth. In other words, philosophical understanding shouldn't be limited to seeing what consistent solutions to different philosophical problems are possible and to overviewing the logical space populated by various philosophical theories. According to the followers of the epistemic tradition, these cases of understanding are important but not enough, as the goal of doing philosophy is to establish the truth of *substantive* philosophical propositions.

Secondly, this kind of philosophical understanding must be *factive* in all of its instances. As applied to "atomistic understanding," this means that "S cannot understand why p if p is false"—"S can understand why p *only* if p is true." And applied to "holistic understanding," this means that "S cannot understand phenomenon X if her beliefs about X are false"—"S can understand X *only* if her beliefs about X are true." That is, this kind of philosophical understanding requires relevant *true* (substantive) *beliefs*. For example: if S believes that objects o_1 and o_2 belong to the same type because they instantiate the same immanent universal, but this belief of S is false (as there are no immanent universals), then S does not understand *why* o_1 and o_2 belong to the same type—S can understand why o_1 and o_2 belong to the same type *only* if her belief that o_1 and o_2 instantiate the same immanent universal is *true*.

Thirdly, this kind of philosophical understanding cannot be *independent of philosophical knowledge* (as compellingly justified true substantive belief). As applied to "atomistic understanding," this means that "S cannot understand why p if she does not know why p"—"S understands why p *only* if she knows why p." And applied to "holistic understanding," this means that "S cannot understand phenomenon X if she knows neither the central propositions $p_1, p_2, p_3 \ldots, p_n$ about X nor how they relate to each other"—"S understands phenomenon X *only* if she knows both that $p_1, p_2, p_3 \ldots, p_n$ and how they relate to each other." Why cannot the followers of the epistemic tradition be satisfied merely with the stipulation that all cases of philosophical understanding must be factive? The reason is that S must be able to *compellingly justify* in the given case that her understanding is *really* factive and is not apparent. As we have seen before, according to the members of this tradition, it is not enough that S knows that p, because S *must also know* that she knows that p. (KK must be met.) Likewise, for the followers of this tradition it is not enough that S's understanding of p is factive, because S also *must know* that her understanding of p is factive. (KFU must be met.) Now, since the assertion that a given case of understanding is really factive needs to be compellingly justified, and since understanding itself (as a mental event) doesn't have any justificatory force, this kind of philosophical understanding *depends* on the appropriate philosophical knowledge.

Of course, many epistemologists of understanding would take exception to the second and third stipulations. According to some of them, there may be cases of understanding that are not factive but are epistemically valuable (e.g., Elgin 2007; Zagzebski 2001), or cases of understanding that have epistemic value independent of knowledge (e.g., Kvanvig 2013; Pritchard 2010). Still, I don't have to deal with these scruples here, as my present task is to characterize the epistemic tradition. And what I want to show is the following: although the followers of this tradition can acknowledge that understanding has a place in the story and has epistemic value, according to them, *the only epistemic value* of doing of philosophy on its *own right* is *knowledge*. And although the goal of the epistemic tradition can be characterized in terms of "understanding," one cannot give a comprehensive definition of it without invoking the concept of knowledge. Here is a possible definition that could perhaps be accepted by the members of the epistemic tradition: the goal of philosophy is to achieve a factive understanding of why things are as they are and not otherwise, and how things are interrelated—*and* also to *know* (and justify compellingly) that this kind of understanding is factive.

3.2 The continuity of the epistemic tradition of philosophy

I think the continuity of the epistemic tradition is based on the continuity of the *philosophical problems* discussed. That is, the followers of this tradition have been discussing *more or less similar* philosophical problems. Neither extreme is right. Nor is the idea of *philosophia perennis*, which says that the historical context of philosophical problems is completely irrelevant, and that *in abstracto* there is a defined set of philosophical problems carved in stone once and for all. Nor is the idea that philosophers respond exclusively to the philosophical challenges of their own times, and consequently philosophical problems cannot be separated at all from the historical context in which they were articulated.

My proposal is to steer a middle course. The historical context of philosophical problems is sometimes (quite) relevant and sometimes (quite) not. Sometimes it can be ignored (without loss), sometimes we have to take it seriously into consideration. The significance of the historical context of philosophical problems comes in degrees.

I don't think it is possible to deny with an impartial mind that, for example, Anselm of Canterbury (in his *Proslogion*) or Thomas Aquinas (in his *Quinque viae*) attempts to do the same (or at least something very similar) as Richard Swinburne did centuries later (see Swinburne 1990); namely to present philosophical arguments for the existence of God as an infinitely perfect, personal, compassionate, and providential being. The difference in their historical contexts—that atheism did not exist in Anselm's and Aquinas' time, while it does in Swinburne's—does not affect their common goal. Neither does the fact that Anselm and Aquinas intended their arguments to be taken as infallible justifications, whereas Swinburne only as a probabilistic (abductive) inference.

I think it is also impossible to deny impartially that Descartes' demon hypothesis and Hilary Putnam's "Brains in a vat" scenario 350 years later *are similar in a relevant way*. They both are based on the conceivability of situations in which the external world does not exist, but these scenarios are subjectively indistinguishable from the one in which it does exist. Descartes and Putman both aim to show that these skeptical scenarios do not or cannot occur. The two scenarios are different in their rhetoric, the arguments are also different, and the skeptical challenge has a different role to play in Descartes' than in Putnam's work. However, they both attempt to refute skepticism—they share their intended conclusion that the mind- and experience-independent world exists.

I don't dispute that the historical context can indeed be important in certain cases. Let's take Plato's theory of forms, which contemporary philosophers take to be a suggested solution to the problem of universals. Plato says: "[T]here are certain forms from which these other things, by getting a share of them, derive their names — as, for instance, they come to be like by getting a share of likeness, large by getting a share of largeness, and just and beautiful by getting a share of justice and beauty" (*Parmenides* 130e–131a). Most contemporary metaphysicians read this passage to mean that if a number of distinct particulars share a property, then they get a share in the same form, i.e., they instantiate the same universal.

Someone could object that the context of Plato's theory of forms is so different from the contemporary one that it makes no historical sense to place it among contemporary metaphysical theories. For example, as opposed to contemporary Platonist realists, Plato's commitment to the existence of forms is conceptually connected to his conviction that the object of knowledge is unchanging (see *Republic* 477a–480a) and, also in opposition to contemporary realists, Plato probably limits his thesis to a certain class of entities by aesthetic-moral considerations, saying that, for example, there are no forms for mud and "anything else totally undignified and worthless" (*Parmenides* 130c–130d).

To this I can only reply that just because the original context of the Theory of Forms is indeed relevantly different from the context of contemporary philosophy, Plato is still a realist. Just because his motivations are different, he still asserts that the type identity of distinct particulars (or at least some of them) is explained by the numerical identity of the appropriate form. The objection is simply based on an exaggeration because, on the appropriate level of abstraction, Plato's solution *is* a solution to the problem of universals. In addition, his view is constantly present in the contest of rival theories.

Another thing about Plato is that it can be seen without any kind of abstraction that what Kebes was eager to find out about by Socrates' deathbed is *exactly the same* question (see *Phaidon* 102b–107b) as the one you would be eager to find out about 2,500 years later if, God forbid, you were standing by your beloved teacher's deathbed—namely, whether the soul of this adored being will go on to live after the death of his body, or everything will become gray and eventually, darkness will take place. If someone keeps on saying that the two historical contexts are different, and so Kebes is interested in something *completely different* than we would be today, they only confirm that they are living in a prison of their own hermeneutic prejudice.

I don't just want to dwell on examples, however. There is a rather negative consequence of the view which denies that philosophers have been dealing with more or less the same problems since the dawn of philosophy—even if there have been new problems born or gone. If there is no continuity in posing philosophical questions but rather, philosophers in every era look for answers to different and unrelated philosophical problems that are completely inseparable from the historical context of their formulation, then what could be the rationale for the history of philosophy? Generally speaking, we have only one reason to engage with the writings of classical authors in the hope of gaining true philosophical benefits instead of pure interest in the history of ideas, namely that we trust that our great ancestors were largely occupied with questions similar to our own.

Overall, then, I think that the *broadly construed* condition of identity (or rather the condition of persistence) of the epistemic tradition is secured by the *broadly construed* identity (more precisely, persistence) of philosophical questions and philosophical problems passed down from generation to generation. I cannot adduce compelling arguments for this thesis, but I think it is the natural and the least partial view.

2

Philosophy as a Failed Epistemic Enterprise

The epistemic failure of philosophy lies in the fact that the followers of philosophy's epistemic tradition have been unable to solve philosophical problems. They could not present well-founded substantive philosophical truths. But they set out to do these things. And since they undertook this task, and since their aspirations were not crowned with success, it is no exaggeration to say that their attempts have failed.

The obvious and indisputable sign of this failure is the permanent disagreement that spreads to all areas of philosophy. For if there is no consensus among philosophers concerning the solutions of philosophical problems, then no philosophical problems have ever been solved. No sane person would call it a solution to a philosophical problem if a group of philosophers said that p was true, another group said that q was true, a third that r was true, and a fourth that s was true whilst p, q, r, and s are mutually incompatible philosophical theses.

All this may seem evident, but in fact, things are not so simple. Let's take the two propositions below:

(1) There is no consensus among philosophers concerning the solutions of philosophical problems.
(2) No philosophical problems have ever been solved.

Proposition (1) merely says that in connection with every philosophical problem, there are at least two (but characteristically more) well-worked-out theories that are incompatible with each other, whose proponents always debate with each other—none of them has succeeded in coming up with any arguments that could convince all sides. In a word, concerning any philosophical problem, there is no consensus among philosophers as to which of the competing theories is true.

Proposition (2) also needs some clarification; (2) doesn't say that *no* philosophers have ever had any *true* substantive philosophical beliefs. Since we can formulate almost every problem of philosophy as a yes-or-no question, and since there were philosophers who said "yes" and, also, philosophers who said "no," it clearly follows that some philosophers were right. If we take the philosophical question "Do immortal souls exist?" or "Do abstract entities exist?" or "Do temporal parts exist?" then either those who thought "Yes, they do" or those who thought "No, they do not" were right. Rather, (2) says that *no* philosophers have ever had *compelling* justification (knock-down arguments or intuitive fulfillments in phenomenology) for the truth of their substantive philosophical beliefs. Hence, *no* philosophers have ever had substantive philosophical *knowledge*—not even those who happen to be "true believers."

Moreover, (2) does not exclude that some philosophers may *know* substantive philosophical theses in the *externalist* sense of knowledge—it is compatible with the possibility that a reliable cognitive process leads to S's belief *p*; that the arguments on the basis of which S believes that *p* track the truth; that S believes in the truth of *p* based on things that make *p* true. However, as we have already seen, the externalist justification of the truth of *p* is not compelling. This is because compelling philosophical justifications would require that we have access to *all* their elements from a first-person perspective (each of their steps must be transparent)—but this condition is not met in the externalist case. Consequently, the externalist knowledge of *p* is not a proper case of philosophical knowledge, and is not the solution to a philosophical problem.

In brief, the solution of a philosophical problem would consist in some philosopher(s) coming up with a compellingly justified substantive philosophical theory, and (2) says that, at least so far, philosophers' efforts have been unsuccessful in this respect.

As for the *relationship* between propositions (1) and (2), they are logically *independent* of each other. From the fact that there is no consensus among philosophers concerning the solutions of philosophical problems, *it does not follow* that a philosopher (or a group of philosophers) has not yet solved any philosophical problem. It is *possible* that a small minority has already solved this or that philosophical problem, and yet no consensus has been reached. So, the essential point is the following: pervasive and permanent philosophical disagreements *do not entail* that some philosophers do not have a compelling justification for their views—it is *possible* that certain "true believer philosophers" have compelling arguments, but the "false-believers" *do not understand* them, and thus are *unable to recognize* their compelling force.

Despite the fact that (1) doesn't logically entail (2), (1) is a *good reason* for accepting (2). Why is that? It is because *if* philosophers have not been able to come up with philosophical arguments in which no points could be disputed by other philosophers (and they haven't), *then* we have every reason to suspect that they have not produced any compelling philosophical arguments—similarly, *if* the community of mathematicians judges a mathematical proof not to be conclusive, *then* we have every reason to suspect that it actually isn't. In other words, insofar as there were compelling philosophical arguments, *then* philosophers *would* recognize their compelling force—similarly to the community of mathematicians recognizing the conclusive force of conclusive mathematical proofs. Or, as Peter van Inwagen puts it: "[i]f any reasonably well-known philosophical argument for a substantive conclusion had the power to convert an unbiased ideal audience to its conclusion (given that it was presented to the audience under ideal conditions), then, to a high probability, assent to the conclusion of that argument would be more widespread among philosophers than assent to any substantive philosophical thesis actually is" (2006: 52–3).

Of course, someone might object that the analogy is wrong, because successful philosophical arguments differ from successful mathematical proofs. Some philosophers may have come up with knock-down philosophical arguments whose comprehension and the recognition of their compelling force requires a kind of intellectual hardware which surpasses most philosophers' abilities *by orders of magnitude*. That is, while some philosophers (thanks to their extraordinary talents) can recognize that this or that philosophical argument is compelling, and so they can recognize that *there are* already solved philosophical problems, most philosophers are unable to do that (due to their substantially more modest abilities).

One can say this, indeed. Moreover, this is, by and large, the only thing that someone could say to give reasons for their reluctance to accept (2) despite their accepting (1). I admit that I cannot present any knock-down arguments for this not being the case. In addition to thinking that there are no philosopher-supermen, and that the above assumption is as implausible as any can be, the most I can say is this: it seems to me that philosophers in dispute with each other understand each other's arguments quite well, they just think that these arguments are bad; and it also seems to me that they perform confidently and well in pointing out the weaknesses of various philosophical arguments.

Let me take a different approach. If X and Y disagree with each other (according to X, p is true, whereas according to Y, not-p is true), then two things may be behind their disagreement. *Either*, it is that neither does X know that p, nor does Y know that not-p. *Or*, it is that while one of them has knowledge, the other is mistaken. By the same token, we can explain the fact of pervasive and permanent philosophical dissensus in two different ways. *Either* there is no consensus among philosophers because philosophical problems are unsolved—*nobody* has ever come up with a compelling justification for the truth of a single substantive philosophical thesis. *Or*, there is no consensus because, although certain philosophical problems have been solved (*some* have managed to come up with compelling arguments), not everyone recognizes the solved philosophical problems as solved and the compelling arguments as compelling.

Now, if we don't think that the majority of philosophers is unable to recognize compelling arguments, and we don't think that philosophers possessing knockdown arguments have intellectual powers that are by far stronger than those of the proponents of rival theories (and, in my opinion, we wouldn't think of either of these), then, in light of (1), we cannot help but accept (2). We must conclude that the supposition that there are no solved philosophical problems *better explains* the fact of pervasive and permanent dissensus than its alternative, namely that there are some solved problems, but not every philosopher recognizes them as such.

In this chapter, I attempt to give a big picture of the failure of the epistemic tradition. Firstly, I illustrate the serious extent of dissensus in philosophy—on virtually any substantive question. In what follows, I discuss whether there has been progress in philosophy, and if so, in which sense of the term—what are the things that we now know but earlier didn't.

Like in the previous chapter, here too, I would only like to assert some platitudes. And it is not easy to do that, just like in the previous chapter. While discussing philosophy's epistemic failure, it is not easy to avoid exaggerations and keep the discussion balanced. Nevertheless, I will try my best to achieve that.

1 A catalog of problems

Let me start with metaphysics, one of the most important areas of philosophy. Firstly, philosophers disagree about *what kind of things there are*. Some philosophers hold that immanent universals exist; entities which can be wholly present at different locations at the same time and more of them can be present at one time in one location in space. Other philosophers deny this—they do not agree that multi-local entities exist. Some philosophers think that we need to introduce abstract entities into our ontology—things that exist outside of spacetime. Others deny this—they do not think we should introduce them. Some philosophers think we should commit ourselves to the existence of possible worlds, while others are anti-realist on this issue. And so on and so forth. If you take the entities posited by philosophers (universals, abstract objects, agents that are not subject to the laws of physics, possible worlds, Cartesian minds [which have no physical properties], tropes, gluons, scattered objects, multi-local particulars, bare dispositions, spatio-temporal parts, arbitrary undetached parts, mentons, gunks, etc.), there is not one of these the existence of which is unanimously agreed on by philosophers. And, vice versa, just think of the kinds of entities which play fundamental roles in our everyday ontology, such as familiar physical objects (desks, chairs, ashtrays) or mental states (beliefs, thoughts, desires)—there is no complete consensus about their existence among philosophers, either. Mereological nihilists deny the existence of the former, while eliminativists deny the existence of the latter.

Secondly, there is disagreement about *what the nature* of the things we consider to exist *consists in*. Let me just give one example. Some philosophers think that physical objects are bundles of universals. Others think they are bundles of tropes, and yet others think that physical objects are not just bundles of properties but also have an additional and separate metaphysical constituent, the substrate. Yet again, others think that physical objects are instances of natural kind universals. There are some who think that the discovery of the nature of physical objects is not the task of metaphysics but of the natural sciences. However, as I mentioned above, there are also quite a few philosophers who deny the existence of familiar physical objects and only commit themselves to that of elemental particles. They think that desks do not exist, only molecules do which are arranged desk-wise.

Thirdly, there is disagreement about *how* the posited kinds of entities (or ontological categories) *are connected to one another*. In other words, there is no agreement even about which other types of entities we must commit ourselves to in consequence of our ontological commitment to a certain type of entity. For example, certain nominalists think that nominalism can only be defended against the counterargument from coextensive properties if one accepts Lewis' genuine modal realism; that is, one may only assert that "There are only particulars and properties do not exist on their own right" if one also asserts that "There are countless other worlds besides our actual world which are categorically identical to this one." Other nominalists do not wish to commit themselves to the plurality of worlds; they think it is too big a price to pay. They think that endorsing nominalism is conceptually independent of endorsing genuine modal realism.

Fourthly, there is also disagreement about *the nature of ontological debates*; there is no consensus among philosophers in meta-ontology either. Some meta-ontologists think that the majority of their ontological debates is verbal—everything depends on how we interpret the existential quantifier. Antirealists accept the thesis of quantifier variance and think that the word "exist" has a number of possible meanings which all play the role of the existential quantifier through certain inferential role properties. In contrast to this, ontological realists claim that although there is a number of possible meanings of the word "exist," it is always interpreted as the so-called "ontologese" language quantifier in ontological debates.

Let's take *epistemology*. Epistemologists disagree about whether in justifying our beliefs about the external world, we should have first-person access to the factors that justify our beliefs or not. Epistemological internalists think that we should, but externalists think that we should not. There is also disagreement about whether there are propositions the truth of which is *a priori* knowable, and if so, whether this can be explained by reference to a semantic fact or a kind of rational intuition. There is no consensus among philosophers about what to do with skeptical arguments concerning the existence of the external world. Should we deny the KK thesis? Or the deductive closure principle? Should we redefine the concept of knowledge perhaps? *Horribile dictu*, shall we concede that skepticism is the right view and admit that we do not have knowledge of the external world?

Consider the *philosophy of language*. Philosophers of language disagree about whether proper names refer via descriptions or without them, directly. The first view is held by those who endorse the description theory of proper names, the second is by those who endorse the direct reference theory. There is no consensus in the fundamental question of whether external factors constitute the meaning of our words and sentences. Semantic internalists think they do not, but semantic externalists think the opposite. Moreover, philosophers of language do not agree about the connection between thought and language either. Some think that language is more basic, others think that thought is more basic, and yet others think that neither have priority.

Let's take the *philosophy of mind*. Philosophers of mind do not agree about whether the existence of conscious experience can be explained within an exclusively physicalist ontology or not. Physicalists disagree about what type of relationship there is between mental and physical properties. Is it identity? Realization? Local supervenience? Global supervenience? Necessary supervenience? Superdupervenience? Constitution? There is also no consensus about what kind of relationship there is between the intentional and the phenomenal properties of conscious experience. Are they independent of each other? This is what separatists think. Or one is more fundamental and the other supervenes on it? This is what prioritists think. But which is more fundamental? According to representationalists, phenomenal properties supervene on intentional properties. Advocates of the theory of phenomenal intentionality have the opposite view, i.e., that it is the intentional properties that supervene on phenomenal ones. Or, perhaps, neither of the above views is correct because these two properties are inextricably bound up. As Colin McGinn puts it:

> [E]xperiences are Janus-faced: they point outward to the external world but they also present a subjective face to their subject: they are of something other than the subject and they are like something for the subject. But these two faces do not wear different expressions: for what the experience is like is a function of what it is of, and what it is of is a function of what it is like.
>
> (1991: 29–30)

Or take *moral philosophy*. Moral philosophers disagree about whether we should define the concept of a morally right action in terms of duties or in terms of consequences. They also disagree about whether the "could have done otherwise" condition is necessary for free will and hence for moral responsibility, or we should assign responsibility even in cases where the person could not have done otherwise. There is disagreement about the extent to which we are (if at all) responsible for our emotions, personality, and beliefs. Moreover, moral philosophers do not even agree about which property renders an act morally evaluable, i.e., what the difference between morally neutral and non-neutral acts consists in. They also disagree whether moral reasons override any kind of other reasons, not to mention the fact that they disagree about what "morality" means in the first place.

Let's turn to *political philosophy*. Political philosophers disagree about why we have political obligations or to put it differently: where does the sovereign's power come from to exercise sanctions on those who fail to fulfil their obligations? Does it come from divine authority? Or from natural superiority? Or is it derived from greater knowledge or expertise? Or, if we skip these old explanations: do we have political obligations because we choose the rules in our "original position" ourselves and accept them as binding? (This is the principle of consent.) Or is it because if the state provides education, healthcare, and public utilities, then we have to reciprocate? (This is the principle of reciprocity.) Political philosophers fail to agree about the extent of the role the state needs to assume in order to relieve inequalities. Some think they do not have to assume any such role, while others think that the role of the state is significant. Those who think it has a significant role disagree about what kind of equality we should establish. That of resources? Opportunities? Capabilities?

Now, let's look at the *philosophy of science*. It is worth dividing the philosophical problems of science into two groups: general and special. As for the former: there is no consensus among philosophers of science about what the correct answer to the problem of induction is, nor about what the correct interpretation of the term "law of nature" is, nor about what the scientific explanation of a phenomenon looks like at all. Or consider the problem of the metaphysical status of unobservable entities (quarks, strings, black matter, etc.). According to realists, observable entities provide sufficient indirect evidence for the existence of unobservable entities, and consequently, scientific theories should be seen as describing this "unobservable world." By contrast, anti-realists (or instrumentalists) say we have no good reason to commit ourselves to the existence of unobservable entities, and consequently, scientific theories are merely useful tools (useful fictions). As for the special problems: there is no consensus among philosophers of physics about whether a determinist or indeterminist interpretation of quantum mechanics is the correct one, nor about whether space-time points exist and whether a wave function collapse exists. But to mention other areas than the philosophy of physics: there is disagreement among philosophers of biology as to what the basic unit of natural selection is. Some say it is the gene, others say it is the cell, yet others say it is the organism, and, according to others, it is the group.

Or consider the *philosophy of art*. Philosophers of art disagree about whether the concept of a work of art can be defined, i.e., if necessary and sufficient conditions can be given of something being a work of art. They also disagree about the property which makes something a work of art. Moreover, they hold different views about the metaphysical status of works of art. Are they universals? Physical particulars? Mental particulars? Abstract particulars? Events? Or perhaps do some artworks belong to one category and other artworks to others? They fail to agree on whether, while interpreting a work of art, we should take into consideration the author's intentions and if so, to what extent. Not to mention some minor issues such as: "Does the consumption of works of art contribute to the development of our self-knowledge?"; "Is there a difference between popular and high art?"

And the list is not finished. The most peculiar thing is that there is no consensus within *phenomenology*, that is, about establishing phenomenological facts. The reason why this is so peculiar is that because one has first-person access to the phenomenal characteristics of conscious experience, you might think that there can be no differences among different phenomenologists' reports—but there are. On the one hand, Berkeley describes the phenomenology of auditory experience as follows:

> For instance, when I hear a coach drive along to streets, immediately I perceive only the sound; but from the experience I have had that such a sound is connected with a coach, I am said to hear the coach. It is nevertheless evident, that in truth and strictness, nothing can be *heard* but *sound*: and the coach in not then properly perceived by sense, but only suggested from experience.
>
> (1713/1998: 194, italics in original)

Heidegger, on the other hand, says:

> What we "first" hear is never noises or complexes of sounds, but the creaking wagon, the motor-cycle. We hear the column on the march, the north wind, the woodpecker tapping, the fire crackling. It requires a very artificial and complicated frame of mind to "hear" a "pure noise". The fact that motor-cycles and wagons are what we proximally hear is the phenomenal evidence that in every case Dasein, as Being-in-the-world, already dwells *alongside* what is ready-to-hand within-the-world; it certainly does not dwell proximally alongside "sensation"; nor would it first have to give shape to the swirl of sensation to provide the springboard from which the subject leaps off and finally arrives at a "world".
>
> (1927/1962: 207, italics in original)

Do I need to comment? I don't think so. Let's look at anxiety. Most certainly, there is something that it is like to be anxious (anxiety has a definite phenomenal character), which is why you might think there can be no differences among the phenomenological descriptions of anxiety—but there are. Searle for one sees it in the following way: "Beliefs, fears, hopes, and desires are Intentional; but there are forms of nervousness, elation, and undirected anxiety that are not Intentional" (1983: 1). Tim Crane, however, says:

> The cases Searle mentions are not cases where one is anxious for another: otherwise it would be directed anxiety. So the intentionalist will say that these are cases where one is anxious for oneself—so in these cases, one's anxiety is directed upon oneself. Being anxious in this way is a matter of having a certain attitude to oneself and one's position in the world: it is to regard the world, for example, as a potentially disturbing place for oneself. This is one way in which anxiety exhibits directedness. And it is an alternative to seeing Searle's cases as examples of mental states which are directed on nothing, as Searle does.
>
> (1998: 241–2)

And here is what Heidegger says about the same subject:

> That anxiety reveals the nothing man himself immediately demonstrates when anxiety has dissolved. In the lucid vision sustained by fresh remembrance we must say that that in the face of which and for which we were anxious was "really" — nothing. Indeed: the nothing itself — as such — was there [...] The nothing reveals itself in anxiety — but not as a being. Just as little is it given as an object. Anxiety is no kind of grasping of the nothing. All the same, the nothing reveals itself in and through anxiety, although, to repeat, not in such a way that the nothing becomes manifest in our malaise quite apart from beings as a whole. Rather we said that in anxiety the nothing is encountered at one with beings as a whole.
>
> (1929/1993: 101–2)

I think that this obscure passage says that the intentional object of anxiety is the nothing (or nothingness), if what we mean by intentional object is "something" which appears or is manifested to us from the first-person perspective. But even if it says something else (and that is a possibility), it definitely says something different to Searle and Crane, as, in contrast to them, he connects the phenomenology of anxiety to the concept of nothingness.

Or, let's turn to the question of whether cognitive phenomenology exists. Those who think it does say that "there is something it is like to think a conscious thought" (Pitt 2004: 2), and this means that "what it is like to think a conscious thought is distinct from what it is like to be in any other kind of conscious mental state, that what it is like to think the conscious thought that p is distinct from what it is like to think any other conscious thought" (Pitt 2004: 2). Those who think there is no cognitive phenomenology believe that there is nothing it is like to think a conscious thought. If we experience something during an act of thinking, then it is not the act (or this act plus the content) itself that has what-it-is-likeness but the connected emotions and other par excellence phenomenally conscious states.

Let me spend more time on this phenomenological problem. Even the fact itself is peculiar that there are differences in views in phenomenology, but this case—if possible—is even more curious. The question here is not *what kind of* phenomenological marks a conscious mental act has, but simply whether a conscious mental act has *any kind of* phenomenal character or what-it-is-likeness. If we agree on anything, this should be it. We might think that the answer to this question must be either "Yes, *trivially* there is cognitive phenomenology," or "No, *trivially*, there is no cognitive phenomenology"—yet there is dissensus about it.

Some philosophers try to argue that there is cognitive phenomenology by pointing out the inherent phenomenal properties of acts of thinking. They provide a strange sentence that one cannot understand at first reading (or hearing), and then ask the reader (or listener) to make an effort to understand it. Once that happens, they say: "WHAT you experienced when you understood the sentence after making a small effort *is* the phenomenal character of thinking the thought at issue." In brief, they identify the phenomenology of thinking the thought expressed by the sentence with the experience of understanding the sentence.

Terence Horgan and John Tienson (2002) present such an argument. Let's take the sentence: "Dogs dogs dog dog dogs." Native English speakers cannot understand this at first sight. In order to understand it, they have to be asked to take one token of the word "dog" as a verb. If they do so, they will understand the sentence, and so will experience the inherent phenomenal character of thinking the thought expressed by it, according to Horgan and Tienson. Their argument is this: since one reads the same sentence several times in a row, only the inherent phenomenal features of an act of understanding a thought can distinguish between the cases of non-understanding and understanding—thus, cognitive phenomenology exists.

However, a possible objection can go along these lines: the rhythm or the prosody of the sentence could contribute to the experience of understanding the above sentence. So, it is better for the advocates of cognitive phenomenology to bring up rabbit/duck type grammatical ambiguities. For example, they could say "Hunting lions can be dangerous." It could either mean "If you hunt lions, they can attack you," or "If hunting lions attack you, you could be in trouble." This rabbit/duck sentence has the same rhythm and prosody when uttered, yet it will have different phenomenal characters depending on what one means by it.

I used the above example to demonstrate that even where you would *most* expect consensus among philosophers (about whether a mental event has phenomenology or not), they have failed to produce one. Needless to say, many philosophers reject Horgan and Tienson's argument—what is more, they think that arguments that employ such ostensive definitions are fundamentally flawed and cannot be taken seriously.

And finally (the icing on the cake), there is a disagreement between philosophers about the *epistemology of disagreement*—including disagreements among philosophers themselves. This question No. $n + 1$ sounds like this: "Can I rationally stick to the truth of proposition p if (1) I know that there are people who think *p is* false; if (2) in my view, these people are my epistemic peers; and if (3) despite the recognized disagreement, it still seems to me that *p is* true?"

There are two opposing camps on this issue. Proponents of conciliationism claim that I should suspend my belief in the truth of *p*, or at least reassess the epistemic status of my belief in the truth of *p* (see e.g., Christensen 2007; Elga 2007; Feldman 2006). In a nutshell, the basic consideration is this: the fact that someone who I recognize as my epistemic peer disagrees with me about the truth of *p has just as much weight as evidence* for me to think that I myself am wrong as the evidence (or set of evidences) on which I originally committed myself to the truth of *p*. By contrast, proponents of the steadfast view claim that I should not suspend my belief in the truth of *p*—I can still rationally stick to the truth of *p* (see e.g., Huemer 2011; Schafer 2015; Wedgwood 2010). In a nutshell, one of the most obvious consideration for it is the following: the fact that someone disagrees with me about the truth of *p* (even if I recognize this person as my epistemic peer) *is not such a great deal* as the evidence on which I originally committed myself to the truth of *p*—the original evidence (or set of evidences) *has more epistemic weight* than what my opponent believes.

This philosophical question No. $n + 1$ is inherently related to other questions as well. For example, to the question "Can there be only one rational doxastic attitude belonging to evidential base E, or can there be more than one such attitudes?" There is no consensus among philosophers about the answer to the latter question either. According to uniquists, there can be only one (see e.g., Greco and Hedden 2016; Matheson 2011; White 2013), whereas according to permissivists there can be several (see e.g., Ballantyne and Coffman 2011; Frances 2014; Kelly 2010). It is easy to see that commitment to uniquism goes hand in hand with conciliationism, whereas commitment to permissivism with the steadfast view. Here is why: if, as a uniquist, I take it for granted that (1) only one rational doxastic attitude can belong to a set of evidences E (or to the total body of evidence), and (2) E is for the truth of *p* and for the truth of not-*p to the same degree*, then I must suspend my belief in the truth of *p*, because the total body of evidence is, in the final analysis, not in favor of *either* option. By contrast, if, as a permissivist, I take it for granted that more than one rational doxastic attitudes can belong to a set of evidences E (or the total body of evidence), then I can rationally stick to the truth of *p*—even though I must concede that *others* can rationally stick to the truth of *not-p*.

Again, this philosophical question No. $n + 1$ is inherently related to the question "When can we say truthfully that two or more people are epistemic peers?" If we don't count as an accurate answer that Hansel and Gretel are epistemic peers if they rely on more or less the same evidential base and have more or less the same argumentative-cognitive skills and have more or less the same resilience to biases, then we cannot speak of consensus about this issue either. All the more so, because according to some philosophers (see e.g., King 2012) in fact we have almost never any good reasons to judge that our interlocutor in a debate is our epistemic peer—rather, we have good reason to suppose that he or she is not so knowledgeable or competent as we ourselves are.

***

Some may now think that I have used a disproportionate number of examples, and I'm afraid that my catalog has been boring. Nevertheless, I see it as having a *sobering* effect when we look at the huge number of philosophical problems towering before us—*unsolved*. The reason I have brought up so many examples is that the abundance of disagreements in philosophy is shocking. This abundance has a *meaning*, just like it has a meaning if someone has just one suit or a whole cupboard full of them.

One last comment. If you have any reservations about the above catalog of problems, saying that I put it together in an armchair, I suggest that you browse two studies by David Bourget and David Chalmers, if you have not already done so (see 2014, 2021). In them, you can read the results of a survey conducted by the co-authors using empirical methods about what philosophers believe. According to the thousands of questionnaires filled out and analyzed, "there is [...] no consensus on the answer to most major philosophical questions" (2014: 31)—philosophers have very different views on various substantive philosophical questions. In addition, in the two studies you can read a great overview of which philosophical issues are such that there is more (or less) disagreement about them, and you can also find out which philosophical views typically go hand in hand with each other. Finally, you may even be faced with the fact that "philosophers hold [...] false beliefs about their colleagues' views" (2014: 29)—they quite often misjudge which the majority belief and which the minority belief is about each philosophical problem.

2 Progress in philosophy

Speaking about an epistemic enterprise, we can say that it makes progress if the players of the enterprise *did not yet* know that *p* at t_1, *but already know* that *p* at t_2. Now, if we consider that philosophers belonging to the epistemic tradition undertook to solve philosophical problems and come up with compelling philosophical arguments for their substantive theses, then it is clear that philosophy *has not made any progress* for the last 2,500 years. One cannot say that philosophers did not yet know how to solve such and such philosophical problem at t_1, but they already know that at t_2—since they have not solved any substantive philosophical problems, and have not come up with any compellingly justified substantive thesis. In short, the community of philosophers has no substantive philosophical knowledge.

As a starting point, let me recall Eric Dietrich's thought experiment. The scenario is the following: Aristotle crops up at a university in the twenty-first century. He goes to a physics lecture first, where he hears about gravity and about how people went to the Moon, and how planets orbit on an elliptic course. He hears about how the same laws of nature govern the "sublunar" and the "supralunar" world, i.e., throughout the universe. Following this, he goes to a biology lecture. He hears about the theory of evolution, genetics, and cells. He hears about inheritance and different biochemical processes, and is shocked by what he hears. He has to admit that the science of this age has long surpassed the science of his. He then goes to a metaphysics and ethics course. Dietrich thinks something like the following happens in there:

> Here he hears the professor lecturing about essences, about being qua being, about the most general structures of our thinking about the world. He knows exactly what the professor is talking about. Aristotle raises his hand to discuss some errors the professor seems to have made, and some important distinctions that he has not drawn. As the discussion proceeds, the metaphysics professor is a bit taken aback but also delighted at this (older) student's acumen and insight. Then Aristotle goes to an ethics class, where he learns of the current importance of what is apparently called "virtue ethics". He recognizes it immediately, but again, the professor seems to have left out some crucial details and failed to see some deeper aspects of the view. Aristotle raises his hand …
>
> (2011: 334)

How it is possible that as opposed to physics and biology, Aristotle would be a competent partner in metaphysical and ethical debates? Dietrich thinks it is because of the following:

> Only one thing: *Philosophy doesn't progress.* Yes, it morphs and transforms to stay current. Our metaphysics today is not Aristotle's metaphysics. Ours is populated, for example, with *possible worlds*, whose existence is bolstered by a robust and large family of logics that Aristotle couldn't have imagined. Our

metaphysics contains ideas like *supervenience*, which is used to explain, among other things, the relationship between mind and brain and the relationship between consciousness and brain. But more important, our metaphysics is for us. It is written in our language *for* us to communicate our twenty-first century ideas in. But that's all; that's the extent of the "progress". The ideas and theories are new or couched in modern language, but no real progress is made, none.

(2011: 335–6, italics in original.)

And even more sharply:

Philosophy *does not even stumble forward*. Philosophy *does not move forward at all*. It is the *exactly the same today as it was 3000 years ago*; indeed, as it was from the beginning. What it does do is stay current; philosophers confuse this with advancing, with making progress. Staying current is not moving forward any more that staying up on the latest fashions or music is movement toward greater social justice.

(2011: 332, italics mine)

I think Dietrich's view is simplifying, distorting, and shows a lack of sensitivity to finer details. Despite the fact that, like him, I find philosophy to be a failed epistemic enterprise, I don't think that philosophy is treading water and that we know *nothing more* than our predecessors did. This is just as unbelievable and unrealistic as thinking that a philosopher at the height of his career knows *nothing more* than when he first started out.

Put differently, *pace* Dietrich, I'm saying that *there are* philosophical propositions which we did not yet know at t_1, but already know at t_2. On the one hand, we have come to know many non-trivial and non-substantive philosophical truths, and on the other, we have come to know that certain substantive philosophical theories or theses are false.

2.1 Successes

First of all, Dietrich ignores that we can identify philosophical problems more precisely than our predecessors, which means that we see the structure of philosophical problems more clearly and in a finer-grained way—and we have worked out numerous new suggested solutions to these problems.

Let's take the problem of moral responsibility and free will for example. Here is a possible reconstruction of this problem:

P_1: All fully developed human beings are morally responsible for their actions in everyday situations.

P_2: People can have excuses. If someone can prove that their action is a result of (bad) luck or external force, then they cannot be held responsible for their action at issue.

P_3: Events are either determined or indetermined, so all actions are also either determined or indetermined.

P_4: If an action is indetermined, it is a matter of luck.

P_5: If an action is determined, then it was brought about by some external force.

These propositions are jointly inconsistent—I will not show this here, as it is trivial. Furthermore, I think that all of these propositions are "epistemically attractive"—we would tend to hold each of them to be true, were it not for the fact that they are inconsistent with one another. Furthermore, concerning this problem, I think it would be convenient to categorize different philosophical theories—independent of their finer details—based on which of the above propositions they reject and for what reason they reject them.

P_1 is rejected by two theories: *hard determinism and hard incompatibilism*. According to the former view, we are not responsible for our actions because the world is deterministic, and so all actions are brought about by external forces (see e.g., Honderich 1988; Wegner 2002). According to the latter, we are not responsible for anything in the moral sense because if the world is indeterministic, then everything happens by chance, but if it is deterministic, then everything is brought about by external forces (see e.g., Pereboom 2014).

P_2 is rejected by theories that hold that it does not follow from the fact that external forces or chance play a decisive role in all actions that agents could be exempted from responsibility.

One such theory is *semi-compatibilism*. It says that while it is true that all our actions are determined because past events and the laws of nature jointly "make" them happen, it does not mean that the agent always has the same role in executing actions. There are deterministic processes in which agents participate in a morally autonomous manner, even if external forces exclude the possibility that they can act otherwise than they actually do. Thus, semi-compatibilists think that free will (the ability to act otherwise) is not a precondition of moral responsibility. It is enough for moral responsibility if the agent has acted the way he did or refrained from action because of the appropriate (i.e., reason-sensitive) psychological process (see e.g., Fischer 2007; Fischer and Ravizza 1998; Mele

1995); or if the action in question appropriately reflects the morally relevant aspects of the agent's self (see e.g., Frankfurt 1971; Scanlon 1998, 2008; Smith 2005). Instead of the decisions and actions themselves, the former strategy considers the deliberation leading up to the decision as the main source of moral responsibility, while the latter considers the morally relevant attitudes, dispositions, desires, and other mental states as relevant. According to semi-compatibilists then, agents cannot be exempted from responsibility based merely on the deterministic/indeterministic nature of the world because they are definitely responsible for the relevant mental processes and/or states leading up to them (at least, in most cases).

Like semi-compatibilist, consequentialist theories of responsibility (such as revisionism, see e.g., Vargas 2013) also denies that deterministic external forces exempt from responsibility on all occasions. They are convinced that we should hold people morally responsible for their deeds and traits whenever moral blame and praise would produce appropriate good consequences such as positive character-change.

However, p_2 is not only denied by semi-compatibilism and consequentialist approaches but also by *event-libertarianism*. Event-libertarians—as opposed to semi-compatibilists but alike to consequentialists—view decisions and actions as the central objects of moral responsibility. They think that just because actions are indeterministic and their outcomes are chancy in some sense, agents remain responsible for their decisions and the consequences thereof—provided that the chance enters the decision process "in the right place" (see e.g., Balaguer 2004; Franklin 2018; Kane 1996; Mele 2006; Nozick 1981). Kane (1996), for one, thinks that if the agent would like to carry out two kinds of action in a certain situation, the action can still remain free if it is up to chance which volition takes over the other accidentally.

P_3 is primarily rejected by *non-causal libertarian* theories. The advocates of these theories think that there are actions without any cause whatsoever. So, we cannot say about any of these actions either that they are the results of indeterministic or deterministic causal processes. (Which is also why these authors use the phrase "undetermined" and not "indetermined" free action.) These actions should be explained by reference to reasons instead of causes—in other words, it is not reasons which cause or compel the choice of a rational agent but he chooses in light of reasons, so to speak (see e.g., Ginet 1990; Lowe 2008; Pink 2017). This means that the agent does not cause the decision but rather brings it forth, and the decisions that cannot be explained causally are the sources of free will and responsibility as basic actions.

P_4 is most vehemently denied by *agent-causal libertarianism* (see e.g., Chisholm 1966; Clarke 2003; O'Connor 2000). According to the advocates of this view, freely formed intentions or freely executed actions have no (or only partially have) events as their causes but the agent himself, seen as a substance. As Randolph Clarke (2003) puts it: inasmuch as the agent as a substance is the direct cause of the intention or action at issue, then this intention or action can hardly be explained with reference to chance in any sense. And this is true even if the causal action of the agent as a substance has not been determined previously.

P_5 is rejected by *traditional compatibilist* theories. Traditional compatibilist philosophers think that, even though free actions are predetermined, their course is not determined by any external force which would compel it, since agents could have acted otherwise despite determination (see e.g., Ayer 1954/1972; Huoranszki 2011; Moore 1912). As they say, the key to free will and moral responsibility is that the following conditional is true: "Agent S could have acted otherwise, had he decided otherwise." It is easy to see that this conditional can be true even if our world happens to be ruled by deterministic laws.

As far as I can see, no important theory is left out of this taxonomy and they can all be categorized on the basis of which proposition out of the above five the proponents of a given theory give up and why. Now, since we did not see the structure of the problems this clearly before, and since we did not know so many possible suggested solutions, this is undeniably progress—*we came to know* something at t_2 that we did not know yet at t_1.

Secondly, Dietrich fails to consider that while we did not know numerous "if …, then …" type philosophical propositions at t_1, we do know these at t_2, and while we were not aware of the *cost-benefit* equations of the potential suggested solutions of philosophical problems at t_1, we do know these at t_2.

Let's take the mind-body problem as an illustration of this. Similar to the problem of free will, this problem is also made up of jointly inconsistent propositions. Here's the well-known proposition triad:

P_1: Conscious experiences are not physical events.

P_2: Conscious experiences can cause physical events.

P_3: Every physical event has a sufficient physical cause.

Let me begin with this: while we did not know at t_1, we do know at t_2 how the inconsistency between these propositions can be dissolved. For instance, *if* we claim that every single human action is (redundantly and systematically) overdetermined, i.e., every single human action has a sufficient mental cause and a numerically different sufficient physical cause, *then* p_1, p_2, and p_3 will not be inconsistent with each other—we can stick to all of them without getting into contradictions. Or, *if* we claim that conscious experiences cause physical events in a different sense than physical events do, meaning that we deny the homogeneity of mental and physical causes, *then* p_1, p_2, and p_3 will not be inconsistent with each other—we can stick to all of them without running into contradictions (see e.g., Crane 1995 about these "if ..., then ..."s).

Furthermore, in the case of the mind-body problem, while we did not know at t_1, we do know at t_2 what kind of benefit and cost it has if we deny one of the three propositions while we stick to the truth of the other two.

I will only mention one possibility for the sake of simplicity. Let's assume that out of the three, we accept p_2 and p_3 and reject p_1. Let's also assume that we reject p_1 in the spirit of the type-identity theory—we claim that types of conscious experience are identical to types of physical events (see e.g., Armstrong 1968; Lewis 1966). If this is what we do, then we have the benefit of being able to explain mental causation—all the way, since our view will definitely not be threatened by the specter of epiphenomenalism. At the same time, if we do this, then it will have the cost of having to respond to hardcore anti-physicalist arguments according to which it is not possible to place conscious experiences within a purely physicalist ontology; we have to come up with a plausible error theory that shows that the "gap" between phenomenal and physical phenomena is purely illusory and we have to say something against the multiple realization thesis—and none of these is an easy task.

Thirdly, Dietrich also ignores the fact that the different philosophical theories have undergone *internal* progress—they were supported by weaker arguments at t_1 and stronger ones at t_2. I think it's hard to deny that if a philosophical theory put forward by a great dead philosopher has contemporary supporters, then they certainly advocate the theory at issue much more forcefully than its original author did. For example, David Armstrong is a better and more consistent Aristotelian with regard to immanent universals than Aristotle was, and Peter van Inwagen is a better and more consistent Aristotelian than Aristotle was regarding primary substances as described in the *Categories* (see Armstrong 1978, 1997; van Inwagen 1990).

Or, let's take one of the current rival views of the ontological status of physical objects, substrate theory, according to which physical objects have a further constituent that is fundamentally distinct from their properties, the substrate (which bears the properties). This theory was first put forward by Locke, and his only argument for it was that without appealing to the concept of substrate, it would be impossible to explain the fact that the properties of physical objects are held together (Locke 1689/1996: 2, 23, 1–2). Now, it is easy to see that the argument made by later advocates of substrate theory is much stronger (see e.g., Allaire 1963/1998). For example, they claim that one should commit oneself to the existence of substrates in order to be able to explain the particularity of objects that are type-identical. For if two or more numerically distinct objects have the exact same intrinsic properties, then they cannot (obviously) be individuated by making reference to them. Since, however, they have a further metaphysical constituent (the substrate), they can be individuated by making reference to it.

All this is undeniable progress. The latter example shows clearly that Locke's arguments for the substrate theory are not the best ones (and also that Berkeley's arguments are not the best ones against it)—and while we did not know this at t_1, we do at t_2.

Fourthly, Dietrich also forgets that many conceptual relations were revealed among different philosophical problems as time went by, and while we did not know them at t_1, we do at t_2 (see Jackson 2017 on this).

Here's one example. While the inherent relationship between the concepts of temporality and modality was not known at t_1, it became clear at t_2. I'm thinking of the following. When a genuine modal realist says that every possible world exists in the same way as our actual world, he takes the word "actual" to be an indexical, as it simply picks out our world, but it does not refer to any entities of special ontological status. Now, this is inherently related to the case when the eternalist says that the present, past, and the future exist and the word "present" is indexical, as it simply picks out the moment when the speaker is speaking, but does not refer to any entities of special ontological status (see e.g., Lewis 1986). Or, from the other direction: when the actualist (to be more exact, the modal ersatz-realist) says that there are no non-actual worlds, only the actual world exists and so "actual" is not merely indexical, as it refers to the ontologically special actual world, this is inherently related to the case when the presentist says that the past and the future do not exist, only the present does, so "present" is not merely indexical, as it refers to the ontologically special present (see e.g., Crisp 2003; Rea 2003).

Fifthly, (and finally), Dietrich also ignores the fact that we can list quite a few substantive philosophical theories and theses such that there was consensus about their falsity at one point of time. And this is progress, too—whereas we did not know at t_1 that not-p, we do know at t_2 that not-p. As Peter van Inwagen says: "There are no knock-down arguments or demonstrations or proofs in philosophy — not at any rate of substantive, positive theses" (2020: 11) and "If there is any philosophical theses that all or most philosophers affirm, it is a *negative thesis*: that formalism is *not* the right philosophy of mathematics, for example, or that knowledge is *not* (simply) justified, true belief" (van Inwagen 2004: 334–5, italics mine).

But here are some more examples: while we did not know at t_1, we do know at t_2 that Augustine's theory of first language learning is *wrong*. Or: while we did not know at t_1, we do know at t_2 that Descartes' theory of mind-body interaction is *wrong*. Another example: while we did not know at t_1, we do know at t_2 that La Mettrie was *wrong* when he interpreted humans as mechanical clockworks. And another one: while we did not know at t_1, we do know at t_2 that Condillac's sensualism, according to which apart from sensory perception itself, all our capabilities develop from sensory perception, is *wrong*. Or: while we did not know at t_1, we do know at t_2 that Leibniz's thesis that "Every true statement is analytic" is *wrong*. Here are two other more recent examples. The first one: while we did not know at t_1, we do know at t_2 that logical behaviorism is an *untenable* view of the human mind. The second one: while we did not know at t_1, we do know at t_2 that emotivism is an *untenable* metaethical theory. Not only does this list contain some other examples but also, I'm rather sure that the community of philosophers will establish consensus on the falsity of other philosophical theories in the future.

2.2 How we should not evaluate these successes—and how we should

The proposition that philosophers have not solved any substantive philosophical problems doesn't entail that there is no progress in philosophy. My aim in the previous section was just to show that—*pace* Dietrich—philosophy does not stagnate, since we know a lot of things we didn't know earlier. Those philosophers who think otherwise are probably deceived because they are focusing their attention *exclusively* on unsolved philosophical problems, and so they lose sight of the many things that they indeed know. As Rebecca Goldstein puts it:

> Philosophical progress is invisible because it is incorporated into our points of view [...] We don't see it, because we see with it.
>
> (2014: 14)

However, it's important to handle these enumerated developments in their right place—we must neither underestimate nor overestimate their significance. On the one hand, it would be short-sighted to deny that philosophers have acquired numerous non-trivial and non-substantive philosophical propositions about which they had no idea before—put into the terminology of "understanding" instead of "knowing", all this means that we understand philosophical problems and their relations to each other *better* than before. On the other hand, we mustn't overestimate the knowledge of these non-trivial and non-substantive philosophical propositions, and above all we mustn't see in these developments a proof of philosophy's success as an epistemic enterprise—since the community of philosophers has not managed to acquire *substantive* philosophical truths, even though this clearly is the goal of the members of the epistemic tradition.

Also, it is difficult to dispute the claim that there are philosophical theories and theses that came to be discredited by the community of philosophers over time. This, too, is undoubtedly progress: earlier we did not know that they are false, but now we already know that they are. Nevertheless, I would warn everyone not to exaggerate the significance of our being able to pick out philosophical theories and theses that are consensually considered false, and not to see them as discredited once and for all or hail their recognition as a great philosophical insight. For this is deceptive, as knowing that something is not in a certain way does not mean knowing how (in what way) it is—and *solving* a philosophical problem clearly means knowing *how something* is and not how it is not.

It seems to me that many consider the discreditation of philosophical theories as real progress in philosophy, since, they think, the filtered-out theories are no longer "living" choices, and this filtering out narrows down the range of possible philosophical theories, which counts as progress in any problem-solving process. But those who think so forget that in the course of its history, philosophy excelled the most in using more and more established "if ..., then ..."-type non-substantive philosophical truths to populate the logical space with more and more consistent theories that are immune to objections, and consequently it did not actually narrow down the range of rival philosophical theories vying for truth. In fact, the opposite happened: concerning most problems of philosophy, there are significantly more "living" philosophical theories in circulation today than there were before.

Aware of the pervasive and permanent disagreement in philosophy, David Chalmers wrote that there are "glass-half-full" and "glass-half-empty" views concerning the question "Is there progress in philosophy?" (2015: 3). I don't really feel the aptness of this "glass-half-full" vs. "glass-half-empty" metaphor. For if we look at the goal of philosophy's epistemic tradition and think that the goal of philosophy is to establish substantive and positive philosophical truths, then that glass is not half full, nor even *half empty*—there is nothing slopping at its bottom. Conversely, if we look at a metaphilosophical vision with more modest ambitions than the goal of the epistemic tradition, and think that philosophy cannot do more than to increasingly populate the logical space with consistent philosophical theories that are immune against knock-down objections, then again, that glass is also not half empty, but it is not even *half full*—it is almost brimming over with the philosophical "juice."

2.3 Delusional optimism

Perhaps the sharpest contrast to the (pessimistic) vision presented above is Daniel Stoljar's (optimistic) vision (2017a, 2017b, 2017c). According to him, "there is progress in philosophy if and only if—that is, not merely if—the questions of philosophy or *suitably related questions* have been answered in the past and it is reasonable to suppose that such questions will be answered in the future" (2017a: 25, italics in original). And he thinks, yes! "some [philosophical] problems have been solved, and we have a reasonable expectation that more (though not all) will be solved in the future" (2017a: 7).

Below, I will first briefly explore Stoljar's optimistic vision, and then explain why I think it paints a false picture of philosophical progress.

According to Stoljar, the common (and false) premise of all pessimistic views about the success of philosophy as an epistemic enterprise and philosophical progress is that the philosophers dealt with the *same* philosophical problems for centuries. Plato dealt with the same problem (the "One over Many") as, for example, David Armstrong (1997); Aristotle dealt with the same problem (the nature of substances) as, for example, David Wiggins (2001); Descartes dealt with the same problem (the mind-body problem) as, for example, Frank Jackson (1982, 1986).

Now, if we accept this "identity view," we will inevitably become pessimistic, according to Stoljar. As he puts it:

> The identity view makes pessimism almost inevitable. After all, Jackson's problem is an open question; philosophers of mind are currently discussing various answers to it, and no consensus has been reached. If it is an open question, however, and if it is identical to Descartes's problem, then Descartes's problem must be open too. But if that is an open question, the history of the mind-body problem is the history of an open question with no progress being made.
>
> (2017b)

By contrast:

> [S]uppose now we reject the identity view. Then the issue of progress looks completely different. For one thing, if Jackson's problem and Descartes's problem are distinct, it doesn't follow that the latter is open if the former is. Hence the simple argument for pessimism I just set out goes away. Moreover, if they are distinct, it is open to us to argue that Descartes's is a solved problem, even if Jackson's is not. And if that is so, we may begin to see discussion of the mind-body problem over the years as in many ways like discussion in other fields: earlier problems raised and solved, contemporary problems still wide open.
>
> (Stoljar 2017b)

According to Stoljar, we must distinguish between three kinds of philosophical questions:

> On the one hand, there are questions that — to put it a bit vaguely — introduce or define or constitute a topic or subject matter — *topic questions*, as I will call them for short. On the other hand, there are questions that outline particular lines of inquiry (whether big or small) within a given topic [...]
>
> If we distinguish the topics or subject matter of philosophy from the big questions that can be asked about those topics, it is certainly hard to deny that philosophers in the twentieth and twenty-first centuries are in many cases discussing the same topics or subject matters as those in the seventeenth. Both Jackson and Descartes, for example, are (in the relevant parts of their works) concerned with the relation of the mental to the physical; they are not making a contribution to mathematics, after all, or trying to compose a symphony. But it doesn't follow that they are asking the same big questions about that subject matter. And indeed, if we pay only a small amount of attention to what they say it becomes quite implausible to suppose that they are.
>
> (2017a: 12–13, italics in original)

According to this, on the one hand, there are "general philosophical topics," such as the relationship between "the mental" and "the physical." On the other hand, there are the "big philosophical questions"—these are none other than *the way* the (great) philosophers formulate these general topics. For example, in connection with the general topic of the relationship between "the mental" and "the physical" we can talk about Cartesian, Leibnizian, Malebranchean, Spinozian, Ryleian, Lewisian, Putnamian, Jacksonian, etc., big philosophical questions. And, of course, there are also small philosophical questions—these are non-substantive ("Is it true that if ..., then ...?" type) questions pertaining to general topics. For example, "Is it true that if intentional properties supervene on phenomenal ones, then zombies cannot be conceived consistently?" Thus, a general philosophical topic subsumes a number of Q_1, Q_2, Q_3 big philosophical questions, and a number of q_1, q_2, q_3 small philosophical questions.

In the light of this distinction, Stoljar sees the relationship between pessimism and optimism as follows:

> The dispute between the optimist and the pessimist does not concern topic questions, for both sides can agree (or so I will assume) that the topics discussed today are in many cases the topics discussed in the past. Nor does it concern small questions, for both sides can agree (or so I will also assume) that small questions can in many cases be conclusively answered, and so progress here is possible. Rather the issue concerns big questions within philosophical topics.
> (2017a: 14)

And here's how he defines his own position and objective:

> From this point of view, the key theses we will be concerned with may be summarized as follows. Optimism in general is the thesis that there is progress on all or reasonably many of the big questions of philosophy. Unreasonable optimism is the thesis that there is progress on *all* of the big questions of philosophy. Reasonable optimism is the thesis that there is progress on *reasonably many* of the big questions of philosophy. It is reasonable optimism that I want to defend [...]
> (2017a: 14–15, italics in original)

Let me present two big philosophical questions or problems that Stoljar says can be considered solved. The first "big philosophical problem" is the way Descartes formulates the general topic of the relationship between "the mental" and "the physical." According to a pessimist, this "problem is still with us, and that philosophers are still banging on about it" (2017c: 108). But, Stoljar says:

> [T]his pessimistic answer pays no attention to the way Descartes formulated the problem. If we do pay attention to this, what emerges is that, contrary to what often seems to be supposed, the Cartesian mind-body problem has been solved.
> (2017c: 108)

Why does Stoljar think that the "Cartesian mind-body problem" has been solved? Because the defining feature of this problem is that Descartes explicitly identifies matter or body with extension. Now, since this identification is a crucial element of Descartes' argument for substance dualism, and since this identification is erroneous, it clearly follows that Descartes' argument is bad. So, "the Cartesian mind-body problem is a solved problem" (Stoljar 2017c: 109).

Let's look at another big philosophical problem: the "Quinean meaning problem." Stoljar classifies this problem (just like the previous one) as a "boundary problem," saying that most philosophical problems are of this nature. Boundary problems are made up of three inconsistent propositions: p_1 states the existence of certain unquestionable facts; p_2 says that *all these facts are of* this and of this nature (either reducible to this and that, or fully explicable in this or that way); and p_3 says that *not all of* these facts are of this and that nature (either reducible to this and that, or fully explicable in this and that way). Here's the structure of the "Quinean meaning problem":

(P_1) There are facts about meaning.

(P_2) If there are facts about meaning, all such facts are necessitated by behavioral facts.

(P_3) If there are facts about meaning, not all such facts are necessitated by behavioral facts.

(Stoljar 2017a: 55)

Why does Stoljar think this problem to have been solved?

> I think it is fair to say, with respect to this problem, that it has been solved by rejecting (p_2), i.e. the boundary thesis. Of course, Quine himself thought that (p_2) was somehow constitutive of meaning, i.e. that if there are facts about meaning they are determined by behavioural facts. But many philosophers and scientists are united in opposing him on this issue.

> Some reject it because it is empirically implausible. Some because it cannot explain the sense in which facts about meaning explain behaviour. Still others because it entails modal claims that are false, e.g. that it is impossible that someone who duplicates a normal speaker in behavioural dispositions could fail to duplicate them in what they mean. For our purposes, however, the crucial point is not *why* it is rejected but *that* it was, and moreover, was rejected correctly. That is enough to show that Quine's indeterminacy problem is a solved problem; moreover, the reason it is a solved problem is that its constituent boundary thesis was rejected.

(2017a: 55, italics in original)

In broad outlines, this is what Stoljar's optimistic vision looks like, according to which the community of philosophers has already solved many big philosophical problems. Now I will tell you why I find this vision delusional.

I don't dispute that philosophical questions *can be* conceptualized in the way Stoljar does. *It is possible* indeed to call what we normally call a big philosophical problem a "general philosophical topic," and *it is possible* indeed to call the way some philosophers formulate a general philosophical topic a "big philosophical problem." And from there, it is really only one step *to declare a solution* to a "big philosophical problem" to be that such and such philosopher's arguments are (for this and that reason) are bad (or at least not compelling), and/or such and such philosopher's philosophical theories or theses are (for this and that reason) are false. But, and that's the crucial point, it is *extremely hard* to get rid of the impression that all this is nothing more than mere conceptual *relabeling*—the result of a highly *tendentious* conceptual engineering.

Here's the thing. Since the general philosophical topics themselves aren't solved (and Stoljar acknowledges this), and since even Stoljar cannot doubt that philosophers (in accordance with their intentions) made attempts to solve these general topics, I think, it indicates to be *strongly out of proportion* to say that we have solved, for example, the big Cartesian or the big Leibnizian mind-body problem good and proper. It would be more correct to say that we have learned much from the failure of Descartes and Leibniz. We have learned, and have already stored it nicely in our minds, that an argument for substance dualism *cannot* contain a premise stating the identity of body and extension; and that the mind is *not* a monad, for our mental life is quite certainly *not* causally closed. These are really important insights—yet, they *are not* the solutions to a "big" philosophical problem. Having learned from the failure of Descartes' and Leibniz's arguments, we now have a clearer understanding of the structure of the mind-body problem—we have a better understanding of which, seemingly plausible, propositions make an inconsistent set that results in this problem. In the wake of Descartes' and Leibniz's failure, competing mind-body theories (including substance dualism!) now present themselves to us as being significantly stronger and more immune to objections than they were in the age of Descartes and Leibniz.

Let me illustrate the tendentiousness of the way Stoljar speaks about solving "big" philosophical problems. Let's suppose that so far medical science has not been able to cure a single patient, even though it has attempted to do so. At the same time, the medical community could show so much success that it could accurately determine the types of different diseases, clearly distinguish them from each other, and there would be a series of well-worked-out theories about the progress of disease types and how they are cured. Moreover, the medical community would have the knowledge of such true propositions as "Physician X (carefully considering all the evidence at his disposal) tried hydrotherapy to cure the patient with tuberculosis, but it did not help him recover"; or that "Physician Y (carefully considering all available evidence) tried to cure his patient with kidney failure with coprotherapy, but he could not prevent his death." Then someone will suddenly appear and try to convince us that, despite all appearances, medicine is not really an epistemic failure, nor an unsuccessful therapeutic undertaking. This is how he would argue:

> Medicine has successfully dealt with a number of medical problems. Among other things, *it has solved* the problem of the treatment of tuberculosis with hydrotherapy and the problem of treating kidney failure with coprotherapy. While we hadn't known it before, we now know beyond a reasonable doubt that tuberculosis cannot be treated with hydrotherapy, nor can kidney failure be treated with coprotherapy.

I think Stoljar acts in a similar spirit as this imaginary person. They both intend the knowledge that this and this predecessor of ours was mistaken to masquerade as a *great* insight. So, in my eyes, Stoljar's vision is a great deal of delusion. To use a simile: whoever (like Stoljar) tends to match a philosophical problem to *every* single consensually rejected philosophical theory, thesis, or argument and say (by making reference to the prevailing consensus) "See, we have solved another philosophical problem" acts like the plumber who deems it a *great success* figuring out that *the reason why* the bathroom is flooded *is not* that a fluky maid sneaked in overnight, intentionally ran the bath until it overflew, and then quietly left—while he doesn't have even the faintest idea *why* the bathroom was actually flooded and *how* he should remedy the situation.

Let me present my concern about Stoljar's vision in a slightly different tone and with a slightly different focus. I think he cannot show that the community of philosophers possesses *substantive and positive* philosophical truths—although *this alone* would entitle him to speak about *the solutions to* big philosophical problems, and *this alone* could give him *a proper reason* for optimism.

Let's revisit Quine's theory of meaning. It is true indeed that we already know that we must give up p_2 from the corresponding inconsistent triad of propositions (see Stoljar 2017a: 55). But what exactly have we come to know? We have come to know a *negative* substantive truth: *not* all the facts about meaning are behavioral facts. We have come to know that *one* of the many meaning theories equally vying for truth, namely behaviorism, is *false*. But, according to Stoljar, such negative knowledge is not *merely* negative. As he puts it:

> To reject the behavourism behind Quine's problem about meaning is not simply to point out that, e.g. this or that behaviourist analysis of meaning is incorrect, but that the entire project of providing a behaviourist analysis of meaning is misguided; again, *it is to expand the possibilities* as to what sort of fact can make it the case that a word means what it does.
>
> (2017a: 70–1, italics mine)

Or, here is another, more general claim:

> [W]hile it is true that rejecting a boundary thesis is negative, there is also something positive that doing so brings in its train. For to reject or modify a boundary thesis of the sort we have considered is to reassess or expand the parameters of the *possible* as regard a fact, or being a knowable fact, or being an understandable proposition. But to expand the parameters of the possible in this sense is to do something positive. To say that inductive inferences need not be justified in a way is itself either inductive or deductive is to say something negative; but *also opens up further possibilities about how such inferences are to be justified*. Or consider the thesis that the US president need not to be male. That is a negative thesis, but it brings something positive along with it, *since it expands the accepted possibilities* on who can be president.
>
> (2017a: 70, italics mine)

So, Stoljar thinks that if we reject one of the three propositions making up a boundary problem and thus acquire a negative ("this is not the case") type of truth, it also has a *positive* result. In fact, by knowing that not-*p*, we can come to know *additional theoretical possibilities* (viz. *other possible solutions to* philosophical problems) that were previously hidden from us.

Fair enough. Knowledge of which consistent philosophical theories are *possible* in connection with various philosophical problems *is* knowledge indeed. However, it is certainly *not substantive* philosophical knowledge, so it is clear that Stoljar's optimistic vision is in fact nothing more than what a pessimist can easily acknowledge. For without further ado, the pessimist can agree that besides acquiring knowledge of certain *negative* substantive truths, the community of philosophers can also acquire knowledge of such *non-substantive* truths. What the pessimist disputes is that we know *substantive* and *positive* philosophical truths, but, apparently, Stoljar cannot assert such truths either. That's why he resorts to tendentious conceptual engineering: to advertising a philosophical problem as solved if we know how things are not (we know that non-*p*), and by knowing non-*p*, we acquire knowledge of further propositions about how things can be.

To use a slightly transformed and supplemented variant of the above simile, this is as if one called a successful solution the work of a plumber who knows that *if* the drain got clogged *then* a plumbing snake should be applied, while *if* the pipe in the wall is broken *then* a mason should be called, and he also knows that the faucet box does *not* malfunction, but he doesn't have even the faintest idea what should be done to restore the water flow.

***

There is only one loose end left—the "identity view." In order to calmly reject Stoljar's entire conceptual ReFrameworking, we don't need to commit ourselves to the idea of the "identity view"—the idea of *philosophia perennis*. We don't have to think that Descartes and Leibniz and Jackson were dealing with *exactly* the *same* problem. We might also think (and this was what I argued for in the third part of the previous chapter) that (for example) the various formulations of the mind-body problem ensure the *temporal continuity or persistence of* the mind-body problem *itself*. If you wish, the various formulations are the *vehicles of* the tradition or "spread" of the mind-body problem.

Let me explain this in a little more detail. As we have seen before with regard to the structure of the free will and the mind-body problems, these problems are constituted by inconsistent propositions, and there is no consensus among philosophers as to which of the propositions at issue should be considered true and which false—there is no argument for either option that has convinced all philosophers, or at least most of them.

Now, the fact that no argument exists that has convinced all philosophers as to which of these mutually inconsistent propositions we should regard as false is difficult to explain otherwise than by supposing that there is much to be said for each of these propositions—there are many philosophical considerations in favor of each, and each is resistant to objections. Let's revisit the structure of the mind-body problem in its simplest form. Premise (1) (conscious experiences ≠ physical events) is not easy to give up: the gap-intuition in favor of it is "vigorous" and "tenacious," and can even be "pumped" further and further—think, for example, of the variety of increasingly sophisticated conceivability arguments. Premise (2) (the thesis of mental causation) is also not easy to give up—few even try it, since parallelism and epiphenomenalism are both very counter-intuitive positions. Premise (3) (the thesis of causal closure) is also not easy to give up—there is good reason to believe that the most successful epistemic enterprise of mankind is physics, and "[t]he success to date of current physics in finding sufficient physical causes for physical effects therefore provides inductive evidence that all physical events, including both unexamined physical events and examined-but-as-yet-unexplained physical events, have sufficient physical causes" (Melnyk 2003: 288).

Having said this, I would like to propose that the mind-body problem is made up of inconsistent propositions, *each of* which is "epistemically attractive" in its own right. *We would tend to* consider *each on its own* to be true rather than false; or, to put it more modestly, we would *be more* inclined to consider each of them true than false—if, that is, they did not happen to be inconsistent with one another. Even more modestly, whichever of these three propositions we deny, we understand exactly why *others* consider it true—why it is "epistemically appealing" to others.

Suppose we are physicalists who deny (1). In this case, we can say that of the three, (1) is the proposition that can be given up at the lowest theoretical cost. We can also say that the gap is actually an illusion (see e.g., Loar 1990; Papineau 2002). However, we cannot say that (1) is a fatal falsehood without any basis, so that all anti-physicalists should have long ago realized the illusory nature of this gap, and since they did not, they are irrational. Whichever proposition we deny of the three, we must acknowledge that we *are aware* of the "epistemic appeal" of the proposition we deny; so much so that we *perhaps* even acknowledge that we ourselves are not (completely) immune to its "epistemic appeal," and reject it in spite of our (even if faintly) existing "epistemic attraction."

Now, I agree with Stoljar that the mind-body problem (or the general topic of the relationship between the "mental" and the "physical") cannot be understood *exclusively* as a combined inconsistency of these three propositions. The number of propositions may also increase, and their content may also change. And so, it is true indeed that there are as many mind-body problems as there are inconsistent sets of propositions corresponding to them—sets are individualized by their elements. And in that sense, it's also true that Descartes and Jackson don't deal with the same problem.

But, sticking to the mind-body relationship, it is *misleading* to conceptualize inconsistent sets of propositions as problems that are completely *independent* of each other, like Stoljar does—and he does so, for otherwise he could not claim that while Descartes' mind-body problem is solved, Jackson's remains unresolved. I think the following story is more plausible: more and more formulations of the mind-body problem (more and more inconsistent sets of propositions) *perpetuate* a definite and characteristic *conceptual tension* in time. This long-standing and well-known tension consists in the fact that, on the one hand, minds/conscious experiences do not appear to be entities of a physical nature, but on the other hand, minds/conscious experiences appear to be physical entities. On the one hand, we do not understand how minds/conscious experiences could be physical [see arguments in favor of (1)], while on the other hand, we do not understand how they could not be [see arguments in favor of (2) and (3)]. No matter what inconsistent set of propositions we assign to the mind-body problem (or general topic), and no matter how fine-grained it is, it is certain that THIS tension will dominate it. And THIS tension spreads further and further in successive formulations of the mind-body problem—every philosopher who begins to examine the mind-body relationship faces THIS tension and tries to do something with THIS tension. This is the sense in which the mind-body problem persists in time.

I propose the following conceptual framework as opposed to Stoljar's. Every (or at least most) philosophical problem (regardless of its particular formulation) is created by a specific (uniquely characterizing) tension—we "come up against" some inconsistent but "epistemically attractive" propositions. Consequently, the solution of a philosophical problem would amount to *nothing short of* proving, by compelling arguments, which of *these tension-inducing*, inconsistent propositions are true and which are false—this is the *only* way to *eliminate* the tension in question. By contrast, the fact that *we already know* for some time that Descartes erroneously identified the body with extension *merely* amounts to the removal of the term "extension" from the first premise of later conceivability arguments and its replacement with other terms that refer to our physical (or perhaps physical plus intentional) properties. By this, however, the tension that keeps the mind-body problem "alive" *has not disappeared* (not even subsided), but rather passed on "intact." To wrap it up, recognizing Descartes' error is *not* the solution to a problem.

Of course, I still don't dispute that someone could say (after all, not being a conceptual contradiction) that "the community of philosophers has solved Descartes' mind-body problem good and proper"—I just find it to be a misleading and tendentious conceptualization. I also don't dispute that one can only say that *there are* some solved philosophical problems if the "identity view" is false—setting aside the option that one also sees philosophical problems as solved concerning which there is permanent dissensus. At the same time (and this is what I am trying to show in this section under the three stars): when we consider the "identity view" (the idea of *philosophia perennis*) false, we can *still* consistently insist that *there are no* solved philosophical problems.

To conclude, I don't share Stoljar's optimism. He fails to show how philosophical progress could be anything more than just gaining knowledge of more and more non-substantive philosophical truths and discrediting certain substantive philosophical theories. All this, of course, is not nothing, and—*pace* Dietrich—it is by no means treading water. At the same time, we must see that the goals the followers of the epistemic tradition of philosophy set themselves are *significantly more ambitious* than the above results, and these philosophers have *failed to achieve* these goals. Like it or not: unless we relabel philosophical questions in the manner of Stoljar, it can hardly be debated that philosophy is a failed epistemic enterprise—the community of philosophers hasn't solved any philosophical problems and doesn't possess substantive and positive philosophical truths.

3 Philosophers' reactions

To sum up what I have said so far, I see things in the following way. The followers of philosophy's epistemic tradition have attempted to solve philosophical problems and promised compellingly justified substantive philosophical truths. Still, there is disagreement in every area of philosophy among philosophers, and this pervasive and permanent dissensus is a salient sign that their efforts have not been successful and their promises were not kept—philosophers are the actors of an epistemically failed enterprise. Put differently, the community of philosophers (in which we belong) has no substantive and positive philosophical knowledge, and philosophy (which we do) has not made the least bit of progress in the sense that it couldn't give a satisfactory answer to substantive philosophical questions at t_1, but could do so at t_2.

Thus, if a philosopher has *substantive and positive* philosophical beliefs, then she has to face the epistemic failure of philosophy and has the epistemic and moral duty to try to account for their epistemic status. She doesn't proceed correctly if she denies or downplays philosophy's epistemic failure—she would severely deceive herself in both cases.

Now, aware of philosophy's epistemic failure, a philosopher can think in the following four ways about the epistemic status of her substantive and positive philosophical beliefs and the closely connected issue of the meaningfulness and goal of doing philosophy.

(1) In contrast with my predecessors and contemporaries, I have succeeded in providing compelling justifications for my substantive philosophical beliefs. I have knock-down arguments for my substantive philosophical theses. The fact of pervasive and permanent philosophical dissensus and the fact that the community of philosophers does not have substantive philosophical knowledge are irrelevant to me. This is because I do have such knowledge. Of course, I am sorry that other philosophers do not understand my arguments and are unable to see their compelling force. Philosophers must not be discouraged by philosophy's epistemic failure. They must stick to the original goal of the epistemic tradition, so they must keep trying to assert compellingly justified substantive philosophical truths.

(2) I cannot rationally stick to my substantive philosophical beliefs. Philosophy's epistemic failure (the pervasive and permanent dissensus) shows that the truth-seeking and justificatory tools of philosophy are inadequate and unsuitable, and so, my substantive philosophical beliefs are inappropriately justified. Consequently, I have to suspend them. Philosophy's only meaningful tasks are to formulate increasingly stronger (preferably knock-down) arguments for meta-skepticism, and to show that every philosopher has the epistemic duty to suspend their substantive philosophical beliefs.

(3) I do not believe that it is possible to find compelling justifications in philosophy. The goals I set for myself must be more modest than that of trying to formulate knock-down arguments for my philosophical beliefs. I must undertake to develop a philosophical theory which is in harmony or equilibrium with my own fundamental pre-philosophical convictions, and I must defend my theory, elaborated accordingly, against various objections. If I successfully accomplish these two tasks, I can rationally stick to my substantive philosophical beliefs, although I cannot provide compelling justifications for them. It is a mistake to

consider philosophy as a failed enterprise. It is alive and kicking without compelling arguments.

(4) My philosophical beliefs are meaningless because philosophical problems are meaningless. Philosophy's only meaningful tasks are to debunk the appearance-creating mechanism that is responsible for the genesis of philosophical problems, and to work out an effective therapy that cures all persons infected with philosophy of engaging with philosophical problems, so they cause them no more unnecessary worry.

Apart from the possibility that we will come to acquire some method(s) in the future that reliably supply us with substantive philosophical truths [which is, by the way, rather closely related to answer (1)], these four reactions nicely delineate an appropriate logical map. The first question is: Are philosophical problems meaningful? They are, according to (1), (2), and (3), but they are not by (4) [I leave out (4) from now on]. The second question is: Can philosophers rationally stick to their substantive philosophical beliefs? They can, according to (1) and (3), but they cannot by (2) [I leave out (2) from now on]. The third question is: Is providing compelling justification the only way for philosophers to rationally stick to their beliefs? It is, according to (1), but it is not by to (3).

In the Part II of this book, I will deal with these four reactions (as metaphilosophical visions), but not in the above order. Firstly, I will examine the reaction according to which philosophical problems and the philosophers' philosophical beliefs are meaningless, and philosophy's only meaningful goal is therapy. Secondly, I will consider the attitude that allows itself to be summarized this way: "In contrast to others, I have succeeded in providing compelling justifications for my philosophical beliefs." Thirdly, I will analyze the view according to which philosophers can rationally stick to their substantive philosophical beliefs even in the absence of compelling arguments. Fourthly, I will deal with meta-skepticism, which says that in the light of philosophy's epistemic failure, the right thing for us to do is to suspend our substantive philosophical beliefs.

In addressing the question of how we should react to philosophy's epistemic failure and what we should do with our substantive philosophical beliefs in the light of this failure, there will inevitably arise some *ethical* aspects concerning our reaction too, such as *to what extent we can be sincere* about it and *to what extent it is consistent with our insights derived from self-reflection on our philosophical activity*. That is, while considering possible reactions, the question emphatically arises: "Can we be sincere about them with a clear intellectual and moral conscience?" It would be very wrong to react to this failure in a way to which we cannot commit ourselves, with hand on our heart. Of course, these "evaluation criteria" can be formulated during the discussion of first-order philosophical problems too, but they have special significance with regard to the question at issue.

Part Two

3

Therapy for Philosophers

The concept of therapy is in the focus of two (meta)philosophical conceptions. Eugen Fischer distinguishes and characterizes them as follows:

> There are two quite different cases in which a thinker may engage in philosophical reflection in pursuit of such a therapeutic aim. He may wish, first and foremost, to solve emotional and behavioural problems that arise in ordinary life, prior to or independently from philosophical reflection. Let's say that philosophical reflection which primarily addresses such problems is constitutive of *philosophical therapy*. Second, emotions and behaviours constitutive of emotional or behavioural problems may arise in the course of and as a result of philosophical reflection. A philosopher who seeks, first and foremost, to solve such problems engages in what I would like to call "*therapeutic philosophy*".
>
> (Fischer 2011: 53, italics in original)

In other words, "the need for therapy may arise both *outside* and *within* philosophy, and [we] can usefully distinguish between 'philosophical therapy' which addresses the *extra*-philosophical need, and 'therapeutic philosophy' which addresses the *intra*-philosophical need" (Fischer 2011: 50, italics mine).

Philosophical therapy has purely practical goals which fall outside of philosophy. Philosopher-therapists try to help people achieve and preserve a happy life and offer remedy to everyday emotional issues and guide those who wish to follow the path of a virtuous life. At the end of the day, philosopher-therapists are life coaches with a philosophical education who apply philosophical methods in their therapy. You could think of methods such as Sextus Empiricus' proposed suspension of judgment, which yields *ataraxia* (peace of mind), or the exercises and meditational techniques suggested by the philosophers of the late Stoa (Epictetus, Seneca, Marcus Aurelius) that lead to a happy and passionless life. Or you could think of the method of conceptual-linguistic analysis practiced often by contemporary philosopher-therapists, which can help dissolve conflicts that create emotional confusion, by e.g., pointing out that the parties mean different things by expressions such as "faithfulness," "selflessness," "housework," "cheating," etc.

The advocates of therapeutic philosophy (the late Wittgenstein and his followers) also try to remedy emotional problems, but only a special kind thereof—those which arise as a result of dealing with philosophical problems. What these two concepts share is that neither is aimed at solving philosophical problems, and that if they succeed, then their success is primarily therapeutic and not epistemic in kind. But whereas philosophical therapy sits well with the epistemic or truth-seeking tradition of philosophy, therapeutic philosophy is a *reaction* to the epistemic failure of philosophy—according to the late Wittgenstein and his followers, the members of epistemic tradition unnecessarily worry while intending to solve philosophical problems, as philosophical problems are meaningless.

Whether we take philosophical therapy or therapeutic philosophy, the real place of philosophy is not in academia. Seeing it from the perspective of these two therapeutic approaches, philosophy that is done within the academic ghetto has shrunk and become poor (see Hadot 1987/1999: 271). Philosophy affects *everyone* and so "philosophy has to be taken out into the world" (Jonge and Whiteman 2014: 449). Advocates and practitioners of philosophical therapy think so because by its nature, philosophy is an activity we do in communities, while advocates and practitioners of therapeutic philosophy think so because no one is immune to harmful mechanisms generating philosophical problems.

In this chapter I deal with therapeutic philosophy. First, based on ample textual evidence, I try to exactly reconstruct the later Wittgenstein's standpoint on philosophy. In what follows, I attempt to show that Wittgenstein's therapeutic philosophy is a bad reaction to the epistemic failure of philosophy.

1 The therapeutic philosophy of the later Wittgenstein

Wittgenstein thinks that philosophy has no positive task, only negative ones: "All that philosophy can do is to destroy idols. And that means not creating a new one — say in the 'absence of an idol'" (*BT* 413). So, philosophical problems should be eliminated, instead of being solved: "The problems are [...] dissolved like a lump of sugar in water" (*BT* 421); "the philosophical problems should *completely* disappear" (*PI* 133, italics in original). He views his own philosophical work as destruction: "it seems [...] to destroy everything interesting, that is, all that is great and important [...] [but] what we are destroying is nothing but houses of cards and we are clearing up the ground of language on which they stood" (*PI* 118).

Why is the task of eliminating philosophical problems assigned to philosophy? Because they are meaningless. Meaningful (genuine) problems clearly should not be eliminated but solved. One such meaningful (genuine) problem is "Is Goldbach's conjecture true?" but "What does butter do when its price goes up?" (see *PI* 693) is a meaningless (not genuine) question, hence it should be eliminated. "What is the best way to relieve poverty?" is a meaningful (genuine) problem, but the mind-body problem, the problem of universals, other minds, the metaphysical status of physical objects, etc., i.e., philosophical problems are meaningless (not genuine).

What makes a question or problem meaningless? That it occurs as a result of some kind of conceptual confusion. Such is the above "What does butter do when its price goes up?" or the question "What kind of an object is the right jab I'm throwing at my opponent?" This is because butter is not a thing that can act and a right jab is not a physical object that can be moved from one place to another.

Wittgenstein thinks that philosophical questions are *just as* meaningless as the question "What does butter do ...?" or "What kind of an object a right jab is ...?" as similarly to these, they arise out of conceptual confusion. The *only* difference is that while we *immediately see* the conceptual/categorical confusion in "What does butter do ...?" and "What kind of an object a right jab is ...?" in the case of philosophical questions, *we do not*. So, while "What does butter do ...?" or "What kind of an object a right jab is ...?" are innocent "grammatical jokes" (*PI* 111), philosophical questions are nothing but symptoms of permanent conceptual confusions we *do not detect*. This is why Wittgenstein also formulates his philosophical aim as follows: "My aim is: to teach you to pass from a piece of disguised nonsense to something that is patent nonsense" (*PI* 464).

How are supposed to imagine this? Let's assume that two people are arguing about what butter does when its price goes up. One of them says: "Butter has always desired to be more valued and now its dream came true." The other goes: "Butter didn't originally wish to be more valued but pork pâté manipulated it, so it finally agreed to having its price increased." In this case your job is not to compare these theories, not to assess which one is more plausible or has greater explanatory force, which one is free from the faults of the other, but simply to show that the above question is a result of conceptual confusion. Wittgenstein suggests that we should do *exactly the same* in the case of philosophical problems, since every philosophical problem is *exactly as meaningless* as the one about the price of butter. The only difference is that in the case of philosophical problems, it will be harder to do that, as it is harder to catch this kind of conceptual confusion at work.

When do philosophical problems arise? Wittgenstein thinks it is "when language is like an engine idling, not when it is doing work" (*PI* 132); "when language *goes on holiday*" (*PI* 38, italics in original). Or, to use other quotes: "The results of philosophy are the uncovering of one or another piece of plain nonsense and bumps that the understanding has got by running its head up against the limits of language" (*PI* 119).

Now, if philosophical problems arise from the misunderstanding of our language, then the misunderstanding of language is a *precondition* of the existence of philosophical problems, which means that there are no genuine philosophical problems. If, having realized the relevant conceptual confusions, we stopped misunderstanding our language, we would also run out of philosophical problems in no time.

1.1 Misunderstanding language and the genesis of philosophical problems

Wittgenstein identifies two specific features of language that are responsible for creating philosophical problems. One cause of linguistic misunderstandings is that we are misled by the surface grammar of language: "A main source of our failure to understand is that we do not *command a clear view* of the use of our words. — Our grammar is lacking in this sort of perspicuity" (*PI* 122, italics in original). This lack of perspicuity is due to "Misunderstandings concerning the use of words, caused, among other things, by certain analogies between the forms of expression in different regions of language" (*PI* 90); "So long as there is a verb 'be' that seems to function like 'eat' and 'drink', [...] humans will continue to bump up against the same mysterious difficulties, and stare at something that no explanation seems able to remove" (*BT* 424).

Another cause for misunderstandings is that certain pictures are embedded in language, which affect or determine how we pose our questions. These questions are meaningless, but they seem to have meaning in the context of embedded pictures: "A *picture* held us captive. And we could not get outside it, for it lay in our language and language seemed to repeat it to us inexorably" (*PI* 115, italics in original).

Let's look at an example of overlooking that despite certain surface grammatical similarities, some expressions function very differently in different contexts. Wittgenstein's most frequently used example is the verb "have" ("haben" in German).

Take "I have an apartment," or "I have a book." They both express a relation between myself and something else (an apartment and a book). Let's now take "I have an image" ("I habe eine Vorstellung" in German). The three sentences share their surface structure. Due to this surface correspondence, we tend to understand the third sentence, too, as expressing a relation between myself and a thing (namely, an image). This way, since we committed ourselves to the existence of the image as a *thing*, we come to understand "I have an image" as "I have something, namely an image" instead of simply taking to mean "I am imagining something."

Wittgenstein thinks we already have a trouble here. For this image, which is related to me is clearly not a public object but something that is essentially private. Let's look at the following wording:

> "[W]hen I imagine something, or even actually *see* objects, I have *got* something which my neighbour has not." — I understand you. You want to look about you and say: "At any rate only I have got THIS".
>
> (*PI* 398)

Et voilà, this is how Wittgenstein thinks the sense-datum theory is born out of a misunderstanding of the collocation of "have" and "image." As a result of the misunderstanding of these two expressions, you think "You have a new conception and interpret it as seeing a new object" (*PI* 401), namely a sense-datum; and "You interpret a grammatical movement made by yourself as a quasi-physical phenomenon which you are observing" (*PI* 401). Finally, this "grammatical movement" leads you to ask questions such as "Are sense-data the material of which the universe is made?" (*PI* 401). This is how a simple and innocent-looking but in fact harmful linguistic misunderstanding generates a meaningless metaphysical question.

Another type of linguistic misunderstanding is when we are misled by the pictoriality of language. Wittgenstein elaborates on this most fully when he discusses the metaphysical problem of time with special regards to Augustine's view. Let me quote a longer passage here:

> "Where does the present go when it becomes past, and where is the past?" — Under what circumstances has this question an allurement for us? For under

certain circumstances it hasn't, and we should wave it away as nonsense. It is clear that this question most easily arises if we are preoccupied with cases in which there are things flowing by us — as logs of wood float down a river. In such a case we can say the logs which *have passed* us are all down towards the left and the logs which *will pass* us are all up towards the right. We then use this situation as a simile for all happening in time and even embody the simile in our language, as when we say that "the present event passes by" (a log passes by), "the future event is to come" (a log is to come). We talk about the flow of events; but also about the flow of time — the river on which the logs travel.

Here is one of most fertile sources of philosophical puzzlement: we talk of the future event of something coming into my room, and also of the future coming of this event. We say, "*Something* will happen", and also "*Something* comes towards me", we refer to the log as "something", but also the log's coming towards me.

(*BB* 60, italics in original)

The question "Where does the present go when it becomes past, and where is the past?" is meaningless, but it seems meaningful in the context where we compare time to a river in which events float like objects do, from left to right—from the past, through the present and into the future. To put it more accurately: it is *only* in this context that it seems to be meaningful. If, however, trying to resist the pictoriality of this metaphor, we could part with the picture of time as a river, then we would instantly recognize the meaninglessness of this question. Just as we can instantly recognize that the questions "Where does the candle's light go after you have put it out?" or "Where does light go once you turn off the light?" (see *BB* 60) are meaningless.

1.2 The role of grammatical investigations

According to certain interpreters, grammatical investigations serve theoretical purposes in the later Wittgenstein's philosophy. They interpret passages such as "*Essence* is expressed in grammar" (*PI* 371, italics in original); "Grammar tells what kind of object anything is" (*PI* 373) as saying that grammatical investigations have positive goals (see e.g., Kenny 1984: 43)—they have to reveal certain essences.

In fact, this is not about *Wesensschau* at all—the later Wittgenstein is not a kind of grammatical Husserl. Grammatical investigations can indeed reveal certain "essences," but this means nothing else than realizing how we actually use certain expressions in ordinary language. The results of grammatical investigation are embodied in uttering *trivialities*—Wittgenstein calls them "grammatical propositions" (*PI* 251). He thinks of sentences such as "Sensations are private" (*PI* 248); "One plays patience by oneself" (*PI* 248); "[T]he smile of an unweaned infant is not a pretence" (*PI* 249); "[A] dog [cannot] simulate pain" (*PI* 250); "This body has extension" (*PI* 252).

The repeated utterance of these trivialities plays the role of reminders of the actual use of our words. These sentences remind us of the fact that we use our expressions *this way* and not otherwise. We need these reminders because only by having these trivial grammatical sentences in mind can we be clear about *where we diverge* from the everyday use of our words when we formulate philosophical problems.

Wittgenstein refers to this role of grammatical investigations when he says "What *we* do is to bring words back from their metaphysical back to their everyday use" (*PI* 116, italics in original); this is the point of the passage that looks enigmatic at first sight, according to which "The work of the philosopher consists in assembling reminders for a particular purpose" (*PI* 127); and this is what he means when he says that philosophical problems are dissolved "by looking into the workings of our language, and that in such a way as to make us recognize those workings: *in despite of* an urge to misunderstand them" (*PI* 109, italics in original).

The trivial nature of grammatical sentences makes Wittgenstein say "If one tried to advance theses in philosophy, it would never be possible to debate them, because everyone would agree to them" (*PI* 128, italics in original), and that "Philosophy only states what everyone admits" (*PI* 599). This is also the reason why he writes "Since everything lies open to view there is nothing to explain" (*PI* 126), and that "There must not be anything hypothetical in our considerations. We must do away with all *explanation*, and description alone must take its place" (*PI* 109, italics in original).

What should one do if one wishes to follow Wittgenstein? In the words of an interesting Harry Potter character, Alastor "Mad-eye" Mordon, what one needs is "constant vigilance!" Why does one need constant vigilance? Because our language *continuously* misleads us and *continuously* prompts us to ask meaningless questions due to its surface grammar, misleading pictoriality and false analogies. Thus, the eliminating of philosophical problems (which is the only purpose of philosophy) cannot happen overnight but is a long process, or to quote Wittgenstein: "*a slow* cure" (*Z* 382, italics in original). Or, to use a more vivid metaphor of his: "Philosophy is a *battle* against the bewitchment of our intelligence by means of our language" (*PI* 109, italics mine), i.e., it is a *constant struggle* with language; *constant resistance* to the temptation to concern ourselves with meaninglessness due to our misunderstanding of language.

From the fact that philosophy is a struggle, it follows that good and meaningful philosophy is not embodied in various studies (journals and textbooks)—instead, its ontological status is *activity*. What should the followers of Wittgenstein do? Two things. On the one hand, they (as interpreters of Wittgenstein) need to show that "Wittgenstein was not taking sides in the muddled controversies [...] and his reflections cannot be fitted into the misconceived pigeon-holes currently in vogue. The premises upon which these latter-day controversies stand would all be rejected by him as dogmas, absurdities, and misunderstandings" (Hacker 1993: 546). On the other hand, they (as the lonely and heroic advocates of therapeutic philosophy) need to show that most of the philosophical studies published and read, or even quoted sometimes, are the meaningless products of misunderstanding language.

1.3 The psychological component

So far, I have intentionally ignored the most important aspect of Wittgenstein's therapeutic philosophy. I only claimed that he thinks philosophical problems are meaningless, as they arise from the misunderstanding of language. At the same time, I passed over in silence the fact that he thinks that philosophical problems can cause unsettling tension, i.e., real *emotional disorders*.

Let's look at Wittgenstein's following phrasings: "What we call a philosophical problem is a kind of particular, individual disturbance" (*PG* 193); "The problems arising through a misinterpretation of our forms of language have the character of *depth*. They are deep disquietudes; their roots are as deep in us the forms of our language and their significance is as great as the importance of our language" (*PI* 111, italics in original).

He also says the following: "The philosopher's treatment of a question is like the treatment of an illness" (*PI* 255); "A philosophical problem has the form: 'I don't know my way about'" (*PI* 123); "The philosophical problem is an awareness of disorder in our concepts" (*BT* 421). And, finally, here are the most vivid metaphors and similes: philosophical problems are "knots in our thinking" (*BT* 422); "bumps" (*PI* 119); "constant irritations" (*BT* 409); and they are "like having a hair on one's tongue; one feels it, but can't get hold of, and therefore can't get rid of it" (*BT* 409).

Or let's take the well-known passage:

> Naming appears as a *queer* connexion of a word with an object. — And you really get such a queer connexion when a philosopher tries to bring out *the* relation between name and thing by staring at an object in front of him and repeating a name or even the word "this" innumerable times.
>
> <div align="right">(<i>PI</i> 38, italics in original)</div>

Richard Rorty is wrong when he attributes irony and sarcasm to Wittgenstein in this and similar remarks of his and calls the *Philosophical Investigations* "volumes of satire" (1979: 369). There is no irony, sarcasm, or satire to be found here. Instead, Wittgenstein describes the symptoms of a peculiar *illness*. A person who keeps repeating the word "this" while staring at an object in order to use his introspection to discover how the word "this" denotes the object in front of him is miserable and ill. He is someone who deserves sympathy and treatment instead of irony and sarcasm.

In light of the above passages, it is understandable what Wittgenstein sees his own duty in: "As I do philosophy, its *entire* task is to shape expression in such a way *that certain worries disappear*" (*BT* 421, italics mine); "The real discovery is the one that makes me capable of stopping doing philosophy when I want to" (*PI* 133).

Now, if dealing with philosophical problems leads to psychological/emotional problems, then philosophy is only legitimate as *therapy* (see *PI* 133). And the goal of this therapeutic philosophy can only be to eliminate those unsettling tensions (those uncomfortable conscious experiences) that arise from dealing with philosophical problems. In other words, it should bring us the "peace of mind" (*BT* 416) we long to have. Therapeutic philosophy done well brings "*peace*, so that [we are] no longer *tormented* by [philosophical] questions" (*PI* 133, italics mine).

It is important to see that Wittgenstein did *not* just consider his own recovery. He did not want to be just the home therapist of philosophers, either, as the emotional disturbances caused by philosophical problems can take a hold of *anyone* at any time if they are not on their guard. No one is immune to linguistic misunderstanding, so it is not just philosophers working professionally on philosophical problems who are exposed to the mesmerizing power of language but *everyone else* is: "Human beings are deeply imbedded in philosophical, i.e., grammatical, confusions" (*BT* 423). Given all this, Wittgenstein thinks that doing philosophy is not just the business of philosophers. It is much more and more important than that. It is an activity that *everyone* ought to carry out on account of being exposed to these dangers.

There is something else I need to stress. The problem is not simply that we are disturbed or lack our peace of mind. If we are deeply unsettled by a mathematical or physical problem as mathematicians or physicists—that is completely in order. All we need to do is solve the problem at hand and we will have achieved, for a while at least, our peace of mind. It is only the disturbance caused by philosophical problems that is pathological. If these cause us to be unsettled, then, as we are battling pseudo-problems, we suffer *senselessly*. So, we need to achieve our peace of mind differently to how a mathematician or physicist does. This is the point at which the therapeutic philosophy suggested by Wittgenstein can come to our aid.

2 The failure of Wittgenstein's therapeutic philosophy

I don't want to dispute that there are meaningless philosophical problems and that their meaninglessness stems from some conceptual confusion. Thus, I don't want to dispute that some philosophers are really deceived by the surface grammar or pictoriality of language, which leads them to put forward meaningless philosophical theses and makes their philosophical beliefs meaningless. But I do dispute that *all* philosophical problems are pseudo-problems arising from the misunderstanding of language and that *all* philosophers who put forward philosophical theses are victims of conceptual confusions. In a word, I don't think that Wittgenstein reacts appropriately to the epistemic failure of philosophy, or that he gives a right answer to the question "What should we do with our philosophical beliefs in the light of the epistemic failure of philosophy?" I have three main concerns about Wittgenstein's therapeutic philosophy.

2.1 Self-defeat

I think that Wittgenstein's therapeutic philosophy is *self-defeating*. Here goes the argument. In order for Wittgenstein to hold that the only task of doing philosophy is to provide therapy, there has to be some kind of *diagnosis* first. And there is one indeed. According to this, philosophical questions and problems are meaningless. But in order not to simply declare this, Wittgenstein needs to give clear criteria of meaningfulness and meaninglessness. But these criteria should also not simply be declared *ex cathedra*, so he has to say *something* about the nature of linguistic meaning. And he does: "[T]he meaning of a word is its *use* in the language" (*PI* 43, italics mine). But that is still not enough. Since an expression can be used wrongly (e.g., somebody may systematically substitute the word "theology" with the word "teleology," or the expression "phenomenology" with the expression "phenomenalism"), Wittgenstein must say (and he says indeed) that "the meaning of a word = its *right* use." Now, the right use of words and expressions presupposes certain *rules*: "right use = right rule-following." The question arises as to what determines right rule-following. Wittgenstein must answer something, and he does say it: right use is not determined by some mental or neural fact but only the standard practice of the language-using community. Furthermore, following a rule is not a disposition manifested in some behavioral pattern but simple conformity with existing practice (see *PI* 198–241; and see esp. Kripke 1982).

The appeal to the right use of words is a crucial point in Wittgenstein's line of thought. The success of the diagnosis depends on it. It is by appealing to the right use of words that he has to show that assertions that *prima facie* seem to be meaningful (e.g., "A physical event is defined by where and when it happens"; "The distinguishing mark of the 'mental' is that the subject of mental phenomena accesses them differently than other people do"; "Ordinary objects persist by being wholly present at different times") are actually meaningless pseudo-assertions. Wittgenstein cannot think the same of the status of this theory of meaning (or rather, conception of meaning) as of philosophical theories in general, viz. that it is meaningless, since one meaningless conception of meaning will surely not ground the criterion that is desired and fundamentally important for his diagnosis. Thus, he must view his own conception of meaning as *meaningful*. But it is not enough for it to be meaningful, it also must be *true*, since a bad and false conception of meaning cannot serve as the grounds for the desired criterion. If, however, he considers it to be true, then there will certainly be such a philosophical problem, philosophical conception, philosophical thesis, and philosophical belief that he considers as meaningful and true—consequently, he cannot claim that all philosophical problems, theories, theses, and beliefs are meaningless. But since he claims this, he is caught in the trap of self-defeat.

I think there are only two ways to avoid the conclusion that Wittgenstein's therapeutic philosophy is self-defeating. One is to claim that "All philosophical theses are meaningless *except* those that feature in the diagnosis needed for the therapy." The other is to claim that "The making of a diagnosis needed for the therapy is *not a philosophical achievement*; everything Wittgenstein says about the nature of linguistic meaning, i.e., everything that is to ground the criterion of meaningfulness is *not a substantial philosophical thesis*, but something else—something that is a *triviality* in an absolute sense, which does not need any justification" (see esp. Horwich 2012: ch. 4).

These, however, seem to be ad hoc maneuvers. Frankly speaking, they cannot easily be taken seriously. Firstly, *why should exactly those* substantive philosophical theses (concerning linguistic meaning) be the *only* meaningful ones that Wittgenstein asserts in establishing a diagnosis needed for his therapy? Secondly, *why should it not be a substantive (linguistic) philosophical thesis* that "The concept of right use has a pivotal role in defining or characterizing the concept of meaning"; or that "The ability of rule-following is nothing but simple conformity with actual practice"? Moreover, *why should it be a triviality* to say that "The concept of use (and not, say, that of truth, inferential role or communicative intention) is fundamental to defining or characterizing the concept of linguistic meaning"; or that "Rule-following is determined only by the standard practice of the language-using community"? All the more so, because both theses are open to several rock-hard objections.

2.2 Convincing force close to zero

My other main concern with Wittgenstein's therapeutic philosophy is simply that the convincing force of his therapeutic exercises is close to zero. Let me start with the sense-datum theory. The orthodoxy is that the strongest argument for the sense-datum theory is the "argument from hallucination." In outline, it goes as follows:

(1) When S hallucinates a red tomato, then S is aware of *something*—it is phenomenologically implausible to describe S's hallucinatory perceptual experience as S is not aware of anything.
(2) The entity that S is aware of during the hallucination cannot be identified with any element in the world that exists independently of S's current perceptual experience but is a mind-dependent entity (sense datum).
(3) If S's hallucinatory perceptual experience is subjectively indistinguishable from S's veridical perceptual experience, then S is in the same type of mental state when S is hallucinating and when S has a veridical perceptual experience.

Therefore:

(C) When S veridically perceives the red tomato, S is (again) directly aware of a kind of mind-dependent entity (sense datum) and only indirectly perceives the red tomato that exists independently of S's current perceptual experience.

Can you see *anything* in this argument that would allow you to draw the conclusion that the proponent of the argument from hallucination is a victim of some conceptual confusion? Premise (1) says *on the basis of the phenomenology* of hallucinations that S is aware of something when S hallucinates. Premise (2) is *a simple stipulation*—it is a definition of the concept of a sense datum as a mind-dependent entity. Premise (3), according to which two numerically distinct but subjectively indistinguishable conscious experiences are the same type of mental events, is *the most obvious suggestion*—what else could determine the type of a conscious experience than factors we can access subjectively? In a word, the concept and theory of sense datum seem to have apparently *nothing to do with* the alleged misunderstanding of "have/haben" and "image/Vorstellung"—thus Wittgenstein's diagnosis is not convincing, and consequently, neither is his therapy built thereon.

As for the metaphysical problem of time: one has to admit that it is not the best way to formulate the question thus: "Where does the present go when it becomes past, and where is the past?" But one can paraphrase Augustine's question as follows: "Does the past exist, and if so, in what sense?" to which one can answer: "Yes, it exists, as do past facts, and past facts exist in the same sense as present ones do." Here is a sketch of a possible argument for eternalism:

(1) For every true contingent proposition, there is (or: must be) something which makes it true. For example, the proposition "Whales are mammals" is made true by the fact that whales are mammals. If this fact did not obtain, then the proposition "Whales are mammals" would not be true.
(2) Propositions about the past can be true. For example, the proposition "Dinosaurs walked the Earth in the Jurassic period" is true. Or, the proposition "Wittgenstein was born in Vienna" is also true.

Therefore:

(C) The past and past facts exist, and they are as real as the present and present facts are. If only the present and present facts existed, then there would be nothing that would make propositions about the past true, so they could not be true.

My question is the same as before: can you see *anything* in this argument that would allow you to draw the conclusion that the proponent of the argument for eternalism is a victim of some conceptual confusion? Seriously, which premise comes from the image of the river of time embedded in our language? Premises (1) and (2) seem to be obvious truths. If I were ill-willed, I would invoke a passage by Wittgenstein himself against his own therapeutic philosophy, saying that our convictions that "There must be something that makes contingently true propositions true" and that "We can assert true propositions about the past," in his own words, "form the *foundation* of all operating with thoughts (with language)" (*OC* 401, italics mine). Consequently, these, as the cases of "pre-knowledge" ("*Vorwissen*"), cannot arise from misunderstanding language.

Of course, in saying this I don't want to claim that all premises of the above two arguments are true, and that the arguments themselves are compelling. All I claim is that, *for the life of me, I cannot see* any conceptual confusion or misunderstanding of language in any of the premises. That is, even if both arguments are strongly controversial, neither of them is meaningless.

A Wittgensteinian therapist could retort that I'm *still* a victim of conceptual confusion. He might say: "It is true that in formulating the 'argument from hallucination' you were not misled by the conjunction of the words 'have' and 'image'—the reason you are mistaken this time around is that you overlook the fact that in the case of hallucinations it is meaningless to say that '*Someone is aware of something*.'" And likewise, he might continue: "It is true that in formulating the argument for eternalism you are not being misled by the image of the river of time suggested by our language—the reason you are mistaken this time around is that you fail to notice that it is meaningless to say that 'Such and such a thing *makes* such and such proposition true,' that is, 'Something *makes* a truth of something else.'" And after rebuking me this way, he could add that "It is no wonder you don't find Wittgenstein's suggested therapies convincing, since you keep using meaningless sentences even in giving reasons for why you don't find these suggestions convincing."

This response is hard to answer—invoking again Wittgenstein's own words: "I have reached bedrock, and my spade is turned" (*PI* 217). All I can say is the following: perhaps one cannot go on like that *infinitely*. To put it mildly, it is not very polite for the Wittgensteinian therapist to counter my misgivings about his offered therapies by saying that I misunderstand language *again and again*. To put it differently, the reason it is extremely difficult to argue with the Wittgensteinian therapist is that he keeps repeating that I don't notice that I speak nonsense *even when* I try to make him understand why it doesn't seem to me that there are any conceptual confusions or linguistic misunderstandings in the above two arguments—he immunizes his standpoint against all objections. Insofar as he were able to place himself in the perspective of "the baffled ones" (let me add that he must be able to do that as a therapist), *beyond a point*, I think, he *would have* to admit that it is rather hard to believe that every philosopher who doesn't see any conceptual confusions in the premises of the above two arguments suffers from fatal blindness, and that Wittgenstein and the Wittgensteinian therapists *are the only ones* who can see something that not a single soul except them can see.

2.3 Undermotivation

I think that Wittgenstein's anti-philosophy attitude that characterized the whole course of his career was engendered by his experience of philosophy's epistemic failure. As he puts it: "Philosophy *really doesn't make any progress*, that the same philosophical problems that occupied the Greeks keep occupying us" (*BT* 424, italics mine). The already analyzed conceptual connection is clear: if philosophers had succeeded in solving certain substantive philosophical problems, then we should count that as progress—at t_1 they did not *yet* know the solution of this or that substantive philosophical problem, but at t_2 they *already* know it. Nevertheless, philosophers have not succeeded in solving a single substantive philosophical problem, consequently we cannot talk about substantive progress in philosophy.

I cannot see any other explanation. If some substantive philosophical problems had been solved by the community of philosophers, and so there would be consensually accepted philosophical theories, then Wittgenstein could not claim that *all* philosophical problems are meaningless. If philosophers had agreed in 1935 that charge, mass, spin, etc., are immanent universals, as physicists did about Maxwell's equations in the same year, then Wittgenstein would not have had any reason to deem the problem of universals to be meaningless.

However, let's take notice that even if we face the epistemic failure of philosophy as forcefully as Wittgenstein did, we still don't have to interpret this failure by saying that philosophical problems are meaningless pseudo-problems arising from conceptual confusion. Considering the self-defeating character of Wittgenstein's therapeutic philosophy and its close-to-zero convincing force, it seems more obvious to say that philosophical problems are meaningful but are unsolvable with the tools of philosophy. I'm not saying that we have to be metaskeptics, all I'm saying is that the commitment to Wittgenstein's therapeutic philosophy is *undermotivated*. After all, if someone, like Wittgenstein does, aims at achieving peace of mind, that is, stopping doing philosophy whenever they want to (see *PI* 133), then they can achieve that goal by suspending their philosophical beliefs as well. This is because the suspension of philosophical beliefs entails "at best" the abandonment of philosophical truth-seeking, which "offers the prospect" of the slow waning of one's cognitive needs for dealing with philosophical problems.

3 Farewell to Wittgenstein

I think Wittgenstein does not react appropriately to philosophy's epistemic failure, nor does he give a right answer to the question of what we should do with our philosophical beliefs in the light of the epistemic failure of philosophy. His view is almost certainly self-defeating. His therapeutic practices have very little convincing force and efficiency. Choosing his therapeutic philosophy would be undermotivated, as there are other, probably more efficient ways of achieving peace of mind.

But, instead of repeating my earlier criticism, I would like to say what it is that I find especially unappealing in the later Wittgenstein's philosophical attitude.

In my opinion, there are only two possibilities, and in my eyes, both are equally insupportable. One is that Wittgenstein *sees,* and in his sincere moments, *even admits to himself* that his therapeutic philosophy is self-defeating because while he supports the diagnosis for his therapies with a substantive philosophical conception of linguistic meaning (from now on, a bit defiantly, I'll call this concept "use theory"), he also thinks that all substantive philosophical theories and all substantive philosophical theses are meaningless. If this is indeed the case, what Wittgenstein does is quite *unethical,* as he hides behind the slogans "Oh no, I'm not in the business a producing any real philosophical theses"; "Oh no, far be it from me to advance any substantive philosophical theses." Thus, he consciously plays down and lies about an existing contradiction that seems ineliminable. In a word, he is a charlatan.

The other (and much more probable) possibility is that Wittgenstein *seriously believes* that the use theory of meaning underlying the diagnosis for his therapies is not a substantive philosophical theory, and as such, it is not in need of any philosophical justification. That is, he thinks that what the use theory of meaning says is something absolutely evident, a triviality. He even introduces it this way: "For a *large* class of cases—though not for all—in which we employ the word 'meaning' it can be defined thus: the meaning of a word is its use in the language" (*PI* 43, italics in original).

However, Wittgenstein must know (and he obviously knows) that there are philosophers who strongly contest the truth of the use theory of meaning. Wittgenstein is not silly, so he obviously sees that the reasoning of *PI* 43 is circular, because he can only appeal to the *use* of the word "meaning" to point out the trivial truth of the use theory of meaning if he has already committed himself to the use theory of meaning—for why would it be of any interest otherwise?

With the above, I want to say that if Wittgenstein *really* seriously believes that the things he says about meaning do not add up to any substantive philosophical theory but—in spite of their controversial nature—are absolutely *obvious*, then it can be strongly suspected (I for myself cannot imagine any other possibilities) that Wittgenstein considers himself a kind of *oracle*, with the spirit or genius of ordinary language speaking through him, someone from whom the truths about linguistic meaning and rule-following are emanated. Which means that he thinks "*I*, Ludwig Josef Johann Wittgenstein, *don't need arguments*; due to my excellence *I can access the working* of ordinary language and *can see it* not through a glass, darkly, but *face to face*; and this being so, *I can safely ignore* the objections of all those who disagree with me." For if he *really does* believe that he says only trivial truths about meaning and he sees that other people disagree with him, then his thought can only be: "Unlike me, they are lost in the labyrinth of language." In a word, he isn't a charlatan but a fanatic.

Now, whether we consider the case that he consciously downplays self-defeat, or the case that he considers himself an oracle, I feel that to me, Wittgenstein's attitude is anything but a model to be followed in accounting for the epistemic status of my substantive philosophical beliefs. And, I think, it cannot be a model to *anyone* who seriously faces up to the fact of pervasive disagreement in all fields of philosophy (including dissensus about linguistic meaning); who doesn't think it would be right to downplay the problem with a philosopher drawing on substantive philosophical theses to support his philosophical view that all substantive philosophical theses are meaningless; and who feels it inappropriate to consider himself an oracle capable of seeing through confusions no one else can see through. Thus, it cannot be an example to anyone who considers charlatanism and fanaticism as equally unacceptable.

4

Philosophy With (Intended-To-Be) Compelling Justification

Here's the second reaction to philosophy's epistemic failure:

> I'm well aware that philosophers haven't fulfilled their promises—they haven't solved philosophical problems. Still, this means only that my predecessors and contemporaries have failed. I, however, have succeeded—I have found the truth and I have got compelling justification for my substantive philosophical beliefs.

This formulation: "*I have found truth*" or "*I, of all people*, am the one who has compelling justification," or perhaps "*We, of all people*, are the ones who have at last succeeded" forms the *essence* of this reaction. It largely says that:

> After thorough investigation, I have realized that there are no philosophers or philosophical schools that are in possession of some well-founded philosophical truths. Even if there are some philosophers who hold the right view, their arguments aren't strong enough—they don't have compelling force. *I myself* had to produce compelling justifications for this or that philosophical thesis. *I myself* had to solve this or that philosophical problem. And, after a number of aborted attempts by others, *I myself* had to create and promote philosophy as an epistemically successful enterprise.

In this chapter, I deal with this reaction to philosophy's epistemic failure, which—not without sarcasm—I will call the "I'm the only one" view. First, I will illustrate the "I'm the only one" attitude with some well-known quotes. In what follows, I will put myself in the place of an imaginary "I'm the only one" philosopher and try to vividly describe the gist of the "I'm the only one" attitude and its main motivations. Finally, I will say why I think that the "I'm the only one" philosophers' reaction to philosophy's epistemic failure is improper and why I think they give a wrong answer to the question "What should we do with our philosophical beliefs in the light of philosophy's epistemic failure?"

A terminological note. You may be bothered by the wording "*I'm* the only one." You may think that typically not *a single* philosopher defends a philosophical position (be it any of them), but *many* do, so it would be more appropriate to use the phrase "*We're* the only ones." I admit that it would be more appropriate in that regard. Still, what makes me prefer the term "I'm the only one" is that it *phenomenologically better captures* the attitudes of those philosophers who are certain that they have acquired substantive philosophical truths. The emphasis is not on whether these philosophers have or do not have comrades. All that matters is that, despite being aware of the permanent disagreements in all areas of philosophy, they judge (or perhaps rather *dare* to judge) that while others are wrong, being in possession of compelling arguments, *they know* substantive philosophical truths.

1 The "I'm the only one" attitude—an illustration

The attitude of the followers of the epistemic tradition (for I'm speaking about them, although not all of them) has always been characterized by the above duality. On the one hand, they were dissatisfied with philosophy's accomplishment up to that point, and often had a very low opinion of some—or even all—other philosophers' activity. On the other hand, they themselves made attempts to turn philosophy into an epistemically fruitful enterprise—not infrequently considering themselves as the Copernicus or Newton of philosophy. They precisely saw philosophy's epistemic failure, but at the same time, they were certain that—in contrast to their predecessors and contemporaries— they will fulfil (or have already fulfilled) their promises and remedy (or have already remedied) the situation. They often sharply criticized the arguments of their predecessors and contemporaries, but thought that their own arguments were flawless and so they might as well create the much-awaited consensus in philosophy. Their characteristic rhetoric was the following: "So far all philosophy" [insert a criticizing phrase here such as "was lost"; "had no solid grounding"; "provided no certain knowledge"], "but now (!) that *I* have entered the story, everything is going to change (!)" [insert a nice fat promise here]. This rhetoric and attitude is familiar to you, isn't it?

Among the great dead philosophers, Descartes voiced his dissatisfaction this way:

Concerning philosophy I shall say only that, seeing that it has been cultivated for many centuries by the most excellent minds [...] and that, nevertheless, there still is nothing in it about which there is not some dispute, and consequently nothing that is not doubtful [...] Then, as for the other sciences, I judged that, insofar as they borrow their principles from philosophy, one could not have built anything solid upon such unstable foundations. [...] And thus I thought that book learning [...] does not draw nearly so close to the truth as the simple reasonings that a man of good sense can naturally make about the things he encounters.

(1637/2000: 49–51)

Or, here's Hume's beautifully written passage:

Nor is there requir'd such profound knowledge to discover the present imperfect condition of the sciences [that is, philosophy], but even the rabble without doors may judge from the noise and clamour, which they hear, that all goes not well within. There is nothing which is not the subject of debate, and in which men of learning are not of contrary opinions. The most trivial question escapes not our controversy, and in the most momentous we are not able to give any certain decision. Disputes are multiplied, as if every things was uncertain; and these disputes are managed with the greatest warmth, as if every things was certain.

(1739/2000: 3)

Let's leap forward and see Husserl's strict diagnosis:

I am not saying that philosophy is an imperfect science; I am saying quite simply that it is still not a science, that is has yet to begin as science, when measured by the standard of whether it possesses a piece, even if a small one, of objectively justified theoretical doctrinal content.

(1910–11/2002: 250)

And now on to the promises! Here's a promise from Kant, presented with drumroll and packed with moderately creative metaphors:

[T]hese Prolegomena will bring [everyone] to understand that there exist a completely new science, of which no one had previously formed merely the thought, of which even the bare idea was unknown, and for which nothing from all that has been provided before now could be used except the hint that Hume's doubts had been able to give; Hume also foresaw nothing of any such possible form in science, but deposited his ship on the beach (of skepticism) for safekeeping, where it could then lie and rot, whereas it is important to me give it a pilot, who, provided with complete sea-charts and compass, might safely navigate the ship wherever seems good to him, following sound principles of the helmsman's art drawn from a knowledge of the globe.

(1783/2004: 11–12)

And the promise goes on (13):

> Here then is such a plan subsequent to the completed work, which now can be laid out according to analytical method, whereas the work itself absolutely had to be composed according to the synthetic method, so that the science might present all of its articulations, as the structural organization of a quite peculiar faculty of cognition, in their natural connection.

But let me quote Kant's account of the successes he achieved two years earlier:

> I have not avoided reason's questions by pleading the incapacity of human reason as an excuse; rather I have completely specified the questions according to principles, and after discovering the point where reason has misunderstood itself, I have resolved them to reason's *full satisfaction*. [...] In this business I have made comprehensiveness my chief aim in view, and *I make bold to say that there cannot be a single metaphysical problem that has not been solved here*, or at least to the solution of which the key has not been provided.

(1781/1998: 101, [Axii–Axiii], italics mine)

And here's Husserl's promise:

> [A]gainst these and all similar ills [i.e., the failure of philosophies] there is only one remedy: scientific critique and in addition a radical science, rising up from below, grounded on sure foundations, and progressing in accordance with the most rigorous method: the philosophical science we are advocating here. Worldviews can quarrel, only science can decide, and its decision bears *the stamp of eternity*.

(1910–11/2002: 291, italics mine)

Let me quote three other passages of Husserl's, since he is probably the most grandiose philosophical promise-maker of all times:

> [I]t lies precisely in the essence of philosophy, insofar as it returns to the ultimate origins, that its scientific work moves in spheres of direct intuition, and it is the greatest step our age has to make the see that with philosophical intuition in the right sense, *the phenomenological seizing upon essences*, an endless

field of work opens up and a science that, without any indirectly symbolizing and mathematical methods, without the apparatus of inferences and proofs, nevertheless obtains an abundance of the most rigorous cognitions, which are decisive for *all* further philosophy.

(1910–11/2002: 294, italics in original)

Or:

> What is the new "revolution" to mean to us? Perhaps the turn away from the idea of rigorous science? And what is the "system" to mean to us for which we yearn, which as ideal is to light the way in the depths of our inquiring work? A philosophical "system" in the traditional sense; as it were, a Minerva that springs already completed and armed from the head of a creative genius — in order then in later times to be preserved in the silent museum of history alongside other such Minervas? Or a philosophical system of doctrine that, after the colossal preparatory work of generations, actually begins from below with *an indubitable foundation* and *rises up* like any sound edifice, wherein *stone is set upon stone, each as solid as the other*, in accordance with guiding insights? On this question minds and paths must part.

(251, italics mine)

It is also worth seeing what Husserl thinks about the utmost significance of his own philosophy, which is supposed to give a new meaning to human existence due to phenomenological reflection:

> [T]he ultimate self-understanding of man as being responsible for his own human being [is] *his self-understanding as being in being called to a life of apodicticity*, not only in abstractly practicing apodictic science in the usual sense but [as being mankind] which realizes its whole concrete being in apodictic freedom by becoming apodictic mankind in the whole active life of its reason — through which it is human.

(1936/1970: 340–1, italics in original)

Finally, let me quote Moritz Schlick's passage, who presented a sneakier way of promising than the above authors, since not only does he emphasize how well he is aware of philosophy's epistemic failure so far, but he also stresses how well he is aware of how many unfulfilled promises have been made previously by different philosophers:

> I refer to this anarchy of philosophical opinions which has so often been described, in order to leave no doubt that I am fully conscious of the scope and

weighty significance of the conviction that I should now like to express. For I am convinced that we now find ourselves at an altogether decisive turning point in philosophy, and we are objectively justified in considering that an end has come to the fruitless conflict of systems. We are already at the present time [...] in possession of methods which make every such conflict in principle unnecessary. What is now required is their resolute application.

(1930–31/1959: 54)

And here's Schlick's optimistic prophecy and the epistemic degradation of those philosophers who disagree with him:

Thus after the great turning point of philosophy shows its decisive character even more clearly than before. It is only, indeed, because of this character that the conflict of systems can be ended. I repeat: [...] we may today consider it as in principle already ended [...] Certainly there will still be many a rear-guard action. Certainly many will for centuries continue to wander further along the traditional paths. Philosophical writers will long continue to discuss the old pseudo-questions. But in the end they will no longer be listened to; they will come to resemble actors who continue to play for some time before noticing that the audience has slowly departed. Then it will no longer be necessary to speak of "philosophical problems" for one will speak philosophically concerning *all* problems, that is: clearly and meaningfully.

(1930–31/1959: 59, italics in original)

Of course, we rarely meet such great promises laced with rhetoric fireworks in the literature of epistemic tradition. The rhetoric and the promise are usually more modest.

As for the rhetoric, it is indeed true that of the followers of the epistemic tradition, only a few describe their successes with expressions such as "complete sea-charts and a compass," a "safely navigating pilot," the "indubitable foundation," the "stamp of eternity," and a "great turning point of philosophy." At the same time, despite their moderate rhetoric, the "I'm the only one" philosophers are *just as certain* that they can compellingly justify their *own* philosophical views and disprove all the rival conceptions as Kant, Husserl, or Schlick were. They are *just as hopeful* about the epistemic success of their *own* philosophical activity as the great dead philosophers, and their belief about the epistemic status of their *own* substantive philosophical beliefs is the same as theirs—apart from the fact that they hardly ever compare their significance to Newton's or Copernicus', thereby thankfully avoiding a comparison out of proportion. You would misunderstand their intentions if you thought that their reserved rhetoric indicates that they don't fully trust in the success of their theory and present their arguments at half-mast, so to say.

As for the promises, it is indeed true that of the followers of the epistemic tradition, only a few give their essays pretentious titles such as, for example, Cudworth (*A true intellectual system of the universe*), or as Spinoza (*Ethica: ordine geometrico demonstrata*), and only a few set such major goals to themselves as the philosophers quoted above. Not all "I'm the only one" philosophers think that they have succeeded in solving some *big* philosophical problem(s) once and for all. Rather, many of them think something like this: "I have only solved just a *tiny piece* of the great puzzle, and by solving this piece I do my share in the great success of philosophy as an epistemic enterprise." For example, if a philosopher thinks that he has succeeded in compellingly justifying the philosophical thesis that there are no abstract artifacts, and interprets his achievement as taking a *small* but *certain* step *forward* on the road to making sure that later generations can compellingly justify the big philosophical thesis that only concrete entities exist, then he is *also* an "I'm the only one" philosopher. This means that the "I'm the only one" attitude doesn't presuppose that the philosophical thesis to be compellingly justified is a significant, comprehensive one—what only counts is that the philosopher must be *sure* that he has compellingly justified his substantive philosophical beliefs.

I wouldn't like to scorn the followers of the epistemic tradition—I'm just trying to throw light on the nature of the "I'm the only one" attitude. Namely, the "I'm the only one" philosophers are not naïve when they embark on a quest for philosophical truths, and they do not underestimate the difficulty of their enterprise. They are well aware that their predecessors and contemporaries have not managed to fulfil their promises, but they are undeterred by this fact. The later "I'm the only one" members of the epistemic tradition know precisely that the promises made by the above-quoted great dead philosophers have remained unfulfilled. They know that—*pace* Kant—nothing at all was "ultimately" developed by the suggested analytic method, and if Kant has a way of observing his successors' (e.g., the German idealists') works from the beyond, he is unlikely to be rubbing his hands with satisfaction. They know that—*pace* Husserl—the ideas he had about the redemptive role of his own phenomenology did not come true, to put it mildly. Husserl thought that by intuitive fulfillment, he would be able to anchor all his insights in a kind of field of evidence, and thanks to his work, a so far undiscovered space will open, every fruit of which would grow out of apodictic soil. In reality (and using another metaphor), as for the apodictic truth-fishing in the transcendental sea of the eidetic phenomenology of essences he introduced, the net hangs off his boat rather empty. They know that—*pace* Schlick—it did not take too long before logical empiricism was crumbled to pieces; and was considered as one of the least tenable theories put on display as a deterring piece in the retrospective hall of the museum of philosophical ideas.

I really don't want to heap scorn. Instead, I would like to draw your attention to the peculiar feature that despite the incredible amount of unfulfilled promises and failures, the epistemic tradition of philosophy has survived and is alive and kicking even today. That is, to the feature that more and more philosophers join this tradition, who try to "force truth into the open" with the tools of philosophy again and again. And they are able to live with the unshakable certainty that—unlike others—they (*of all people*) have succeeded in doing so.

2 Dialogue with an "I'm the only one" philosopher

One participant of the dialogue is Sophie. Of her, it is enough to say that she is not a constructive (theorizing) character, yet she considers it very important to clearly see the epistemic status of her philosophical beliefs, and she does her best not to deceive herself. The other participant of the dialogue is a figure in the epistemic tradition—a full-fledged "I'm the only one" philosopher. Of him, it is enough to say that he is unshakably certain that he knows substantive philosophical truths and that he has compelling arguments for his philosophical view; moreover, he doesn't hide his extra-high epistemic self-conviction. I will call him "Philonous" for the sake of the game.

> *Sophie*: I gather that you've worked out a metaphysical theory in detail on the nature of possible worlds, right?
>
> *Philonous*: Yes, I have.
>
> *Sophie*: And what does the nature of possible worlds consist in?
>
> *Philonous*: I'm an actualist, an ersatz-realist to be exact. I claim that there is only one world that contains concrete particulars (physical objects and physical events)—the actual world, the one we live in. Also, there are abstract entities in our world besides the concrete particulars—they represent the ways our world could be. Thus, I consider possible worlds abstract entities.
>
> *Sophie*: And what do you make of the fact that your view (i.e., that possible worlds are abstract entities) is just one of the great many rival philosophical views? The other views (modal deflationism, modal fictionalism, robust

modal realism, modal combinatorism, and modal dimensionalism) are logically incompatible with ersatz-realism, but they are also well-supported by philosophical arguments. Don't you think you should take your confidence back a notch?

Philonous: I don't understand why I should bother. As opposed to my interlocutors, I'm in an *epistemically privileged* position.

Sophie: What do you mean by that?

Philonous: I simply mean that the arguments for my view exactly suit the ontological landscape of reality. They provide me with access to its natural joints. But, if you don't like these metaphors, I can put it this way: my view is free from the mistakes of rival views and unifies their advantages. My arguments have shown this—beyond all doubts, that is, compellingly.

Sophie: But apart from appealing to your alleged epistemically privileged position, can you show me at least one independent argument for your having no reason to worry about the others' views?

Philonous: Of course I can. When I have to decide whether I can believe with all certainty in the existence of abstract entities that represent possible situations, I only have to consider the issues which are *inherently* connected with this question. It would only be reasonable to "take my confidence back a notch" if I discovered a seemingly irresolvable *internal* difficulty within my own theory. However, I don't see any such difficulty. I can show beyond all doubts that all alleged difficulties are based on mistakes or on misunderstanding.

To put it differently, if I couldn't answer the question "What distinguishes the actual world from the innumerable non-actualized possible worlds?" or if I couldn't explain the concept of transworld identity, or, if, as I am committed to the existence of abstract entities, I couldn't answer the question "How we, persons existing in space-time (concrete particulars) can have access to these abstract entities that are outside of space-time?" then—I concede—I would start having some doubts about the truth of ersatz-realism. But, excuse me, I don't care at all if the philosophical views held by others are incompatible with mine, because it is evident that this fact is not one of the difficulties with my theory. This has nothing whatsoever to do with it, being neither in favor of nor against it.

Sophie: But how is it possible that your confidence is not shaken if you recognize that there are rival theories that were also worked out by smart philosophers, and they don't accept your arguments as compelling? Why do you think that it is *precisely your* own theory that is epistemically privileged? How can you justify that it is *precisely your* own theory that carves nature at its joints, and all other views misrepresent them? If *you* can consider yourself an epistemically privileged person, then you must allow for the possibility that the advocates of other views can do so as well. Or, if *you* can consider your arguments compelling, then you must allow for the possibility that the advocates of other views can consider their own arguments compelling as well.

Philonous: Of course, all my interlocutors would vindicate the epistemic privileged position to themselves. But it is only *I* who can do it *legitimately*, because my arguments *do support* my view compellingly, and I can make irrefutable objections to the rival theories. Those who think otherwise than me haven't understood the arguments for my view. Although I pointed out the mistakes of their arguments, it was in vain because they failed to recognize them. It is not my responsibility if they cannot see the compelling force of my arguments, just like it is not my responsibility if they cannot notice the fatal pitfalls in their arguments. Sophie, the thing is that my interlocutors are *not* my epistemic peers. All of them are my epistemic inferiors.

Sophie: Excuse me, but I still can't believe you. Imagine a mathematician who comes up with the proof of a conjecture. After reading his paper, his colleagues conclude that the proof is insufficient, or at least not compelling. What's the difference between you and this mathematician? Your papers are read by your colleagues who conclude that your proof is insufficient, or at least not compelling. Perhaps is it the case that your arguments are more difficult to follow than a mathematical proof? It's hard for me not to suspect that you keep advertising your epistemically privileged position so intensively so you don't have to face the fact that you—like other members in the epistemic tradition—have failed to produce compelling philosophical arguments.

Philonous: Sophie, we're going in a circle again and again. I can only tell you that I already told you before. I can see *clare et distincte* that the premises of my argument are unassailable and I can see *clare et distincte* that the conclusion logically follows from its premises. That is, my argument is compelling, and whoever denies its conclusion must be irrational.

But, as you've been nagging me so much, let me tell you how things stand. Let's suppose that you enter into a debate with a philosopher, an avid follower of Marquis de Sade who cannot see that it's morally wrong to cause suffering to others out of sheer pleasure. You try to convince him with all kinds of arguments, but he is adamant that you're wrong. He brushes off your arguments and requests you to produce some additional ones, which would prove beyond all doubt that it is *precisely your* own view that carves the moral world order at its joints.

Sophie, you better admit that you couldn't produce any additional argument like that, moreover, you wouldn't think that any such further argument is necessary in this situation. You would simply think that the Marquis' follower doesn't understand your arguments—he lacks the ability of philosophical insight. You would say "I know I'm right, I know that my interlocutor is wrong, because I can see *clare et distincte* the truth of the proposition 'It's morally wrong to cause suffering to others out of sheer pleasure.'" But you might as well say that "My interlocutor lacks *moral sense*." Now, what I think of my interlocutors is similar: it's that they lack the appropriate *philosophical* sense. If you wish, their "philosophical device" is faulty. If you wish, they're "epistemically ill-equipped." And don't give me the line that whereas you would argue for some obvious truth in the above imaginary situation and your interlocutor would deny some obvious truth, I'm arguing for some non-obvious truth and my interlocutors deny some non-obvious truth. You shouldn't do that because, in the light of my arguments, the truth of ersatz-realism is as evident to me as the truth of the proposition "It's morally wrong to cause suffering to others out of sheer pleasure" is evident to you.

Sophie: Well, then let me also tell you how things stand in my opinion. I think the thing is that you're a victim of a peculiar defect. My diagnosis is that you're incapable of self-reflection, and unable to see yourself from the outside. You're aware that there are others who hold views incompatible with your own view—you must obviously be aware of that, as you're arguing against them. Still, you're unable—please note the emphasis—to *step out* of your philosophical cave and see your own view *as just one* among many others that are also well underpinned by philosophical arguments.

If you were capable of self-reflection (as you're not), then you would immediately *realize* that your philosophical view is just one among many. If you could see the various views—among them, your own—from the outside, you would immediately *realize* that yours *doesn't have a privileged status*. Thus, if you were capable of self-reflection, your certainty that it is *precisely your* arguments that are compelling would vanish into thin air (for you would now think "Indeed, why *precisely my* arguments?"); and you wouldn't think it evident that it is *precisely your* arguments that "map" the ontological landscape of reality (for you would now think "Indeed, why *precisely my* arguments?").

Let me go further. If you could put yourself in your interlocutors' perspective (as you cannot), you would see that they may be just as certain that they're right as you—the situation is *symmetrical*. You would realize that their "certainty-awareness" is subjectively *indistinguishable* from yours. Furthermore, if you could put yourself in their perspective, you would understand at last that their and your philosophical views carry *equal weight,* and they aren't your epistemic inferiors, who cannot see the compelling force of your arguments due to some fault in their "philosophical device" or "epistemic equipment"—rather, these philosophers are your epistemic peers. For you must concede that you cannot non-circularly justify that the intuitions your interlocutors draw on in developing their philosophical theories are less solid than those on which your own theory is built.

Let me give you an example. If you were able to put yourself in Lewis' perspective, you would immediately see that robust realists are able to reduce modalities (they're able to provide truth-makers with proper metaphysical status for our ordinary, literally true modal statements), thus Lewis' theory—at least in this respect—*performs better* than the ersatz-realism you hold, which cannot do that. To put it simply: there are a number of important and fundamental intuitions and pre-philosophical convictions about modalities that are more consistent with rival theories than with yours.

Here's a vivid passage which, in my opinion, sheds light on the situation:

> Suppose, thousands of people, each of whom wants to go to São Paulo, randomly board all flights departing Dallas-Fort Worth. Suppose they fill all departing seats, but are not told where they are going. Of these thousands, a few hundred in fact will land in São Paulo. Most will arrive somewhere else. Philosophy seems like this in many respects. It may bring some people to the proper destination, but it dumps most somewhere else. Actually, matters are worse than that. Travelers will know whether they have arrived in São Paulo. In philosophy's case, some may indeed arrive at truth. However, they will not have discernibly better grounds for believing this than their mistaken peers. They may believe themselves to have better grounds, and their peers believe this about themselves as well. However, *from the outsider's perspective* [that is, on the 'level' of self-reflection], *they look the same.*
>
> (Brennan 2010: 3–4, italics from Sophie)

Philonous: Dear Sophie, you're saying what you're saying with truly impressive vigor—too bad that it's altogether false. You're wrong to claim that I'm incapable of self-reflection. I am capable of it, and I did reflect on my own activity—I've reviewed my own view in the multitude of the many rival theories. However, my self-reflection *has not* revealed what *you think* it should have revealed, namely that my view is just one among many.

Rather, it has revealed that my view is *the only true one* among many other false ones.

You're also wrong to claim that I'm unable to put myself in my interlocutors' perspective. I've already done that on several occasions, and thoroughly investigated the kinds of evidence, pre-philosophical intuitions, and fundamental convictions which my interlocutors appeal to in constructing theories. However, this "putting myself in others' perspective" *has not* produced the result that *you think* it should have. Rather, it has produced the result that most of my interlocutors' pre-philosophical intuitions and fundamental convictions are delusional.

In a word, your whole reasoning is flawed, and, frankly speaking, unappealing. For—and now *you* note the emphasis!—you *presuppose* that my self-reflection *can only reveal* that my view is just one among many epistemically equal views. Moreover, you also *presuppose* that "my putting myself in my interlocutors' perspective" *can only reveal* that their intuitions are not weaker than mine. Let me ask you a rhetorical question: why do you think everything should work out just as you expect it should?

Furthermore, when you "suggest" that I've wrongly judged the epistemic status of my view because in fact it is of equal weight as the others, and when you "suggest" that the degree of my certainty cannot be higher than my interlocutors'—well, I can tell you that *you're the one* who judges wrongly because *you yourself* are unable to see the compelling force of my arguments for ersatz-realism.

I doubt that there are many "I'm the only one" philosophers who would put it this bluntly. I admit that my depiction of Philonous' figure as an "I'm the only one" philosopher was a bit exaggerated—the sentences that I made him utter were "a little" harsh. Still, I believe that Philonous' attitude well represents that of those philosophers who—although being aware of the fact of permanent disagreement in all areas of philosophy—are certain that they know substantive philosophical truths. At least deep in their heart, they must assess the epistemic status of their substantive philosophical beliefs in the way Philonous does.

This is because they cannot really do otherwise. For if they think that they possess substantive philosophical truths, they *must also* think that the reason they possess them is not that they happen to be the lucky winners of an epistemological lottery draw; rather, they think the reason is that they have compelling justifications for their philosophical beliefs at issue. Furthermore, if they think that they have compelling justifications for their substantive philosophical beliefs, then they must think what Philonous thinks. Namely, that their views correctly represent the structure of reality; that the arguments for their views "map" its ontological landscape; that their views are free from the mistakes of the rival ones, and unify their advantages. And, indeed, that those who disagree with them do not understand their arguments—they are irrational because they don't recognize their compelling force. Being aware of the pervasive and permanent dissensus in philosophy, no one can think that one knows compellingly justified substantive philosophical truths unless one considers one's own position as epistemically privileged and degrades one's interlocutors as one's epistemic inferiors.

Using another terminology, the "I'm the only one" philosophers are advocates of the steadfast view. Of course, they do not embrace the variant of the steadfast view that goes hand in hand with permissivism—the "I'm the only one" philosophers don't allow for rational disagreements concerning philosophical problems. In their opinion, there can be *only one* rational view on a philosophical problem. Nor do they embrace that version of the steadfast view which says that S can rationally stick to the truth of belief *p* because the evidence (or set of evidences) on the basis of which S originally committed himself to the truth of *p* has more epistemic weight than the fact, recognized by S, that some philosophers who are his epistemic peers deny that *p* is true. In the eyes of the "I'm the only one" philosophers, the latter wording is weak, insincere, and unprincipled—for according to them, a philosopher can only rationally stick to the truth of *p*, while being aware that others think *p* to be false, if he *does not consider those others his epistemic peers*. The "I'm the only one" philosophers think that the only right variant of the steadfast view which can be upheld sincerely is that which enjoins one to *epistemically degrade* all those who disagree with him—this is the only way for one to rationally stick to the truth of one's substantive philosophical beliefs.

3 The lesson of the dialogue—epistemic blindness

If I had to, I would bet a lot that you side with Sophie and not Philonous in their debate. For there is something displeasing and almost irritating in Philonous' attitude. It is probably clear from the dialogue what the most displeasing factors are, but let me make them explicit.

(1) You may find it displeasing and irritating in Philonous' attitude that he is not the least swayed by the fact that other philosophers do not consider his arguments as compelling. You may think that Philonous has the epistemic duty to take his self-confidence back a notch. Instead, he keeps obsessively repeating that his arguments are compelling, and he knows that with all certainty because he *clare et distincte* sees the compelling force of his arguments. However, Philonous can retort that no argument or justification can be invalidated by the fact that others hold it flawed. Since he really *clare et distincte* sees the compelling force of his arguments, he has no reason, not to mention epistemic duty, to take his self-confidence back a notch.

(2) You may also find it displeasing and irritating in Philonous' attitude his unwillingness to concede that the rival theories about the metaphysics of possible worlds are of equal weight as his ersatz-realism, and his view that the advocates of rival theories are his epistemic inferiors. Philonous, however, might reply that the reason he does not concede that the rival theories are of equal weight as his is that they are not of equal weight as his. His theory is true, and all other theories are false. And he rightly considers his interlocutors as his epistemic inferiors because they believe falsehoods, and are unable to see the compelling force of the objections against their views.

(3) You may also think that Philonous does not understand the concept of self-reflection, and—although he is convinced of it—he has not carried out a single self-reflective act during his career. For had he carried out one, he should have realized that his view is really just one among many and is not privileged. Philonous, however, might reply that he does understand the concept of self-reflection precisely and he has already carried out several self-reflective acts. But his self-reflective acts have made him see the incontrovertible truth that his view is not merely one among many in the multitude of views, but a privileged one, because it is true.

(4) Finally, you may also find it displeasing and irritating in Philonous' attitude that he is unable to put himself in his rivals' perspective. He merely says that he is able, but in fact he is unable to do that, and he merely says he has done that, but in fact he has not. For had he done that, he should have realized that his rivals also drew on strong intuitions in working out their theories, and there are some intuitions that are consistent with those rival theories but not with his own. Philonous, however, might answer that he does not merely

say so but he did put himself in his opponents' perspective. But his putting himself into their perspective has resulted in his seeing without a doubt that the intuitions on which the rival theories are based are all delusional, and deceive those who draw on them in constructing theories.

So, this is how I see the main lesson from the debate between Sophie and Philonous and from the contrasts listed above. Philonous is the unshakable champion of the "I'm the only one" view. He has answers to every objection. He is able to neutralize all of them, and what he says is unassailable from his own perspective. Philonous is absolutely consistent. If his arguments are really compelling, then it is really irrelevant that others doubt them. Philonous is absolutely sincere. He sincerely believes that he *clare et distincte* sees the compelling force of his arguments. He also sincerely believes that the theory he holds is epistemically privileged, and thus that his interlocutors are all his epistemic inferiors whose intuitions and fundamental pre-philosophical convictions are delusional.

At the same time (and now take it as a wink!) *we both precisely know* that Philonous' resistance to Sophie's objections and his consistency and sincerity are not virtues but rather symptoms. *We do not believe him* that he is capable of self-reflection or that he is able to put himself in his opponents' perspective and to really weigh the intuitions on which the rival theories are based.

For, as Sophie has rightly pointed out, Philonous' belief in his epistemically privileged position stems from his special deficiency. I call this deficiency *epistemic blindness*. Philonous is blind. He is not inattentive, like a man who accidentally leaves his king in the hitting position during a game of chess. He does not make any logical fallacies, either. He does not ignore the arguments brought up against his view. He is simply blind to others' epistemic perspective, to the "epistemic attractiveness" of considerations and arguments for rival theories.

And, of course, he is blind to his own deficiency. His own epistemic blindness is *hidden* and *undetectable* for him. He is unaware of his incapability of self-reflection. He is unaware of his incapability of putting himself in others' perspective. As an "I'm the only one" philosopher (in his dark philosophical cave), Philonous can do philosophy throughout his entire career, secure in the conviction that his philosophical position is epistemically privileged and that the truth of his ersatz-realism is beyond dispute—without having second thoughts for a moment.

Now (and take it again as a wink!), *both of us can precisely see* Philonous' blindness. We see that he does not have the faintest idea as to what Sophie finds wanting in his activity. Philonous' epistemic blindness is *transparent*—and being so, it is frightening. Philonous' mind *darkens* whenever he judges himself to be epistemically superior to everybody else. What is *fatal* about his blindness is the fact that he cannot do anything against it, as he is unaware of it. Philonous is a sick fanatic, an epistemic narcissist who is unfortunately able to make himself believe that Sophie's misgivings are all groundless and irrelevant (see Bernáth and Tőzsér 2020: esp. sec. 2). In fact, it is his consistency and "unassailable" arguments against Sophie that actually block the way to realizing his own blindness.

Let's suppose that Sophie, as a last desperate move, tries to parody Philonous. She points out that Philonous' self-confidence to shrug off all criticism is ridiculous and at once pathetic. She lists the great many names of those who, coming before Philonous in the history of philosophy, made self-confident promises, the great many names of those coming before him who already said "All philosophies have so far been wide of the mark, but mine is a game-changer." She brings it to Philonous' attention that this promise-making can be continued infinitely, because philosophers foolishly tend to believe that the more often they repeat a promise—while bringing up the past breakings of promises with a resentful or apologizing tone—the more convincing it will be, for the more truth it includes of the past. In a word, she tries to appeal to Philonous' sense of humor or self-irony.

It might be that on watching the parody, Philonous would laugh at himself together with Sophie and realize that his awareness of his epistemic privilege is comic indeed. But knowing Philonous' character, it is not too probable. A more probable scenario is that Philonous would say to Sophie: "The punch line is off, because I'm not one among many who broke their promises, but rather, I'm the only one who has kept it." To make Philonous laugh, it would be necessary to enable him to see himself *from the outside*—but nobody could force him to do so. Although *we know* that Philonous' self-confidence is comic, he is incapable of self-reflection, so there is a danger that his own comic nature remains forever hidden to him.

4 Farewell to the "I'm the only one" view

Although I consider the "I'm the only one" view an improper reaction to philosophy's epistemic failure, I have some residual bad feeling. For, after all, what if I'm wrong, and an "I'm the only one" philosopher who is able to compellingly justify his substantive philosophical theses has already been born? I have to admit that I wasn't entirely correct in saying above "we both precisely *know*" that Philonous' epistemic confidence merely stems from his inability for self-reflection and for putting himself in other's epistemic perspective, and in saying that "both of us can precisely *see*" that Philonous is in fact a fanatic suffering from epistemic blindness, or a comic figure. *All* I've done is wink at you and reject this reaction by appealing to your presumed agreement.

Now I have to say something to that. And *the most* I can say is this: I reject the "I'm the only one" view as a reaction to philosophy's epistemic failure because *I don't want to be a man like Philonous*. May I say, I don't feel it right to become a man who takes views with absolute self-confidence on questions surrounded with permanent dissent, and doesn't have the slightest doubt about things not being the way he believes them to be—who imagines himself to be epistemically superior to everybody else. And I don't feel it right to become a man who thinks that all his interlocutors are unable to recognize the compelling force of his arguments, thinks that their "philosophical device" and "epistemic equipment" are faulty, and simply declares that their intuitions and fundamental pre-philosophical convictions are deceptive—who considers everybody disagreeing with him his epistemic inferior. I feel that it would be wrong—not just a bit, but *very wrong*—to become a man like this, and that's why I reject the "I'm the only one" view.

Of course, this is anything but an ordinary philosophical argument. But, as I see it, like solipsism, the "I'm the only one" view or attitude is irrefutable and unassailable. Just as the solipsist does not think that other persons' epistemic perspectives are relevant because he thinks they don't exist and so he renders himself virtually immune to any objections, the "I'm the only one" philosopher does more or less the same. To put it differently, the "I'm the only one" view—just like solipsism—looks "as a little frontier fortress that will undeniably be forever invincible, but whose garrison can never leave, so we may go safely past it and not be afraid to leave it behind us" (Schopenhauer 1818/2010: 129). And if it is invincible, then—beyond winking and parody—I cannot do anything but tell you why I feel that this infinitely consistent and unassailable attitude is *morally wrong*, and why I feel that for me, the "I'm the only one" philosopher is *not a role model*, and his reaction to philosophy's epistemic failure is *not an example to follow*. In some instances, the most one can do is to make a personal confession in rejecting a philosophical view or attitude.

Thus, in rejecting the "I'm the only one" view, I do not place the main emphasis on the point that—in light of the pervasive and permanent dissensus in philosophy—it is almost certainly the case that no "I'm the only one" philosophers have so far succeeded in coming up with compelling arguments for their substantive philosophical theses. (Who knows, perhaps some of them have succeeded—I cannot rule out this possibility.) Rather, the main emphasis is on the "I'm the only one" philosophers' extra-high epistemic self-confidence and the epistemic degradation of their interlocutors—and that is why I find their attitude unacceptable, even if it stems from their epistemic blindness.

***

Now I make a leap. It is a well-known fact in the history of philosophy that Descartes (as one of the "I'm the only one" philosophers) sent the manuscript of *Meditations* to six philosophers, asking them to formulate objections to the line of thought of his work. On the one hand, this is a very sympathetic and fair gesture—Descartes insisted on having his book published with these objections and the replies to them. On the other hand, however—and this is a lesser known fact—he made only one change in the original text in response to the criticisms. He revised this sentence

> The second reason for doubt was that since I did not know the author of my being, I saw nothing to rule out the possibility that my natural constitution made me prone to error even in matters which seemed to me most true.
>
> (1641/1991: 53)

by inserting *seven* words (five in Latin) in brackets into it "in response" to Arnauld's criticism:

> The second reason for doubt was that since I did not know the author of my being (*or at least was pretending not to*), I saw nothing to rule out the possibility that my natural constitution made me prone to error even in matters which seemed to me most true.

That's all he did. By the way, he thought that *each* of the close to 100 objections were misguided. *None of them*, he thought, was powerful enough to make him change the "perfect" line of thought of the *Meditations*.

What I want to illustrate through this example is the "I'm the only one" philosophers' attitude towards other philosophers who disagree with them. Descartes considered the objections of Hobbes, Arnauld, Gassendi, and others as relevant and took their epistemic perspective seriously *only to the extent* that he was able to incorporate their objections to his own "flawless" philosophical theory, which enabled him to articulate it in an even more powerful and elaborate form. That's why he published his book with his replies to those objections.

Just as in the case of Wittgenstein, Descartes' attitude is not an example for me to follow. Obviously, I'd like to have such intellectual hardware that Descartes had (who wouldn't?), but I wouldn't like to have the same attitude as his to my own philosophical beliefs.

5

Philosophy Without Compelling Justification

Several philosophers think that there can be no compelling justifications for our substantive philosophical beliefs. Thus, in their opinion, it is not right to react to philosophy's epistemic failure by sticking to the original goal of the epistemic tradition. Nor it is right to react to it by committing ourselves to meta-skepticism—to suspend our substantive philosophical beliefs and thereby end the standard (ordinary) practice of philosophy. David Lewis puts it this way in the preface to Volume 1 of his *Philosophical Papers*:

> The reader in search of knock-down arguments in favor of my theories will go away disappointed. Whether or not it would be nice to knock disagreeing philosophers down by sheer force of argument, it cannot be done. Philosophical theories are never refuted conclusively […]
>
> It might be otherwise if, as some philosophers seem to think, we had a sharp line between […] "intuition", which must be taken as unchallengeable evidence, and philosophical theory, which must at all costs fit this evidence. If that were so, conclusive refutations would be dismayingly abundant. But whatever may be said for foundationalism in other subjects, this foundationalist theory of philosophical knowledge seem ill-founded in the extreme. Our "intuitions" are simply opinions; our philosophical theories are the same. Some are commonsensical, some are sophisticated; some are particular, some general; some are more firmly held, some less. But they are all opinions, and a *reasonable goal for a philosopher is to bring them into equilibrium*. Our common task is *to find out what equilibria there are that can withstand examination* but it remains for each of us to come to rest at one or another of them.
>
> (1983: x, italics mine)

I would like to point out two things in the above quote. Firstly, according to Lewis, the foundationalist theory of philosophical knowledge is ill-founded. Our intuitions, pre-philosophical beliefs, and fundamental convictions *do not need* any justification. Nonetheless, the intuitions, pre-philosophical beliefs, and fundamental convictions have a *decisive role* in philosophical theorizing—philosophers draw on them and elaborate them in constructing their theories. As Lewis puts it in another context:

> It is not the business of philosophy [...] to justify these preexisting opinions, to any great extent, but only to try to discover ways of expanding them into an orderly system. A [philosophical] analysis [...] is an attempt at systematizing our opinions [...] It succeeds to the extent that (1) it is systematic, and (2) it respects those of our pre-philosophical opinions to which we are firmly attached.
>
> (1973: 88)

Gary Gutting sees things similarly:

> On any account, philosophy is concerned with our convictions — beliefs about fundamental human issues [...] According to the view that I've called philosophical foundationalism, the project of philosophy is to provide compelling arguments for or against our convictions, so that our beliefs [...] can be put on solid rational basis. But, I have maintained, one of the most important achievements of recent philosophy has been to discredit this foundationalism. Philosophers themselves have good reason to believe that our convictions do not require [...] compelling philosophical justifications [...]
>
> Prior to philosophical reflection, our convictions are not very well articulated and can be profitably regarded as expressing general *pictures*; that is, general schemes for thinking about some major aspect of the world. One of the main projects of philosophical thinking is the development of the precise and detailed formulations of important pictures that I called *theories*.
>
> (2009: 225, italics in original)

Secondly, Lewis distinguishes between the task of *individual* philosophers and the *community* of philosophers. The task of individual philosophers is to develop theories that are in harmony or equilibrium with *their own* pre-philosophical convictions and to defend and protect this equilibrium. Although Lewis does not say, he obviously thinks that insofar as philosophers can do that, they can rationally stick to their philosophical theories, that is, their considered philosophical beliefs. And the task of the community of philosophers is to present *more and more* well-formulated philosophical theories which are resistant to objections, thereby showcasing the possible views about philosophical problems. In short, philosophy aims to populate the logical space with consistent philosophical theories, stable equilibria.

This metaphilosophical vision stands in contrast with the epistemic tradition in both respects. On the one hand, the followers of the epistemic tradition are foundationalists—they consider their fundamental convictions as justified (moreover, compellingly justified), on which they build their philosophical theories. On the other hand, the goal of individual philosophers and the philosophers' community is the same in the epistemic tradition—to acquire substantive philosophical knowledge, and to come up with compellingly justified substantive philosophical truths.

As far as I can see, this kind of metaphilosophical vision that has given up on seeking compellingly justified philosophical truths but wishes to refrain from suspending beliefs is increasingly popular among contemporary philosophers. More and more philosophers interpret their own activity within the metaphilosophical vision described above, which is a humbler ambition than that of the great dead philosophers. It is no surprise that this is so. What this vision suggests—contrary to both the search for compelling philosophical arguments and a general suspension of judgment—neither seems hopeless, nor is depressing but something that philosophers *are able to* actually do and philosophy is *capable of* doing.

Following Lewis, I will call this metaphilosophical vision *equilibrism*. In this, I differ from the terminology in which "equilibrism" is used to denote a narrower metaphilosophical vision than the one delineated above (see Beebee 2018). As for terminology, according to equilibrism, philosophy is not an epistemic or truth-seeking enterprise. To put it more precisely, it is not an epistemic enterprise in the sense defined in Chapter 1 of this book, in that it should present compellingly justified substantive philosophical truths. Apart from this, equilibrism is, of course, also a cognitive (or, if you wish, a *quasi*-epistemic) enterprise because it gives us knowledge of what equilibria are possible and which equilibrium we should commit ourselves to in the light of our own pre-philosophical convictions.

In this chapter, I first outline the metaphilosophical vision of equilibrism. In doing so, I will try to introduce it in its most convincing form possible, and underline those features that make it attractive to many philosophers. Secondly, I will present my concerns about this vision. I will try to show that, however attractive and lucrative the commitment to this vision that gives up on seeking compellingly justified philosophical truths may seem, it is actually a wrong reaction to philosophy's epistemic failure—the equilibrist doesn't give a right answer to the question "What should we do with our philosophical beliefs in the light of philosophy's epistemic failure?" Finally, I will briefly deal with that version of equilibrism which says that the good strategy is not to *believe* in our substantive philosophical theses but only to *accept* them—and present my misgivings about it.

1 Equilibrism as a metaphilosophical vision

Let's first see the goal of individual philosophers and that of the philosophers' community, and then where the attraction of equilibrism lies.

1.1 The goal of individual philosophers

According to equilibrism, every philosopher has two clearly distinguishable tasks. The first is to come up with a philosophical theory. Whether this theory has Hegelian ambition or concerns only an isolated and partial problem; whether it includes some positive view or a negative one; whether it has an existential stake or not—these are all completely irrelevant. Now, a philosopher's theory construction is successful if she can come up with a consistent theory that is in equilibrium with *her own* pre-philosophical convictions—those which she is not willing to (or cannot) abandon. In short, if she can develop her own pre-philosophical convictions into a philosophical theory.

To use a very simple example: if Esther's fundamental pre-philosophical conviction is that mathematical theorems are truths that are discovered instead of being invented by mathematicians, and Esther constructs a philosophical theory according to which there are abstract entities (there is a Fregean "third realm"), then she has already completed her first task. She now has a philosophical theory that is in equilibrium with her pre-philosophical conviction. What happens if Ester's pre-philosophical convictions change with time? Well, then she would have to start the work *again from scratch*—she would have to work out a philosophical theory which is in equilibrium with her *changed* pre-philosophical convictions.

The second task of philosophers is just as important. What is more, they spend most of their time completing this task, since it is not enough to find or construct a philosophical theory that is in equilibrium with their pre-philosophical convictions. They must defend this equilibrium as well, as it is threatened by more than one thing. The equilibrium they reach, to use Gary Gutting's expression, needs *intellectual maintenance* (see 2009: 225; 2015: 258).

Intellectual maintenance has two components. Firstly, philosophers have to defend the theories that are in equilibrium with their pre-philosophical convictions against objections. They have to do this because philosophical objections ultimately have the intended conclusion that it is *not rational* to stick to the philosophical theories at issue. For this reason, the bulk of philosophers' work is *defensive* in nature—they have to show that none of the objections against their theories are compelling, and so they can *continue* to rationally stick to them. If a philosopher is unable to find a weak point of the objections brought up against her theory, she cannot rationally stick to it anymore, so she has to give it up. In this case, the previously created equilibrium is upset. She continues to have so and so pre-philosophical convictions, but she can no more rationally believe the philosophical theory that elaborates them.

Here's an example. Let's suppose that Judith has the fundamental pre-philosophical conviction that God, as an infinitely perfect being, exists. Of course, Judith is well aware of the objections to the existence of God: the arguments from evil and from divine hiddenness. It is relatively easy for her to respond to the latter, because according to her elaborate vision of the history of salvation (similar to Fichte's [1806/1999]), one of the necessary stages in the development of the human race is when it does not perceive its own supernatural/divine origin. The argument from evil, however, is a challenge to her. She does not hold the kind of theodicy to be convincing which explains the evil in the world by appealing to man's free will, nor the one which says that every evil is the logical precondition for something greater good. She thinks that due to the great many senseless and horrible human and animal sufferings, one cannot rationally stick to the view that our world is the best of all possible worlds, no matter which theodicy one chooses, and she thinks that this belief of hers is incompatible with her belief in the perfection of God. After lengthy consideration, Judith finally concludes that she can only resolve this incompatibility by committing herself to theistic modal realism (see Almeida 2008), according to which our world is just one among infinitely many (taken in the Lewisian sense) concrete universes created by God. And since God has created a multiverse (a plurality of worlds), and since we do not have good reasons to suppose that it is *precisely* our world that should be the best among them, she thinks that God's perfection is compatible with the fact that our world is not the best of all worlds. In short, after committing herself to theistic modal realism, Judith can continue to rationally believe in the existence of God as an infinitely perfect being—for she can show that the argument from evil does not have compelling force.

The second part of the intellectual maintenance of philosophical theories does not have to do with possible objections but with the cognitive household of philosophers, as the (naturally fragile) equilibrium they reach may be upset otherwise than by certain objections. It can also be upset if a philosopher realizes that her theory x is in equilibrium with her pre-philosophical convictions c_1, c_2, and c_3 and theory y that she also holds is in equilibrium with her pre-philosophical convictions c_4, c_5, and c_6, but y cannot be reconciled with one of c_1, c_2, and c_3. In short, the intellectual maintenance of philosophical theories assigns philosophers the task of dissolving these types of conceptual tensions.

Let me give you an example of this as well. Let us suppose that Andy's pre-philosophical convictions are that the physical world is causally closed and that there is mental causation. Unsurprisingly, he embraces a version of the reductive physicalist theory of mind. Moreover, let's suppose that Andy has already defended reductive physicalism against the well-known objections, so he has finished this phase of intellectual maintenance. However, during his reflective self-monitoring he realizes that one of his pre-philosophical convictions is that humans possess moral responsibility, and concludes that only the theory of agent-causation can be in equilibrium with this pre-philosophical conviction, because only this theory ensures proper (increased) control. Nevertheless, he finds that agent-causation seems hardly compatible with the causal closure principle, which he needs in order to rationally stick to his belief in reductive materialism. In this case, the intellectual maintenance of Andy's beliefs should result either in his rejection of one of the two philosophical theories, or perhaps in the reconciliation of them, against all odds (see e.g., Timpe and Jacobs 2016).

It is hard to say about this description of philosophers' activity that it is unlifelike and "phenomenologically" implausible. In fact, I think it gives an accurate picture of what philosophers actually do. With regard to this activity, the following is worth stressing from the viewpoint of equilibrism.

The goal of the intellectual maintenance of a philosophical theory and philosophical argumentation is not to *"force the truth into the open"*—the goal of philosophers is not to convince *everyone* with their arguments. Of course, philosophers can and do have positive arguments for their philosophical theories, but these cannot be compelling. The fundamental role of philosophical argumentation then is *to defend* theories—and a defensive philosophical argument, as opposed to any positive one, *can be successful*. Philosophers can successfully defend their philosophical theories against objections (if they can show them not to be compelling), and so they can form a right to rationally stick to their philosophical theories. According to equilibrism, this is the *only* sense one can talk about successful philosophical arguments.

To sum up (and this is what I take to be the most important message of equilibrism): philosophers' activities are essentially *egocentric*. I don't use this word in a morally condemning sense, of course. Instead, what I want to stress with this expression is the following. According to equilibrism, the goal of individual philosophers cannot be more than (1) to construct philosophical theories that are in equilibrium with *their own* pre-philosophical convictions which they are unable to abandon and which form an essential part of their *personal* integrity and cognitive economy, and (2) to defend and maintain these equilibria in ways that are reassuring *to themselves*, thereby preserving them intact.

Make no mistake, however. The above does not imply that equilibrism would like to ease the rigor of philosophical argumentation or to lower professional standards in any sense. Philosophers must do the intellectual maintenance of their philosophical theories with the *same* professional conscience as those philosophers do who aim at coming up with substantive truths, try to support their theories with compelling arguments, and make attempts to solve philosophical problems.

Equilibrism also attributes *epistemic duties* to philosophers. They *must* respond to all relevant objections that are known to them; they *must* strive for consistency; they *must* carefully weigh all evidence that is accessible to them, etc. That is, they *must* proceed the same way *as if* they were seeking the truth themselves. The difference between those philosophers who act in the spirit of the epistemic tradition and those who act in that of equilibrism is only to be found in how they interpret their own activity. While philosophers who set themselves less humble goals than equilibrism think that their work is to formulate arguments which compellingly justify the truth of their philosophical beliefs, equilibrists think that their work aims at no more than to create and preserve the integrity of their own equilibria.

1.2 The goal of the community of philosophers

The goal of the community of philosophers can be defined as a function of the individual philosophers' goal. In this sense, if the philosophers' goal is not to present substantive truths and justify them compellingly but to develop theories which are in equilibrium with their own pre-philosophical convictions and can be shown to resist even the strongest of objections, then, as Lewis puts it, "[The] common task is to find out what equilibria there are that can withstand examination" (1983: x)—to present "the menu of well-worked-out theories" (1983: xi). That is, the goal of the community of philosophers is to map the logically possible and consistent philosophical views—to populate the logical space with stable equilibria.

The goal of the community of philosophers can easily be formulated differently, using different emphases and terminology—and maybe it is worth doing so, as the descriptions given above may seem narrow and alien to certain philosophers. Here are a few "more ceremonial" definitions: the goal of the community of philosophers is to form *perspectives* which conceptually "organize" the world; to develop *viewpoints* which "give meaning" to phenomena. Or, to be even bolder: the goal of the community of philosophers is to come up with "productive discourses," "narratives," "forms of meaning," "spaces of meaning," "dimensions of meaning," "constitutive connections in meaning," etc., all of which resist objections and can help those who are open to it to understand and conceptually articulate the world and themselves within it.

1.3 The attraction of equilibrism

One of the main attractions of equilibrism stems from the fact that according to this metaphilosophical vision, *philosophy is not a failed enterprise*, consequently philosophers need not see themselves as participants in a failed epistemic enterprise. The goal that equilibrism sets to the individual philosophers and the community of philosophers is such that the tools of philosophy are *suitable* for attaining it; moreover, philosophy has *excelled* in attaining it. From the viewpoint of equilibrism, philosophy is one of the most successful intellectual enterprises of all time. From the very start, it has been able to satisfy our innate cognitive need for giving a conceptually well-articulated and consistent form to our fundamental pre-philosophical convictions.

Just think about it. Seen from the ambition of the epistemic tradition, we are bound to admit that philosophy has failed and stagnates—what we didn't know at t_1 we still don't know at t_2 because we haven't solved a single substantive philosophical problem, we haven't succeeded in finding the answer to a single substantive philosophical question, nor in presenting a single substantive philosophical truth. However, if we part company with this view in the spirit of equilibrism, we can see that philosophy is successful and making progress—the community of philosophers is able to develop an increasing number of philosophical theories, that is, an increasing number of ways for us to think consistently about the nature and knowledge of reality or about morally right action; and, thanks to its activity, the cost-benefit equations of these philosophical theories are becoming clearer and clearer. In Lewis' words: "what we accomplish in [philosophy]: we measure the price; [and] [...] that is something we can settle more and less conclusively" (1983: x). True, we don't possess any substantive *sub specie aeternitatis* truths, but the fact that we have come to possess several important non-trivial and non-substantive truths richly compensates for it. This is because knowing the costs and benefits of various philosophical theories amounts to the recognition of many true propositions of the "If ..., then ..." type and relevant conceptual distinctions, and as such, it qualifies as a case of *philosophical knowledge* (see Gutting 2009: 226–31).

I can also put it this way: because according to equilibrism, the goal of the community of philosophers is not to present well-founded substantive truths, philosophers do not have to struggle with *feelings of inferiority* towards scientists—philosophy is *not a competitor* to the natural sciences. Only the advocates of the epistemic tradition think that it is—and needless to say, that it stands on the losing side. And if so, the well-known malicious comment from Stephen Hawking and Leonard Mlodinov seems correct:

> Philosophy is dead. Philosophy has not kept up with modern developments in science, particularly physics. Scientists have become the bearers of the torch of discovery in our quest for knowledge.
>
> (2010: 5)

According to equilibrism, their criticism misses the point, because the goal of philosophy is not to acquire knowledge of the world, but to map those conceptual perspectives (equilibria) which form the foundation and starting points for us to think consistently about the world.

At first sight, one could think that equilibrism is in trouble because it sets different goals to individual philosophers and the community of philosophers. For if the goal of individual philosophers is to work out and defend their own equilibria, then, presumably, they are not motivated by working out one possible equilibrium among many. But this is not so. Quite contrary, the equilibrists—unlike the "I'm the only one" philosophers—do not suffer from epistemic blindness and do not see their interlocutors as their epistemic inferiors. For them, other philosopher's views that are inconsistent with theirs are of the highest importance. In fact, equilibrists are *happy* to see their opponents formulating stronger and stronger arguments because it helps them to hold their own equilibria in even stronger forms which are even more resistant to objections. And the fact that the community of philosophers continues to populate the logical space is useful and beneficial to equilibrists because they can reliably "price" their own theories by comparing them to other theories. It is in comparison with other theories that the virtues and weaknesses of their theories "show up" sharply, which helps them to see the points where their theories need improvement and the ways to improve them.

So, equilibrism is that variant of the steadfast view which goes hand in hand with permissivism. Moreover, it is its friendliest and most lenient form. For, according to equilibrism, if a philosopher successfully meets the requirement of intellectual maintenance, then she can rationally stick to her substantive philosophical beliefs. Furthermore, if a philosopher thinks that her interlocutors (like her) have successfully met the requirement of intellectual maintenance, then she must think of them that they are as rational as she is—regardless of the fact that their substantive philosophical beliefs are incompatible with hers.

But equilibrism has another two attractions that deserve mentioning. One is that it seems that *a philosopher's performance can only be judged on the basis of equilibrism*. Let's take Leibniz, for example. I think there is a massive consensus within the community of philosophers that his central claims are mistaken. It isn't true that our mental life is causally closed. It isn't true that there are no causal connections among substances, nor is it true that their states (perceptions) develop from an entelechy. It isn't true that all truths are analytic. Despite all that, we rank Leibniz among philosophy's greatest figures. Now, if this is the case, then the high ranking of Leibniz's philosophical performance has hardly anything to do with whether his claims are true or not. The only thing it has to do with is that he came up with a very consistent metaphysical theory (or theories) that reconciles diverging propositions—the equilibrium that he worked out had not earlier been present on the logical map of philosophical theories.

Another attraction of equilibrism is that it is able *to legitimate the doing of philosophy*—more precisely, the way it is being done in academic circles. You don't have to agree with Dennett on the point that philosophy is just "luxury decoration on society" (as quoted by Goldhill 2016: 2). The equilibrist may think that philosophy can have a serious *social value*, namely, putting the outsiders' minds in order. To use Gutting's example: "an atheist who thinks all arguments for God's existence are demonstrably fallacious *may need* a clever philosopher to show what's wrong with a sophisticated version of the cosmological argument or the design argument from fine-tuning" (2015: 258, italics mine). In other words, the social value of doing philosophy lies in its capacity to help articulate one's fundamental convictions in a conceptually organized manner.

To sum up: equilibrism is especially attractive and motivated, because it seems to be the *only* metaphilosophical vision that, unlike the epistemic tradition, does not set hopeless goals to philosophers and, unlike meta-skepticism, it does not offer them a bad deal. Here's a possible consideration in support of equilibrism that appeals to your sincerity:

> Put your hand on your heart! Can you imagine that the following report will ever be published in *Nature*: "X university's philosophy research group has recently confirmed that charge, mass and angular momentum are Aristotelian immanent universals; multi-local entities, which can wholly and perfectly be present at different locations in space at the same time, and more than one of which can be present in one place at a time. It is only a matter of months before they find a solution to the metaphysical nature of physical objects and have their hypothesis confirmed that physical objects are bundles of universals plus a fundamentally distinct entity, a substrate as a bare particular". No, you cannot. And, put your hand on your heart once more! Are you willing to give up all of your philosophical beliefs because of philosophy's failure as an enterprise to find the truth if you can see clearly that they are built on your fundamental convictions, which are the constitutive elements of your personal integrity and cognitive household? No, you aren't.

2 Why I cannot identify with equilibrism

Naturally, the strongest argument against equilibrism would be if I could come up with some (undoubtedly) compelling argument for a substantive philosophical thesis. In this case, I could say that any commitment to equilibrism is *undermotivated* and we have no reason to attribute goals to philosophy that are humbler than finding the truth, since philosophy is capable of attaining these less humble purposes. But an equally strong argument against equilibrism would be if I could come up with a compelling argument for meta-skepticism. In this case, I could say that equilibrism is *untenable*, because every philosopher has the epistemic duty to suspend their substantive philosophical beliefs—no matter whether it would damage their cognitive household. But I don't have such compelling arguments, so I cannot show equilibrism to be either undermotivated or untenable. On the contrary, I think that equilibrism is a rather strongly motivated metaphilosophical vision. It is no accident that it is gaining in popularity.

My main concern to equilibrism is this: as an equilibrist, *one cannot seriously and sincerely believe in the truth* of one's substantive philosophical theses—*one cannot take epistemic responsibility for the truth* of one's substantive philosophical beliefs.

2.1 Two kinds of philosophical problems

I will start from afar. One can make a distinction between two kinds of philosophical problems. One category includes problems concerning which *there is a truth simpliciter*, i.e., *things are a certain way independently of our (linguistic or mental) representations*. These problems are either about what type of entities there are or about what their nature consists in.

Some examples: "Do the past and the future exist along with the present?"; "Are there abstract entities?"; "Are there multi-local entities?"; "Are there worlds that are causally and spatio-temporally disconnected from ours?" Or, "What is the connection between our conscious experience and our brain states?"; "Is it true that our actions were not predetermined by the universe's initial conditions (plus laws) but are not accidental either?"

I think all the questions listed above are such that you would be surprised if God did not know the answers to them. You would be surprised if God said: "*I do not know* if I created one world or a multiverse"; "*I do not know* whether the past and the future exist or only the present does, even though I created time"; "*I do not know* what the relationship is between the mind and the body, even though I created all living beings, including humans," etc.

The other kind of philosophical problems includes those concerning which there are *no truths simpliciter—these philosophical problems and the features on which they are based do not exist independently of our linguistic or mental representations*. Thus, these problems are exclusively about *how to conceptualize* certain phenomena—*how to understand and how to make sense* of them for ourselves. These problems contain concepts that do not directly refer to anything existing independently of these concepts—characteristically, the focal points of these problems (either they are things, categories, or whatever else) are carved out according to these concepts *as a result of* concept formation.

Some examples: "What is the definition of art?"; "What is modernity?"; "How should we classify different speech acts?"; "What is the difference between science and pseudo-science?"; "To what extent does the correct interpretation of a literary text depend on its author's intentions?"; "What does civil disobedience consist in?"; "Do works of absolute music have meaning?"; "How can we define the concept of labor?"

I think you would be surprised if God would be able to answer these questions. You would be surprised to hear from Him, for example, that "*I know* that the institutional theory of art is false, since a work of art is rendered as such by virtue of its perceptual properties and these perceptual properties are structural universals." And before you would object (knowing your mind), He would go on: "Duchamp-type ready-mades are not counterexamples—these are only *quasi*-artworks, since revealing their punchlines substitutes for the perception of their perceptual properties."

In what follows, I will call the former set of issues *factual* philosophical problems and those of the latter sort *conceptual* philosophical problems.

Now, this categorization of philosophical problems is *universal* and *exclusive*—every single (meaningful and not merely verbal) philosophical problem is either factual or conceptual, and there is no philosophical problem that belongs to both kinds, just as there is no philosophical problem that belongs to neither. Thus (and I consider it very important to emphasize this point), *the metaquestion* "Which philosophical problems are factual and which are conceptual?" *is itself a par excellence factual philosophical question*—since this categorization of philosophical problems is based on their (in)capacity to allow formulating propositions that can be made true or false by a reality existing independently of our conceptual framework.

2.1.1 Non-trivial cases

This categorization of philosophical problems is intuitively clear, though not unproblematic. In contrast to the evident cases listed above, several philosophical problems do not allow us to reassuringly decide whether we should categorize them as factual or rather as conceptual. Such harder cases are, for example, the following: "Are proper names rigid designators?"; "Are meanings in the head?"; "Is there metaphysical necessity above and beyond logical necessity?"; "Are holes material objects?" I'm sure that if I were to list these philosophical problems under the heading of factual versus conceptual philosophical problems, then I couldn't expect a relatively stable consensus.

It is also an interesting and important question whether *normative* philosophical problems belong to the category of conceptual philosophical problems or rather to that of factual ones.

I see it as follows. Let's suppose that Mike thinks that no moral values and facts exist in their own right (independently of our concepts)—Mike denies the (concept-independent) existence of a moral world order. He thinks that we do not discover but rather "create" moral values and facts—in his opinion, moral rightness or wrongness is ultimately a matter of agreement. Consequently, *normative* ethical questions such as "Is it morally *right* to do X?" or "*Must* X be done?" are *conceptual* to Mike—our answers to them depend on our conceptual framework and cannot depend on anything else. However, let's suppose that according to Claire, some moral values and facts exist in their own right (independently of our concepts)—according to her, there is a (concept-independent) moral world order. She thinks that instead of "creating" moral values and facts, we discover the truth of the proposition "It is morally wrong to cause pain to others out of sheer pleasure," just as we discover the truth of the proposition describing the value of the gravitational constant, or the truth of the proposition "If an integer n is greater than 2, then the equation '$a^n + b^n = c^n$' has no solutions in non-zero integers a, b, and c." Thus, *normative* ethical questions such as "Is it morally *right* to do X?" or "*Must* X be done?" are *factual* to Claire—our moral duties depend on the facts of a moral world order (existing independently of our concepts).

Now, it is easy to see that the question which of them is right is also a *factual* philosophical question. Their debate concerns *whether there exist or not* facts independently of our concepts, which determine what counts as morally right.

Here's another example. Let's suppose that David has contextualist or social constructivist views about propositional knowledge. He thinks that the question "What conditions must obtain for S to know that p?" is not a factual one—our answer to this question depends only on our (context-dependent) conceptual framework, and cannot depend on anything else. Thus, *normative* epistemological questions are *conceptual* to David. But let's suppose that Meryl thinks about propositional knowledge in the spirit of the classical definition of knowledge (more precisely, some expanded and corrected version of it). That is, according to Meryl, the question "What conditions *must* be met for S to know that p?" is a factual one—because the concept-independent fact that these conditions are met either obtains, in which case S knows that p, or does not obtain, in which case S does not know that p. Thus, *normative* epistemological questions are *factual* to Meryl—there is a kind of "epistemic world order" (similarly to the moral world order), which determines what conditions must be met so we can speak about knowledge (and not mere true belief).

Also, it can be easily seen that the question which of the two is right is a *factual* philosophical question. Their debate concerns *whether there exist or not* facts independently of our concepts, which determine what counts as a case of propositional knowledge.

With the above, I would like say that (even if the terminology may seem strange at first sight) normative philosophical questions, too, are either factual or conceptual. If there is a concept-independent moral and/or epistemic world order which makes our moral and/or epistemic statements true, then normative philosophical questions are factual. By contrast, if there is no concept-independent moral and/or epistemic world order, then normative philosophical questions are conceptual—the choice of those moral and/or epistemic statements to which we commit ourselves depends only on our conceptual framework.

2.1.2 Two bad objections

There are certainly some who dispute the validity of the above categorization of philosophical problems. Now, it is *evident* that those who do so do not think that all philosophical problems are factual—they think that all are conceptual.

On the one hand, they can claim that this categorization is wrong because there are no facts that exist independently of our concepts, and so there are no philosophical problems concerning which there would be truth simpliciter (independent of our conceptual framework). I can answer this objection as follows: even if it were true (although I think it is certainly untrue) that there are no facts existing independently of our concepts, the ones who formulate this objection must concede that they have committed themselves to the truth of a par excellence factual philosophical thesis, namely global anti-realism, which leads them to contradict themselves.

On the other hand, they can argue by singling out a philosophical problem which seems par excellence factual (for example, the question "Is there a God?"), and then go on saying that "Even though this problem seems to be a factual one at first sight, if we go deeper, we have to see that it all depends on *what we mean by the concept of 'God.'*"

I can answer this objection by saying that although it is true that the question "Is there a God?" needs some conceptual clarification and specification, this isn't an impossible task. Here's a somewhat more precise phrasing: "Is there anything that has the following properties: it created the world; it is a person and not a kind of principle; it is not indifferent to the fate of humanity; its abilities and knowledge exceed our abilities and knowledge to an inconceivable extent?" If they keep responding to this that the question "Is there a God?" is a conceptual one, as everything depends on what we mean by "the creation of the world," "the fate of humanity," etc., then I can only say to this, using Wittgenstein's well-known metaphor again, that "my spade is turned" (*PI* 217) and they are just provoking me. If they sincerely meant what they said, then they could reiterate the "What do you mean by this and that term?" question *endlessly* about the existence and nature of every posited entity, and if they did this consistently, they would have to conclude that there is no question the response to which could be "yes" or "no."

Using a different approach, concerning those who deny the existence of factual philosophical problems in the above spirit, we must primarily appeal to their truthfulness. It is worth asking them to be truthful and admit that (after some conceptual clarification) *everybody precisely understands* the question "Is there a God?"—no less than the question "Are there intelligent aliens similar to us in the universe?" Also, they should admit that *everybody knows exactly* that the answer to these questions is either a simple yes or a simple no, which means that both questions are factual.

To sum up, I do not think it can be seriously thought that all philosophical discourse *en bloc* and *sui generis* is not fact-stating, and there is no single philosophical problem concerning which the question of truth or falsehood comes up simpliciter and so there are no factual problems at all.

2.2 Insincerity

I came up with the above classification of philosophical problems because I think that equilibrism cannot be sincerely held concerning factual philosophical problems. But before I can show this, I must first explain why it can be sincerely held concerning conceptual philosophical problems.

The point is the following. Insofar a philosophical problem is a conceptual one, you *can be satisfied* with focusing on whether the philosophical theory you have chosen or elaborated is in equilibrium with your pre-philosophical convictions. The reason why you can be satisfied with this is that there is nothing *besides* your pre-philosophical convictions (which you think you're unable to reject) that you should conform to or take into account during the construction of your philosophical theory. Furthermore, if a philosophical problem is a conceptual one, you *can be satisfied* with the intellectual maintenance of the achieved equilibrium. The reason why you can be satisfied with this is that it is out of the question that things may be different to the way as your philosophical theory says they are—because the things at issue *are not in any way at all* in themselves, independently of your conceptual framework. Thus, regarding conceptual philosophical problems, you don't need to worry that your pre-philosophical convictions may turn out to be false and misrepresent the nature of those things your philosophical theory is about.

Let me put it differently. If you take sides regarding a conceptual philosophical problem, then you can *sincerely believe* in your philosophical theory. This is because, if it is really the case that the things at issue are not in any way at all, independently of our conceptual framework, then, in fact, *it only matters* to what extent you are able to bring your philosophical theory into equilibrium with your pre-philosophical convictions, and how successfully you can intellectually maintain your philosophical theory. If you fully discharge these two epistemic duties, you can sincerely believe from your egocentric perspective that you should "piece together" or articulate your theory *in this way and not in another one*. You will not have to ask the question that "This and that are my pre-philosophical convictions, and this is my theory which is in equilibrium with them—but could it be the case that I'm wrong and my theory is simpliciter false?"

I will go further. No matter how you take sides regarding a conceptual philosophical problem, *you don't need to feel insecure* knowing that other philosophers have other pre-philosophical convictions and correspondingly they conceptualize the phenomenon at issue differently than you. That is, you don't need to begin to have doubts because of the philosophical disagreement between you and other philosophers. For if a phenomenon is not in any way at all in itself, then you can safely think that other philosophers' other equilibria can be just as plausible, enlightening, and productive, etc. as yours.

What's more, if entity *e* is not in any way at all in itself, then the pluralism of philosophical theories (equilibria) of *e* is nothing short of a blessing. It is welcome because the question of truth *simpliciter* will not arise about the philosophical theories concerning *e*, and consequently it would be unnecessary and meaningless to discredit even a single one of them. Each equilibrium "shows," "brings out," "elucidates," "captures," etc., *something* about *e*—each offers us a consistent conceptual framework/perspective/viewpoint for thinking about *e*. Thus, by discrediting any of these equilibria, we would only divest ourselves of a possible perspective in which (or on the basis of which) *e* can be interpreted.

By contrast, with regard to factual philosophical problems, the situation is entirely different, because in this case the aim is to hit upon truth. Just think about the following.

Firstly, if Sarah takes sides regarding a factual (and so non-conceptual) philosophical problem, the truth-conditions of the proposition "Sarah achieved the desired equilibrium and successfully defended it against objections" are different to the truth-conditions of "Sarah's philosophical theory is true." The first proposition can be true even if the second is false and vice versa. It follows that in contrast to conceptual philosophical problems, in the case of factual philosophical problems, the following *always remains an open question*: "Sarah's philosophical theory is in equilibrium with her pre-philosophical convictions and she has intellectually maintained her theory through fully discharging her epistemic duties, but is her philosophical theory *true*?" This question is open because—according to the equilibrist—Sarah doesn't have (and cannot have) justification which would show that her pre-philosophical convictions, i.e., the basis of her philosophical theories, are *not* false.

Secondly, every philosopher's aim may be put in such a general way that they would like to know what they should believe. However, note that the proposition "Sylvia knows what she should believe" is ambiguous. On the one hand, it can mean that "Sylvia knows what she should believe *depending on* what her pre-philosophical convictions are." On the other hand, it can also mean that "Sylvia knows which proposition(s) she should believe in order to believe something *simpliciter true*." Now, while only the first meaning of "Sylvia knows what she should believe" is in play in the case of conceptual philosophical problems, in the case of factual philosophical problems both possible meanings are in play, and it is the second one that is relevant.

Thirdly, every philosopher's aim is to work out a philosophical theory in which they can rationally believe. However, note that the proposition "Sonia rationally believes in theory T" is also ambiguous. On the one hand, it can mean that "Sonia rationally believes in theory T because T is *in equilibrium with* her pre-philosophical convictions and her other beliefs, and no knock-down objections can be brought against T (or at least, Sonia isn't aware of any)." On the other hand, it can also mean that "Sonia believes in T rationally because she has good reasons to think that her justification of T is *truth-conducive*." Now, while only the first meaning of "Sonia rationally believes in theory T" is in play in cases of conceptual philosophical problems, in cases of factual philosophical problems both possible meanings are in play, and it is the second one that is relevant.

The three above-mentioned differences clearly show that while you can commit yourself to your philosophical theory with a clear intellectual conscience if the philosophical problem is a conceptual one, provided you fulfil the expectations of equilibrism (by developing and intellectually maintaining a philosophical theory which is in equilibrium with your pre-philosophical convictions), you cannot do that regarding factual philosophical problems. After all, you're not an "I'm the only one" philosopher, you don't believe that you have knock-down arguments for your philosophical theory, so you may ask the questions quite emphatically, unnervingly, and strongly appealing to your intellectual conscience: "What if I'm wrong?"; "What if things stand otherwise than I believe they do?"; "What if my philosophical theory is false?" Even if you have fulfilled all the epistemic duties prescribed by the equilibrist, when you take sides in a factual philosophical problem, *it does not seem to be an unnecessary and meaningless worry or too pedantic* to ask yourself: "Can I *seriously and sincerely* believe in the simpliciter truth of my philosophical views if the most I can provide them with is egocentric 'justification'?"; "Can I *firmly* trust in the simpliciter truth of my philosophical views merely on the basis of the fact that they are in equilibrium with my pre-philosophical convictions and no compelling arguments can be brought up against them?"; "Can I take *epistemic responsibility* for the simpliciter truth of my philosophical views if my fundamental pre-philosophical convictions on which my views are based are unjustified, and the most I can say for them is that I cannot discard them without damaging my personal integrity and/or my cognitive household?"

I would be surprised if someone dared to call these questions irrelevant without further ado. I would also be surprised if someone disputed that these questions may arise in the equilibrist in the most natural way—developing unnerving doubts in her. All this, I think, clearly shows that equilibrism is *insensitive* to the difference between conceptual and factual philosophical problems. On the one hand, *you can be content* with the intellectual maintenance of your considered philosophical beliefs in relation to conceptual philosophical problems, because there is no question of truth or falsehood in relation to them independent of your own conceptual framework—the only thing at stake is the preservation of the integrity of your own equilibrium. On the other hand, *you cannot be content with* the intellectual maintenance of your considered philosophical beliefs in relation to factual philosophical problems, because what is at stake in relation to these problems is not only to preserve the integrity of your own equilibrium but also to find truth independent of your own conceptual framework.

Let me put it differently. If S believes that p concerning a conceptual philosophical problem, then S's p-belief does not aim at some truth that is independent of her own concepts—rather, it aims at some truth that can be inferred from S's conceptual framework. This is because each and every belief that is in line with S's own fundamental pre-philosophical convictions can be inferred from S's pre-philosophical convictions and her conceptual framework. By contrast, if S believes that p concerning a factual philosophical problem, then

S's *p*-belief aims at some truth that is independent of her conceptual philosophical framework. However, in this case, the truth of S's belief cannot be inferred from her pre-philosophical convictions and conceptual framework.

To sum up, concerning a factual philosophical problem if S believes that *p*, then S believes that *p* is true simpliciter—*p* describes things as they actually are. So, if *all* S can say is "(1) these and these are my fundamental pre-philosophical convictions (which are unjustified but I cannot abandon them), (2) *p* is in equilibrium with these and these pre-philosophical convictions of mine, and (3) there are no knock-down arguments against *p*" (and these three claims are the *most* the equilibrist can make), then *S cannot take epistemic responsibility for the truth* of her belief *p*.

But let's go more into depth. Here's a confession of a disillusioned equilibrist:

> I take it for certain that the mind-body problem is a factual philosophical problem—that things stand one way or the other, independently of my conceptual framework. I also take it for certain that if God exists, then He knows the nature of this relation. He knows the truth about it.
>
> What do I know? The only thing I know is which philosophical view I should commit myself to so it can be in equilibrium with my pre-philosophical convictions. *As it happens*, one of my pre-philosophical convictions is that our conscious experiences can cause physical events—it seems to me untenable that our conscious experiences are epiphenomenal. My other pre-philosophical conviction is that conscious experiences are non-physical—I simply cannot conceive how an entity whose nature is essentially subjective could be placed in the framework of a purely physicalist ontology. Now, the only variant of dualism with which these two pre-philosophical convictions of mine are in equilibrium denies the principle of the causal closure of the physical.
>
> Earlier, as equilibrist, I thought that if I can show that none of the arguments against my dualism is compelling, and I can clearly see that my dualism doesn't contradict any of my fundamental pre-philosophical convictions, then I can, in good conscience, commit myself to the truth of my dualism. That is, earlier, I was an equilibrist because I was concerned *exclusively* with the intellectual maintenance of my personal-cognitive integrity. Now, however, I can clearly see that it isn't enough to cherish my pre-philosophical convictions and my dualism which is in equilibrium with them. What has changed?
>
> Firstly, I realized that if the most I can say is that "I'm a dualist because dualism is in equilibrium with my fundamental pre-philosophical convictions, which I

de facto have," then I'm actually in no better epistemic situation than the one who *rolls a dice to decide* which view she should commit himself to. While I can say that "There is such and such relation between mind and body *depending on* what my pre-philosophical convictions are," she can say that "There is such and such a relation between mind and body *depending on* the result of my dice roll."

Apart from the fact that my decision about which propositions I hold true is based on contingent factors similar to the result of a dice roll (for this must be the case if I decide about them on the basis of my pre-philosophical convictions) seems to be an irresponsible act in itself, I must also realize that I will quite probably come to adopt mistaken views with the use of this "method." There are several different configurations of pre-philosophical convictions, and correspondingly there are several possible equilibria. There is only a slight probability that of all pre-philosophical convictions, it is precisely mine that are true and that it is precisely the equilibrium corresponding to them that is true.

In other words, the community of philosophers has worked out several epistemically *equivalent* and mutually *inconsistent* equilibria concerning the mind-body problem. Now, if—as equilibrism says—these equilibria are epistemically equivalent (they stand an *equal chance of being true*), then I have no good epistemic reason to commit myself to the truth of *any* of them. This is because it would certainly not be a proper epistemic reason for me to say that "*As it happens*, these and these are my pre-philosophical convictions, consequently *I* must hold dualism to be true out of the several epistemically equivalent equilibria."

Secondly, I was confronted with my former insincerity most acutely and painfully when I finally asked myself, "*Why* are my fundamental pre-philosophical convictions what they are and not others?" I thought that this contingent fact should have a contrastive causal explanation, and, through my self-reflective monitoring, I have come to the conclusion that the factors determining my fundamental pre-philosophical convictions *have absolutely nothing to do with* whether they are true or false. Now, if my fundamental pre-philosophical convictions on which my dualism is based are *biased*, then *I cannot trust them*, and therefore I cannot seriously and sincerely believe in my dualism that elaborates on them—I cannot take epistemic responsibility for its truth. Of course, this doesn't by itself mean that my dualism is false—just because my pre-philosophical convictions are biased, my dualism may still be true. But it does mean that even if dualism is true, I believe it to be true not for the reasons why it is true, but because of certain bias factors. And that's not as it should be.

Take, for example, my fundamental pre-philosophical conviction that our conscious experiences cannot be physical. What bias factors explain this pre-philosophical conviction according to my self-reflection? Well, from an early age, I grew up in a highly religious environment—and the religious point of view inexorably became part of me. Because of my childhood socialization, I believe in the existence of God and the truth of the conditional that "If God exists, then the mind (or soul) cannot be physical, for it is immortal." Furthermore, in my youth, I was indelibly influenced by Plato's "Allegory of the Cave," according to which the visible (physical) world is not the ultimate reality—there is a more fundamental existence than the physical. This reading experience strongly shaped my epistemic character: I constantly felt (and sometimes still feel) that I am homeless in this "visible" (shadow) world, and that the physical story is not only incomplete, but just the surface of existence. And I confess that this pre-philosophical conviction of mine was further strengthened by the fact that during debates, my scientist-physicalist interlocutors often displayed such an intellectual arrogance and disdain for everyone who didn't categorically preclude the existence of the supernatural, which literally filled me with revulsion.

Of course, I'm not saying that the pre-philosophical convictions of all dualists are determined by precisely these bias factors. Nor am I saying that these factors are the *ultimate* causal explanation for my pre-philosophical conviction that our conscious experiences cannot be physical. In a word, I'm not saying that my self-reflection can gain access to the ultimate biases that determine my pre-philosophical convictions. But I do claim that *such* factors (arising from my environment, upbringing, etc.) had a decisive effect on the formation of my epistemic character, and they determine my pre-philosophical convictions to be what they are and not to be different. And I also claim that all philosophers are in the same situation (no matter what their positions are, including physicalism)—the content of their fundamental pre-philosophical convictions results from a combination of certain contingent, causally effective factors that have nothing to do with truth and are not under their control.

Finally, I asked myself one last question: what would it really mean to take epistemic responsibility for the truth of my dualism? And here is what I have concluded: it would mean that *I would dare* to bet high stakes (say, ten years of my life) that dualism is the right mind-body theory. It would mean that *I would dare* to try convincing the people who matter most to me to commit themselves to dualism. It would mean that as an epistemic authority, *I would dare,* in every possible forum, to stand up for the truth of dualism. But (and that's crucial!), I had to admit to myself that I *wouldn't dare to do any of these*. Having realized their biasedness, I could not trust any of my fundamental pre-philosophical convictions to be veridical, hence in the truth of my dualism based on them.

These two revelations were a flash to me that made me quite uncertain. Thus, I need to seriously consider the possibility of becoming a meta-skeptic—even if it is a terrible thought that the suspension of my dualism would collapse my cognitive household.

Take a deep breath and put your hand on your heart before you answer the following questions! Do you think that the above confession is nothing more than a philosopher's excessive worry, groundless lack of self-confidence, meaningless self-recrimination and causeless complaint? Do you think that the uncertainty of this person is totally unfounded if she thinks that she is not superior in terms of accuracy over the one who decides by rolling a dice which substantive philosophical theory she commits himself to? Do you think that this person distresses herself completely unnecessarily when, by her self-monitoring, she concludes that her fundamental pre-philosophical convictions are biased; and since they are biased, she cannot trust them, and therefore cannot take epistemic responsibility for the truth of the theory based on them? And do you think that it was completely groundless for this person to think that perhaps it would be right for her to suspend her belief in the truth of dualism, since she wants to avoid being mistaken about the solution of the mind-body problem at all costs?

I think that you cannot answer these questions with a definite yes if you have a bit of intellectual empathy. And if you realize that you cannot answer them with a definite yes, then you must also realize what the insincerity of equilibrism's ethos consists of concerning one's beliefs about substantive and factual philosophical issues.

***

So, what's the source of the trouble? I will try to present it as simply as possible. Here's what is on the equilibrist's mind:

> The goal that the followers of epistemic tradition set themselves is too ambitious: to compellingly justify substantive philosophical theses. Now, since (1) this goal is unattainable, and since (2) I don't want to (cannot) stop doing philosophy, *I must settle for a more modest goal.* This more modest goal, and at once the *most* I can achieve, is to intellectually maintain my considered philosophical beliefs—to keep my equilibria intact.

In this section (especially with the fictitious confession above), I tried to show the following: despite our firm belief that the goal of the epistemic tradition is unattainable, we *still* cannot be satisfied with what equilibrism can offer "in its place," "in exchange for it." If the most we can bring up for the truth of our considered substantive factual philosophical beliefs is that which equilibrism allows us, then *doubts come to us galore*, in a *completely natural way*—and we are completely *defenseless* against them. And those doubts don't arise from the fact that our philosophical theories are threatened by knock-down objections (we can overcome them if we're smart enough)—rather, they arise from our realization that the *most* we can achieve (namely, keeping our equilibria intact) *isn't actually enough*.

How should I put it? Although facing the failure of epistemic tradition initially seemed a viable option, and even the *only* viable option, equilibrism cannot *make up for* what we have lost—namely, our confidence in the possibility of substantive philosophical knowledge and in our ability to solve philosophical problems. Just as it seems a hopeless undertaking to seek compelling justification for our substantive factual philosophical theses, so too, trying to commit ourselves to their truth without compelling arguments does not offer any prospects. There are times when we clearly see that something is impossible for us to achieve, and that the most we can achieve cannot satisfy us—and equilibrism is precisely this latter option.

2.3 Epistemic schizophrenia

Let's suppose that you realize that as an equilibrist, you cannot commit yourself to your substantive factual philosophical views with epistemic responsibility. Nevertheless, you also realize that you're unable to discard these philosophical views. On the one hand, you clearly see that the merely egocentric justification of your views doesn't entitle you to seriously and sincerely believe in their truth; on the other hand, you cannot hold your beliefs to be irrational and suspend them—you keep sticking to them.

Let's not sugar-coat, this is *writhing* indeed. I will christen it right away: *epistemic schizophrenia*. Now, I think that this epistemic schizophrenia overwhelms *every* equilibrist who is sufficiently reflective and sincere to confess to herself that her philosophical views are built on her unjustified pre-philosophical convictions, and who, for this very reason, entertains doubts about her ability to sustain her views with epistemic responsibility, but also realizes her inability to give up her philosophical views without her personal-cognitive integrity falling apart.

Philosophy Without Compelling Justification 143

Let me show how wicked epistemic schizophrenia can be in another dialogue—this time with a real philosopher, instead of a fictitious one. The interlocutor is, again, Sophie, but I'm going to quote the answers to her questions from actual papers by van Inwagen:

> *Sophie*: The other day I got involved in a lengthy and rather depressing debate with Philonous about the epistemic status of his philosophical view. The take-home message from our discussion was that he is incapable of self-reflection and of putting himself in the perspective of his opponents. He thinks that all those philosophers who disagree with him are his epistemic inferiors—meaning that they don't understand his arguments and they're unable to recognize their compelling force. I know that you're not an "I'm the only one" philosopher, yet you have definite views on certain philosophical issues. You think that possible worlds are not concrete physical objects; that physical objects are not four- but three-dimensional entities; and that free will is incompatible with determinism. Let me put this question to you, too: aren't you made uncertain by the fact that the views that some other very smart philosophers (Lewis, for example) hold on these issues are incompatible with yours?
>
> *van Inwagen*: So you wonder, "How can I believe (as I do) that free will is incompatible with determinism or that unrealized possibilities are not physical objects or that human beings are not four-dimensional things extended in time as well as in space, when David Lewis—a philosopher of truly formidable intelligence and insight and ability—rejects these things I believe and is already aware of and understands perfectly every argument that I could produce in their defense?" (1996: 138)
>
> *Sophie*: Exactly. But, for the sake of simplicity, let's take only the problem of free will and determinism. What do you think of the significance of Lewis holding a view different from yours? Do you think that your belief in incompatibilism is rational while Lewis' belief in compatibilism is not?
>
> *van Inwagen*: "It seems more plausible to say (to revert to the example of David Lewis and myself) that David and I have the same evidence in the matter of the problem of free will, and to concede that this entails that either we are both rational or neither of us is" (2010: 27).
>
> *Sophie*: And what do you say to that?
>
> *van Inwagen*: "The position that we are both rational [...] is hard to defend. If I suppose that we are both rational, I hear W. K. Clifford's ghost whispering an indignant protest [...]

If you and Lewis are both rational in accepting contradictory propositions on the basis of identical evidence, and *you* accept one of these propositions—incompatibilism—on the basis of evidence, that does not direct you toward incompatibilism and away from compatibilism. (For, if it did, it would have directed *him* away from compatibilism, and it would not have been rational for him to be a compatibilist.) But of all the forces in the human psyche that direct us toward and away from assent to propositions, only rational attention to relevant evidence *tracks the truth*. Both experience and reason confirm this. And, if you assent to a proposition on the basis of some inner push, some 'will to believe', if I may coin a phrase, that does not track the truth, then your propositional assent is not being guided by the nature of the things those propositions are *about*. If you could decide what to believe by tossing a coin, if that would actually be effective, then, in the matter of the likelihood of your beliefs being true, you might as well do it that way" (2010: 28, italics in original).

Sophie: Let me tell you in my own words the nature of your doubt, step by step. (1) You're aware of the fact that Lewis has a view that is the opposite of yours—namely, he's a compatibilist. (2) You suppose that both of you have the same evidential basis. (3) You think that if the evidential basis is common yet your views are different, then the only explanation for it is that the common evidential basis doesn't sway you toward or away from any view. (4) You think that if both of you expound your mutually incompatible views drawing on the same evidential basis, then the theory construction or line of argument of at least one of you is affected by "forces" that don't track the truth. (5) You think that these "forces" operate in an undetectable way, and you cannot rule out the possibility that it is you who is being misled by them. (6) Since you cannot rule out the possibility that these "forces" deceive you, you cannot rationally (at least, concerning belief-accuracy or truth-conduciveness) believe that incompatibilism is true and that your Consequence Argument for it is compelling. (See van Inwagen 1975.)

From the viewpoint of equilibrism, the reason for this difference of views between you lies elsewhere. According to it, the difference of views between you persists because your fundamental pre-philosophical convictions are different. Thus, it is not the case that you both start out constructing your philosophical theories on the basis of a given and shared set of evidence, and subsequently, at some point of theory construction, some "mysterious force" starts to operate undetectably and leads both of you (or at least one of you) astray. Rather, the case is that you and Lewis take different pre-philosophical intuitions at "face value" during theory construction, and presumably it is at this point where some "forces" or bias factors come into play that don't track the truth.

But all this is not so relevant to our present conversation, since as I see it, the essence is the following. Let's suppose that you're right from God's perspective and Lewis is wrong. But, as you cannot rule out the possibility that it is not you who is misled, at some point of your argument, by that "mysterious force" of which Clifford's ghost is speaking, after all it is a *matter of chance* that you're right and Lewis is wrong.

I know that you're completely aware of all the above. Then, how is it possible that you still stick to incompatibilism and don't suspend your belief?

van Inwagen: "I am unwilling to listen to the whispers of Clifford's ghost; that is, I am unwilling to become an agnostic about everything, but empirically verifiable matters of fact. (In fact, I am unable to do that, and so, I think, is almost everyone else; as Thoreau said, neither men nor mushrooms grow so.) And I am unable to believe that my gnosticism, so to call it, is irrational. I am, I say, unwilling to listen to these whispers. *But I am unable to answer them*" (2010: 27, italics from Sophie).

This is also *writhing*—epistemic schizophrenia. I am asking you to have empathy and try to imagine what it like is to live through this "battle"! Try to imagine yourself in van Inwagen's place—you're unable to give up your incompatibilism, while you have to hear the continuous reproachful whispering of Clifford's ghost. What can come out of this? Something like this may do:

If I assume that determinism is true, then by that I state (or I may be guided by "will to believe") that given the world's initial condition and the laws of nature, nothing can happen differently to how it actually happens. If, however I state that nothing can happen differently to how it actually happens, then I also have to state (oh, it may just be my heart's voice): every action, on account of being a physical event, is forced by other physical events that do not fall under the agent's control. And if every action as a physical event is forced by other physical events that do not fall under the agent's control, then I have to say this (although I am so afraid that this is only a result of "some inner push"): when, for example, Franz Joseph signed the document declaring war on Serbia in 1914, this was something he had no way to avoid—his hand had to move the exact way it did.

You cannot just wave aside again this line of thought that is quite "impregnated" with cognitive unrest, and cannot say that its author is troubled by unnecessarily self-recrimination and meaningless worry. It would be a sign of excessive insensitivity, wouldn't it?

This cannot end well. If a philosopher's doubt triumphs, then she will become a meta-skeptic. She suspends her substantive philosophical beliefs and gives up on seeking philosophical truths. And if a philosopher finally gives in to an irresistible urge to stick to her view at any cost, then she cannot but try to put Clifford's ghost's (or Sophie's) words out of her head and retire to her philosophical cave—even if it is (at least initially) accompanied by a hellish intellectual remorse.

* * *

Still, perhaps neither of the above cases should occur. Let's assume that someone argues as follows:

> I don't believe that my arguments for the truth of my philosophical views have compelling force. Neither do I believe that the rival views are underpinned with arguments weaker than mine. In spite of all these, I think that *I can confidently believe* that, in contrast to my interlocutors, *I am* the one who is *right*. I can do so because *beyond/above* my philosophical arguments, but in accordance with them, I have some further *private evidence* for the truth of my philosophical views. Referring to it, I can attribute privileged status (extra weight) to my own view—saying that my interlocutors don't have THIS evidence. So, against the equilibrists I can claim that my philosophical views aren't *merely ones* among many other equilibria because they *aren't merely* elaborations of my fundamental pre-philosophical convictions—I have *further* evidence for the truth of my views. And I can say to the whispering of Clifford's ghost that my private evidence *does* track the truth—it directs me towards assenting to truth propositions.

It seems that van Inwagen himself tries to get out of this trouble in a similar way (at least, some passages attest to it):

> Well, I *do believe* these things [my first-order philosophical views]. And I believe that I am justified in believing them. And *I am confident that I am right*. But how can I take these positions? I don't know. That is itself a philosophical question, and I have no firm opinion about its correct answer. I suppose my best guess is that *I enjoy some sort of philosophical insight* (I mean in relation to these particular theses) that, for all merits, is somehow denied to Lewis. And this would have to be an insight that is incommunicable — at least, I do not know how to communicate it — for I have done all I can to communicate it to Lewis,

and he has understood everything perfectly everything I have said, and he has not come to share my conclusions.

(1996: 138, italics mine)

It is hard to say anything to these proposals. If a philosopher's confidence is *seriously shaken* in the truth of his beliefs, then I'm afraid that he can hardly regain it by citing some private evidence. Just think about it. What could he say (how *more specific* he could be) about the *nature* of this private evidence, which could convince him and restore his confidence? If he can say no more about this private evidence that it is *he* who *experiences* it and what *he* experiences counts for much more than someone else's experience (e.g., Huemer 2011)—then it surely won't be enough. He might as well say: "The fact that I believe in the truth of *p* is *further* evidence for the truth of *p*, above my arguments—please give me back my confidence!"

The most he can say is this: the experience of this private evidence has a *specific phenomenology*. For example: "When my philosophical theory appears to me in its completeness, alongside my arguments for it, an *inner voice* always *starts speaking* inside me, and *assures* me: 'Yes, that's true', 'Yes, this is how the pieces come (must come) together!'—like God, taking a glance of what He had done, 'He *saw* it was good.'" To give another example: "An inner voice *has been showing me the way* right from the start for working out my philosophical theory; it '*has been with me*' all along; it '*has accompanied me*'; it '*has guided* me' during the argumentation; it *has indicated* the *right* direction to me: '*Don't go that way!*'; '*Avoid* that!'; 'Try to find it *this way!*'; and it *has assured* me at each and every step of the *correctness* of these steps."

I don't dispute that there are such inner voices, inner compasses, and inner "truth-signalers," neither do I dispute that these have an important role in shaping our philosophical beliefs. But, no matter how we would like to avoid it, we always *come across* the question *whether we can trust* in them. Can we *seriously and sincerely believe* in the truth of *p* based on an inner voice that assures us of the truth of *p*?

This doubt has two sources—it is easy to figure out what they are. One is: what should I do if my interlocutors, too, appeal to private evidence? I can afford to ignore it, saying "The inner guiding voice speaks in only those who, like me, believe that *p*—by contrast, in those who believe that non-*p*, this voice remains silent." I can also say: "The inner guiding voice speaks in my interlocutors, too, except that it tells them falsities." However, they can say these things just like me—the whole debate would turn into a farce. The other is: why should I believe that the inner voice is reliable? *For all I know*, the inner voice which assures me of the truth of *p* might be private evidence which really signals the truth of *p*; or, it might be a mere "will to believe," or again, some different "inner push" that does not track the truth. This is an especially nagging issue, since the latter *also* "show" me the "truth" and *also* "signal" the "right" direction to me. However, I have to admit that I don't have the *right criteria* to tell apart the private evidence which (reliably) signals the truth of *p* to me from the various bias factors.

Each of these issues is banal (they couldn't be more banal)—so, all the more it is painful that we can hardly answer to them in good conscience. And if we cannot do that, then our trust in the truth of our beliefs will not be restored—we keep sinking deeper into the pits of epistemic schizophrenia. *Earlier* we had to face that we cannot believe in the truth of our substantive factual philosophical views with epistemic responsibility if *all* we can say is that they are elaborated versions of our fundamental pre-philosophical convictions (which are unjustified but I cannot abandon them), and there are no knock-down argument(s) against them. *Now* we have to face that there is an inner voice assuring us that the way things are is the way we think them to be. But, since we are *at a loss* when we are requested to justify that this inner voice signals the truth to us, rather than being a mere bias factor which has nothing to do with the truth, we cannot keep believing in the truth of our substantive factual philosophical views with epistemic responsibility.

Of course, independently of all that, some philosophers *might convince themselves* (even permanently) that they have a kind of private evidence which *reliably* signals them the truth of *p*, and consequently they can believe in the truth of *p in cognitive peace*. Once again, it is hard to say anything to this. I feel like shrugging my shoulders, saying: "*Look*, to what length some will go in order to regain their trust in the truth of their philosophical beliefs—and *look*, how much success they achieve in this regard!" But I feel that irony would be misplaced at this point. Rather, here is how I see it: if a philosopher "achieves success," then that is one of the saddest things that can happen to him in his career.

3 Philosophy without philosophical beliefs

Here's the core idea in brief. The advocates of Lewis-style equilibrism would like to stick to their philosophical *beliefs*—what is important to them is that *they can believe* in their philosophical theories. As Lewis puts it in his "maxim of honesty": "never put forward a philosophical theory that you yourself cannot *believe* in your least philosophical and most commonsensical moments" (1986: 135, italics mine).

The advocates of Lewis-style equilibrism admittedly don't possess any compelling justifications for their philosophical theories. However, the intellectual maintenance of their considered philosophical beliefs (if you wish, the mere egocentric "justification" of their philosophical theses) is not enough for them to seriously and sincerely believe in the truth of their philosophical theories.

The failure of Lewis-style equilibrism clearly shows that the philosophers' beliefs are the source of all troubles. But it also clearly shows the solution: to be able to commit themselves to a philosophical theory, philosophers *should not believe in it* (what is more, it is even counter-indicated for them to do that), but rather *merely accept it* (see e.g., Barnett 2019; Beebee 2018). The reason is that the mere acceptance of a philosophical theory means a *less binding and looser* commitment. We could say, "no belief, no cry."

3.1 Belief vs. acceptance

Here's one formulation of this suggestion:

> I suggest [...] that something like van Fraassen's view about "acceptance" of scientific theories can be made to solve the problem. Constructive empiricism faces a similar problem to equilibrism: given that science does not aim at the truth, and hence knowledge, of scientific theories — it only aims at empirical adequacy — how can we make sense of the fact that scientists *do* (and indeed *must*, for the purpose of pursuing that aim) make assertions that apparently express belief in claim about unobservables for which they have no justification? Van Fraassen's answer, in short, is that "acceptance" of and belief in such claim are two distinct phenomena — and that only acceptance is required [...]

> Roughly, then, the idea is that in "accepting" a scientific theory that is ontologically committed to unobservables, the scientist does nor (or, at least need not) adopt the attitude of *belief* towards what the theory says about those unobservables [...]

> [I]f we are not entitled to *believe* that claims of our own theories, in what sense can they truly be said to be *our* theories? How can we sincerely endorse the claims those theories make? Acceptance, I take it, is supposed to deliver sincerity. The attitude of acceptance does not, of course, constitute sincere *belief*, but it

is sincere nonetheless. The working scientist adopts a theoretical view, works hard to accommodate the existing evidence and explore further consequences of her theory, makes adjustments where necessary, and so on. And she can do all of this entirely sincerely while yet merely accepting rather than believing her own theory [...] All of this, I suggest, amounts to the scientist's *taking a view* in as much of a sense of "taking a view" as is required of her for the purposes of playing her part in the progress of science.

If something like van Fraassen's notion of acceptance really can constitute a legitimate sense in which one might "take a view", then it can, I think, be applied to the working philosopher no less that to working scientist. The aims of science [...] and the aims of philosophy [...] differ, of course: the aim of empirical adequacy in science is very different to the pluralist aim in philosophy of discovering the equilibrium positions that can withstand examination. But in each case the acceptance of a theory that one cannot rationally believe serves a purpose relative to that aim. In the case of science, the aim of empirical adequacy demands that theories that posit unobservables are developed and tested, and in the case of philosophy the aim of the discovery of equilibria demands that we take on board a set of core assumptions and methodological prescriptions in order to develop and scrutinize an equilibrium position of our own that can withstand examination.

(Beebee 2018: 20–2, italics in original)

The thing is the following. Let's make a difference between belief in a theory and acceptance of a theory (see e.g., Cohen 1989, 1992; Engel 1998; van Fraassen 1980). Putting subtleties and related major and minor disagreements aside, and concentrating solely on factual philosophical problems, I would like to point out the following differences between the concepts of belief and acceptance.

Firstly, if we believe that p, then our p-belief aims at *truth*. For example, if we believe that mereological sums do not exist, it means that we hold true the proposition that "Mereological sums do not exist." By contrast, if we merely accept that p, then the acceptance of p does not aim at truth—we accept p solely for practical purposes. For example, if we merely accept that mereological sums do not exist, it means that we hold mereological nihilism as a possible philosophical equilibrium to be productive, rich in prospects, progressive, etc.—something that yields a lot of "juice" when squeezed.

Secondly, if we believe that p, then we must be able to give reasons as to why we hold p true. For example, if we believe that free will is incompatible with determinism, then we must be able to argue for the truth of incompatibilism and the falsity of compatibilism. By contrast, if we merely accept that p, then we do not need to have reasons for the truth of *p*. For example, if we merely accept that free will is incompatible with determinism, then we must only be able to argue for the claim that incompatibilism as a philosophical equilibrium is productive, rich in prospects, progressive, etc.

Thirdly, if we believe that *p*, then our *p*-belief is *not a result of our deliberate decision* (or just very rarely is)—we do not have control over our beliefs (or have only minimum control over them). For example, if we believe in the existence of God, then we did not decide that from that moment on, we hold true the proposition "God exists." By contrast, if we merely accept that *p*, then it is always a result of our deliberate decision—we have strong control over what we accept. For example, if we accept that God exists, it means that we made a conscious decision that from now on, we will work on developing and defending a theist equilibrium, and take sides in other philosophical issues in its spirit.

Fourthly, if we believe that *p*, then our *p*-belief *has personal significance to us*. For example, if we believe that phenomenal consciousness is not a physical property, then this belief of ours cannot be detached from several other beliefs, and is (or can be) an integral part of our personal and cognitive identity. By contrast, if we merely accept that *p*, then our acceptance of *p* has no personal significance to us. For example, if we merely accept that phenomenal consciousness is not a physical property, then it has nothing to do with the system of our beliefs—it may even be possible that we actually believe anti-physicalism to be false.

To sum up, as opposed to our belief in a philosophical theory, to accept a philosophical theory is nothing else but to commit ourselves to a well-defined *working hypothesis*, of which we *believe* (because this is the *only thing* we must *believe* in) that it is sufficiently productive, rich in prospects, progressive, etc., *to be worthy* of our further development and defense, and to provide us a framework for doing philosophy.

What is the significance of this distinction? Here's the answer: if we start from the assumptions (1) that we cannot appropriately justify our philosophical theories to be able to seriously and sincerely believe in their truth, (2) that belief in a philosophical theory is not a necessary condition for commitment to it, (3) that we are free to accept any philosophical theory (equilibrium), and (4) that doing philosophy is a valuable thing, which we should not eliminate, then it is *advisable* that we show an attitude of acceptance towards philosophical theories instead of an attitude of belief. The reason is that there is *nothing at stake* for us in merely accepting a philosophical theory, it is *not* an integral part of our system of beliefs, it does *not* involve taking a personal stance, and it has *nothing* to do with our intuitions, pre-philosophical beliefs, and fundamental convictions—consequently, *it cannot happen* that we are suddenly visited by cognitive unrest or the disease called epistemic schizophrenia. In other words, it is advisable that we merely accept philosophical theories instead of believing in them because this is the only way for us to achieve *complete cognitive peace* to do our share in implementing that great and noble goal of the community of philosophers, that of populating the logical space with stable and increasingly sophisticated equilibria.

Taking a different track, in contrast to Lewis' (let me call it "human-faced" from now on) equilibrism, according to the "no belief, no cry" equilibrism, our appropriate reaction to philosophy's epistemic failure should be just to *pretend* having any philosophical beliefs—while we don't believe in the truth of a single substantive philosophical thesis. The proper conduct for us during philosophical discourse is to act *as if* we had philosophical beliefs—while we don't have any. The right attitude for us is to interpret philosophical discourse *in a fictionalist manner*—that is, as it is inevitable, we should keep *saying* that "I believe that *p*," but we *don't assert* it literally. Thus, we can sustain our usual philosophical discourse and don't have to worry about the uncertainty of our philosophical beliefs.

3.2 Phalanstery of philosophers

I don't want to dispute that the "no belief, no cry" equilibrism offers an attractive alternative to many philosophers. I also concede that if the "utopia" of the "no belief, no cry" equilibrism came true, then philosophers would not live in cognitive uncertainty any more indeed, as they would have no philosophical beliefs, "the source of all troubles." At the same time, I cannot identify with the "no belief, no cry" equilibrism. I will try to briefly tell you why I am so averse to and displeased by this metaphilosophical vision.

(1) Let's imagine how work would go on in the "no belief, no cry" "utopia." Since, according to this metaphilosophical vision, philosophy's exclusive goal is to populate logical space with consistent equilibria that resist objections, there is no doubt that the most suitable candidates for this task would be those philosophers who *do not at all have* any philosophical beliefs. For if a philosopher does not have philosophical beliefs that are significant to him (or, what is more, have existential stake), then, after all, he can work with complete cognitive peace of mind in the "assembly hall" of *any* equilibrium.

Of course, there could be some "malfunctioning" in the "no belief, no cry" "utopia," too, as the following dialogue illustrates:

Philosopher No. 123422: Dear equilibrium construction manager, I have a small problem. Ashamed as I am, I have to confess this: it seems that I still have some residual philosophical beliefs. One example is that a political community does the right thing if it benefits the least advantaged in allocating resources. Another one is that there are no abstract entities. Yet another is that the mind is part of the physical world. I can "vividly" believe all the (just-mentioned) propositions, and my personal-cognitive integrity would be damaged if I had to give up any of them. But, as I take it for sure that there can be no compelling arguments in philosophy, and as I've realized that the Lewis-type "human-faced" version of equilibrism necessarily gives rise to cognitive unrest, I cannot see how I could do my part in the works of implementing philosophy's ultimate goal, the construction of equilibria.

Equilibrium construction manager: God save us from you constructing philosophical equilibria related to these fundamental convictions of yours. If you don't want to catch the disease called "cognitive unrest" or "epistemic schizophrenia," just let go of your cherished pre-philosophical convictions and the equilibria that elaborate them!

Philosopher No. 123422: But what should I do, then?

Equilibrium construction manager: Don't worry! We will surely find some philosophical problems that you don't have any solid intuitions about. For instance, do you have any solid pre-philosophical convictions about the problem "The ship of Theseus"?

Philosopher No. 123422: None at all.

Equilibrium construction manager: Great! Starting from tomorrow, you will be busily building the equilibrium which says that the original ship is identical with the reconstructed ship—of course, in the spirit of mereological essentialism. But if you deem the topic of mereological essentialism to have already been thoroughly dissected by your predecessors, and think that you would not benefit much from it, then feel free to choose an equilibrium that promises more new insights. For example, the one which says that the original ship undergoes fission. Still, the best you can do is to obtain a thorough taxonomy of the "Ship of Theseus" problem (let's say the one written by Gallois [1998]) and choose the philosophical equilibrium from which you think you can squeeze the most philosophical "juice."

I don't know about you but for me, the vision of "no belief, no cry" equilibrism is not a pleasant, serene, sunny, and peaceful utopia, but a horrible and frustrating dystopia. Of course, I cannot rule out that my unwillingness is idiosyncratic, and perhaps even self-destructing in a certain sense. The most I can say is this: I have some "vivid" substantive philosophical beliefs that are important to me, and I think that a person like me *would not prefer to live* in this "utopia." The reason is that I consider it my epistemic duty to try to account for my substantive philosophical beliefs in the light of philosophy's epistemic failure—and if I worked in the "no belief, no cry" utopia, doing philosophy in the spirit of "no belief, no cry" equilibrism, then I would continuously and definitely feel that *I do not do* what I should do, and what I should do is *not what I do*.

To put it bluntly, in my eyes the "no belief, no cry" equilibrism is a *superficial* metaphilosophical vision, which downgrades doing philosophy to a lightweight, no-stakes intellectual game, transforming it into a kind of charade, so to speak. Within the framework of this game, no concepts such as "eutrophication," "flirtatiousness," or "troubadour poetry" should be drawn and expressions such as "Karamazov brothers," "globalization," "Sally-Anne test" shouldn't be shown without words. Instead of these very difficult riddles, this charade, made in the spirit of "no belief, no cry" equilibrism, would include very difficult riddles such as "Argue for panpsychism, show that photons have proto-consciousness!"; "Argue that there can be aliens who have very different geometry than ours!"; "Argue that any combination of temporal parts of any objects from any time, no matter how scattered and disparate, composes an object!"

If the utopia of "no belief, no cry" equilibrism were realized, the doing of philosophy would not be much different from this charade. I don't dispute that this charade would be a fun and exciting pastime for many, but I am quite certain that those philosophers who have substantive philosophical beliefs would *feel homeless* in this world. They would feel that they're not of this world.

(2) Let's imagine, however, a philosopher who—unlike me—would like to live in this "utopia." He might say this:

> I like the vision of "no belief, no cry" equilibrism because I experience it as a kind of liberation. I don't believe that there could be knock-down arguments in philosophy, and I don't sympathize with the "human-faced" version of equilibrism either. For me, the "no belief, no cry" vision is the only option to commit myself to a philosophical theory with cognitive peace of mind. This is because it requires me no more than to accept a working hypothesis, and do my job in accordance with it day after day.
>
> The reason why I can do my job with complete cognitive peace of mind by accepting the working hypothesis that I've chosen or I've been assigned is

that for me, the work of building (or assembling) equilibrium *x* is no more significant than the work of building (or assembling) equilibrium *y*. I believe neither in *x* nor in *y*. And as I don't have any philosophical beliefs, I don't mind, and even consider as another challenge, if in the meantime the community of philosophers expects me to accept another working hypothesis (one whose content is incompatible with the earlier one) and the construction of a corresponding equilibrium.

But that's not all. The vision of "no belief, no cry" equilibrism strongly attracts me because it offers a moral redemption at once. I don't have to lie to myself any more when trying to account for my decision to continue my professional philosophical activity, even though I no longer believe in any substantive philosophical theories.

I don't know about you, but in my eyes the above is a clear proof that the "no belief, no cry" equilibrism is in fact nothing else but an open and sophisticated yet displeasing form of that opportunism that tries to divert attention from the unresolvedness of philosophical problems and the misery of those burnt-out philosophers who have lost all their substantive philosophical beliefs by reassuring them that "although you have failed both intellectually and morally, you can keep on doing everything as you did so far."

As you can see, I used some morally condemning expressions—I called the "no belief, no cry" equilibrism superficial and unprincipled opportunism. At the same time, I have to admit that whether a philosopher likes or dislikes the "no belief, no cry" equilibrism is, like so many other things, dependent on *value choice* at the end of the day—being a matter of *taste*, if you wish.

I fully admit that someone could think that populating the logical space, knowing possible equilibria, and the clarification of the philosophical-logical relations among them is *a value in itself* for which it is *worth* doing philosophy. I don't think it is. I cannot see why the production of increasingly more precise and detailed maps of philosophical equilibria would be a value in itself if one *doesn't want to believe at all* in the truth of a single substantive philosophical theory or equilibrium. In my eyes, for example, there is no special value in a philosopher's ability to make fine-grained distinctions among different kinds of supervenient dependence; he has the highest resolution picture of the advantages and difficulties of various theories of supervenience—while he *does not* (and *does not want to*) *believe* anything at all about the mind-body relationship, or, if he believes anything about it, his belief *has nothing on earth to do* with his above-mentioned ability.

Of course, someone could say (see e.g., Barnett 2019), that we should only *temporarily* be "no belief, no cry" equilibrists—until one or other equilibrium gains the upper hand over its rivals. As soon as this happens, we may begin to believe in their truth with clear conscience.

However, I cannot commit myself to this proposal either. Let's suppose that at some point in his career Thomas decides to do no more than accept certain substantive philosophical theories because he sees that he cannot identify with the "human-faced" version of equilibrism. In my opinion, Thomas can seriously think that his decision is just a temporary one (and not final), *only if he strongly believes* that sooner or later (hopefully, in his life) the "Epistemic End of Days" (MacBride 2014: 231) will arrive—*only if he strongly believes* that one day someone (hopefully, he himself) will come up with some knock-down argument(s) for a given equilibrium, or refute all its rivals with knock-down arguments, and so he will be able to safely discredit them all. Thus, Thomas has good reason to think that he is just a temporary (and nor a permanent) "no belief, no cry" equilibrist *only if* he at the same time believes that there can be compelling justifications in philosophy.

Now, since like the "human-faced" equilibrists, I think that there can be no compelling justification for our substantive philosophical theses, any commitment to this optimistic version of the "no belief, no cry" equilibrism is not a viable alternative to me.

4 Farewell to equilibrism

I don't want to repeat my misgivings about the human-faced or the "no belief, no cry" variants of equilibrism—I wish to say something different.

Recall the section in which I listed the main motives for choosing equilibrism. Among them, I mentioned the fact that equilibrism is capable of legitimating the received way of doing philosophy. To illustrate this, I quoted the passage below from Gutting: "an atheist who thinks all arguments for God's existence are demonstrably fallacious may need a clever philosopher to show what's wrong with a sophisticated version of the cosmological argument or the design argument from fine-tuning" (2015: 258). In what follows, I will confine myself to reacting to this point, because this is where the insincerity of the human-faced equilibrism is especially clear.

Let's take again the mind-body problem as a factual philosophical problem. Let's suppose that Alex, an outsider, is deeply interested in how the mind and the body are related to each other. What can the community of philosophers offer her? Two things. Firstly, it can show her which philosophical view she should endorse in light of her fundamental pre-philosophical convictions in order to avoid logical/conceptual contradiction with herself. Secondly, it can enlighten Alex about how she should address the objections against her view.

Nonetheless, this is not what Alex expects. She does not turn to the clever community of philosophers in order to be enlightened about what she should think in harmony with her fundamental pre-philosophical convictions and how she could neutralize objections. For example, if Alex is uncertain but inclined to believe in the immortality of the soul, it will not comfort her that the community of philosophers shows her beyond doubt that no materialist objection is compelling. Or, if Alex is uncertain but inclined to believe that the soul is not immortal in any sense, it will not comfort her that the community of philosophers shows her beyond doubt that none of the anti-physicalist objections are compelling.

The equilibrist, of course, may say (what she has *always* said) that Alex cannot expect more than this from the community of philosophers. Alex, however, may retort (and I'm convinced that any outsider who is sincerely curious would retort with this as well) that if the community of philosophers cannot provide more than this, it would be more *righteous* or at least *sincere* for it to confess that it *does not have a clue* about what the relationship is between the mind and the body—because they *actually* do not have a clue.

But let me dramatize this further. I think that the insincerity of equilibrism is even more obvious when an outsider turns to the community of philosophers for an answer to a philosophical question which has great existential importance to him. Let's suppose that Sammy had a long but immoral life. He enjoyed torturing others and tortured many people in an extremely cruel way. Furthermore, let's suppose that Sammy feels that the end is near. And let's also suppose that Sammy firmly believes in the truth of the conditional that "If God exists, sinners will be condemned to eternal damnation." (He believes this as firmly as he believes that the plane which he boarded does not crash and almost as firmly as he believes that there is a mind-independent reality.) However, he is uncertain about the existence of God. Of course, Sammy would not like to be condemned to eternal damnation, so he turns to the community of philosophers (for whoever else could he turn to?) in order to learn what he should believe regarding the existence of God and the afterlife.

Now, let's suppose that Sammy is told: "First you should explicate your fundamental pre-philosophical convictions about supernatural beings and the mind-body problem, and then we will tell you in which theories of philosophy of religion and philosophy of mind *should you* believe, given these convictions." If this is the answer from the community of philosophers to his question which has extreme importance to him, then Sammy rightly retorts that it did not help him at all, because he *did not* get a real answer to his question. He got to know certain relevant aspects of the problem, but he did not get to know the most important thing which was the reason he asked anything in the first place. Namely, he did not get to know whether he does have reason to worry or not.

If the community of philosophers (as it did in Alex's case) addresses this problem by saying that one should not expect more from philosophy than this, it is abundantly clear that what the equilibrist can provide Sammy is *not more than* what a thoroughbred meta-skeptic is able to provide. The answer "If these are your fundamental pre-philosophical convictions, then you should believe this and that" *has the exactly the same value* for Sammy as the answer "We are unable to tell you what you should believe."

What is more—and in my view, this is the main trouble—if the equilibrist was successful and Sammy was satisfied with the above "if ..., then ..."-type answer, then the equilibrist would "teach" Sammy only how he *does not have to be aware* that he is *still as ignorant as he was before* regarding a question which has great importance to him. Thus, it was even *worse* for him than if he had met a meta-skeptic. Sammy could not receive a reassuring answer from him either, but the meta-skeptic could raise Sammy's awareness of his ignorance and its consequences. In contrast to the equilibrist, the meta-skeptic *would not mislead* Sammy.

6

Meta-skepticism

According to meta-skepticism, philosophers *cannot rationally believe* in the truth of their philosophical theses, views, and theories, so *their epistemic duty is to suspend* their philosophical beliefs.

This definition of meta-skepticism is incomplete as yet—it needs completion at two points. Let's first see what the meta-skeptic means by saying that philosophers cannot *rationally* believe in the truth of their philosophical theses.

Rational belief is a broad concept that encompasses many different kinds of belief, and a rather elusive concept at once, since "rational" has several mutually contradictory definitions. Perhaps the most inclusive definition is this: S's belief in p is rational if S *does well* to believe that p. This can be interpreted in a number of ways.

Firstly, "S rationally believes that p" can mean that S does well to believe that p because S's belief in p has some *useful consequences or benefits* for S (or for someone else). For example, a candidate does well to believe she has prepared for the exam (even if it's not true) because by having this belief, she will probably better perform than by having the contrary one. I call this concept (which appeals exclusively to useful consequences and benefits and has nothing to do with justification) *pragmatic* rationality.

Secondly, "S rationally believes that p" can mean that S does well to believe that p because S's belief in p is *coherent* with other beliefs of S—p fits S's worldview which is a constitutive element of S's personal identity. For example, a Young Earth believer does well to believe that the presence of fossils under the ground is a deception, because this fits well her belief system, while the theory of evolution is incoherent with it. I call this concept (which appeals exclusively to the coherency of S's belief system) *pure coherentist* rationality, and the corresponding justification *pure coherentist* justification.

Thirdly, "S rationally believes that p" can mean that S does well to believe that p because S's belief in p is not only coherent with S's beliefs, but p does not have any defeaters (or, at least, S is not aware of any). For example, Bellarmino did well to believe that the Sun revolves around the Earth because this belief was coherent with his belief system *and* (at the time) it had no defeaters. I call this concept (which appeals to the coherence of S's belief system *plus* the absence of defeaters) *supplemented coherentist* rationality, and the corresponding justification *supplemented coherentist* justification.

Fourthly, "S rationally believes that *p*" can mean that S does well to believe that *p* because the justification S has for *p* gives S good reason to believe that *p is true*. That is, S rationally believes in *p* when S has good reason to believe that the justification of *p* is *accurate* or *truth-conducive*. For example, Suzie does well to believe that the Earth is round because, besides the fact that her body of evidence strongly indicates that the Earth is round, the scientific community unanimously agrees on this fact (true proposition). I call this concept (which appeals to accurate or truth-conducive justification) *epistemic* rationality, and the corresponding justification *epistemic* justification. (For the sake of simplicity, in what follows, unless indicated otherwise, I will use only this concept of rational belief.)

Now, when the meta-skeptic claims that "Philosophers cannot rationally believe in the truth of their philosophical theses," he doesn't mean it in the sense of "all-inclusive" rationality. He may allow that philosophers can (in the pragmatic or in the pure coherentist or in the supplemented coherentist sense) rationally believe in philosophical theses. At the same time, he maintains that they cannot rationally believe in the truth of their philosophical theses in the sense that *they have good reason* for thinking that they have accurate or truth-conducive justification for their philosophical beliefs.

Thus, the meta-skeptic disputes that philosophy's truth-seeking and justificatory tools are adequate and suitable for establishing truth and for the compelling justification of philosophical theses. And if they are not adequate and suitable, then the use of these tools doesn't give philosophers any good epistemic reason to hold their philosophical beliefs to be true. Consequently, they cannot rationally hold their philosophical beliefs to be true.

The meta-skeptic is dissatisfied with all kinds of externalist justification (which merely appeal to some reliable cognitive process). According to him, even if (similar to chicken-sexers) there were some chosen philosophers who always believe the right philosophical propositions to be true thanks to some philosophical super-skill that is *inaccessible* to them (like chicken-sexers accurately determine the sex of a given chicken as female or male), they could not rationally believe in the truth of their philosophical theses. The reason is that—primarily in the light of the permanent dissensus in all areas of philosophy—they, *too*, would have good epistemic reasons to doubt whether their philosophical skills are reliable and whether their philosophical beliefs are true.

Let's now turn to the second half of the meta-skeptical thesis. The meta-skeptic does not necessarily dispute that philosophers may have good epistemic reasons to believe in the truth of some *non-substantive* philosophical propositions. He can allow that S can rationally believe in the truth of propositions like the following: "If physical objects are bundles of immanent universals, then the principle of the identity of indiscernibles is true." Or: "Conceptualism about perceptual content has the virtue of being able to easily account for the role of perceptual experiences in our beliefs about the external world, but it has a hard time accounting for the phenomenology of perceptual experiences, for example for the phenomenological fact that perceptual experiences are finer-grained than the concepts under which they are subsumed." In a word, S does not have to suspend her non-substantive philosophical beliefs of this kind.

Another interesting issue is whether the meta-skeptic would expect philosophers to suspend those beliefs of theirs concerning which we cannot talk about truth simpliciter—their philosophical views on *purely conceptual* philosophical problems. The meta-skeptic can be hardline, or alternatively, he can be lenient. If he is hardline, he can say that "Because S cannot have good epistemic reason to believe, for instance, the proposition that 'Works of art are expressions of the artist's emotions', S must suspend this belief." But if he is lenient, he can say that "If S's philosophical belief p does really nothing but enables S to conceptually 'piece together' the 'world', then for all I care, S may believe that p, and S need not suspend p." From now on, I will focus on the lenient variant of meta-skepticism—considered as a more consistent version of it.

An even more interesting issue is whether the meta-skeptic would expect philosophers (or any sane person) to suspend their belief in the external world or other minds, and in the possibility of reliable cognition at all. No, he wouldn't. But of course, the reason why he wouldn't expect them to do so is *not* that according to him, there are compelling philosophical arguments for their beliefs of this kind. On the contrary, our insistence on these beliefs has nothing to do with any kind of philosophical consideration—nobody believes in these propositions on the basis of philosophical arguments. The meta-skeptic can acknowledge that we have some (even if very few) beliefs which we can rationally insist on due to their special *content*. I call these beliefs with special content *inherently warranted* beliefs. Not in the sense that belief p warrants (justifies) itself or p is warranted (justified) just by virtue of being p (like our beliefs about our own mental states do, see e.g., Alston 1976), but simply in the sense that *one would be mad to deny p*.

Even though philosophers disagree about the grounds of their inherently warranted nature, there is a kind of agreement that the lack of these beliefs would make the practice of epistemic justification absurd in the first place. This is because the very motivation to justify our beliefs is closely connected to their truth even if it is hard to tell what their precise connection consists in. Just think about it! What would justifying our beliefs mean if no minds or nothing at all existed besides our minds? Or if our minds were incapable of reliable cognition? Let's suppose that someone argues that there is only one mind, there is no external world, and no one is capable of reliable cognition. Although we might be tempted to think that this kind of talk provides some evidence for these claims, the sane approach would be to reject them even if we cannot present any arguments against their truth.

Since our insistence on these inherently warranted beliefs has nothing to do with philosophical considerations, the meta-skeptic does not dispute that *everybody* is *entitled* to sustaining these beliefs. In this way, he can accept that there are at least three substantive and factual philosophical theses in which any philosopher (or, in fact, *anyone*) can believe—we do not have an epistemic duty to suspend them.

Thus, the meta-skeptic does *not* claim that philosophers have the epistemic duty to suspend *all* of their philosophical beliefs. What he *must* claim is this: philosophers have the epistemic duty of suspending *only those* substantive and factual beliefs which they reached or hold solely on the basis of philosophical considerations—but they have to suspend those beliefs *without exception*.

Taking these remarks into account, I would like to give the following definition of meta-skepticism as the fourth reaction to philosophy's epistemic failure:

Meta-skepticism: (1) Philosophers cannot (in the epistemic sense) rationally believe in the truth of their substantive and factual philosophical theses because they have no accessible and good epistemic reasons for thinking that their substantive and factual philosophical theses are appropriately justified, therefore (2) philosophers have the epistemic duty to suspend their substantive and factual philosophical beliefs that are based solely on philosophical considerations.

It is important to emphasize that although meta-skepticism is, of course, a *normative* philosophical view, in the meta-skeptic's eyes (1) and (2) are *not conceptual but factual* philosophical theses—*independently* of our conceptual framework, it is *true simpliciter* that philosophers' substantive factual beliefs are irrational, and *independently* of our conceptual framework, it is *true simpliciter* that they have to suspend them. Which means that according to the meta-skeptic, it is a *fact* (existing independently of our conceptual framework) that philosophers' substantive factual beliefs are not justified appropriately enough to entitle them to rationally stick to them, and it is a *fact* (existing independently of our conceptual framework) that philosophers have the duty to suspend them. In a word, according to the meta-skeptic, we do not have to accept (1) and (2) because they follow from our conceptual framework, but because (1) and (2) are made true by the epistemic world order.

To be sure, most philosophers don't consider meta-skepticism an attractive alternative. There are three well-known and rather serious worries which make them think that meta-skepticism is an untenable metaphilosophical view.

Firstly, meta-skepticism is a *self-defeating* view—the propositional content of this view *defeats the belief* in its propositional content. According to the meta-skeptic, philosophers cannot rationally believe in the truth of their substantive factual philosophical theses, consequently *the meta-skeptic cannot rationally believe* in the truth of the substantive factual philosophical thesis that "Philosophers cannot rationally believe in the truth of their substantive factual philosophical theses," *either*. Furthermore, according to the meta-skeptic, philosophers must suspend their belief in the truth of their substantive factual philosophical theses, consequently *the meta-skeptic, too, must suspend his belief* in the truth of the substantive factual philosophical thesis that "Philosophers must suspend their belief in the truth of their substantive factual philosophical theses."

Secondly, the meta-skeptical view requires us to do something psychologically impossible (or at least extremely difficult), namely to suspend even those philosophical beliefs that are essential parts of our personal integrity and constitutive elements of our cognitive household. We simply cannot go down this road—*we cannot live our lives* as consistent meta-skeptics.

Thirdly, even if somehow it were psychologically possible for us to suspend those substantive factual philosophical beliefs, we would be much worse off if we committed ourselves to meta-skepticism. It *offers no prospects* and *narrows down our intellectual options*, in particular the scope of our philosophical activities and stances, without offering anything in exchange. This means that adopting the meta-skeptical strategy is the worst possible business.

The above three worries do not have equal weight. The first one is the most serious because if all possible arguments for meta-skepticism undermine their own conclusions, then it is not rational to adopt meta-skepticism. But if it is possible to formulate a non-self-defeating and perhaps compelling argument for meta-skepticism, then the second and third worries are *eo ipso* invalidated. This is because if there are compelling arguments for the thesis that philosophers have the epistemic duty to suspend their substantive factual philosophical beliefs, then—however difficult and painful, and however hopeless it may be—they *must* suspend them.

In this chapter, I first expound and characterize the general argumentative strategy of meta-skepticism, trying to show what premises a meta-skeptic can use in his argument to support his view in the most promising way. I give a detailed analysis of the meta-skeptic's theses (1) and (2), and say what he can do with the problem of self-defeat. In what follows, I put myself in the meta-skeptic's perspective to describe what he sees as the mistake of those philosophers who stick to their philosophical beliefs, and what kind of "training" he offers them so they can suspend their philosophical beliefs. Finally, I try to show that the meta-skeptic doesn't react well to philosophy's epistemic failure, and doesn't give a right answer to the question "What should we do with our philosophical beliefs in the light of philosophy's epistemic failure?"

1 The meta-skeptical argumentative strategy

1.1 The main argument for meta-skepticism

Before presenting the argument, I would like to make some preliminary clarifying remarks. First, the meta-skeptic must give *compelling* argument(s) for his view. Why cannot he be satisfied with non-compelling arguments? Because non-compelling arguments—as you could see in the discussion of equilibrism—can at most provide egocentric "justification," and so the meta-skeptic could be allowed to say just this much: "*In my opinion*, philosophers cannot rationally believe in their substantive factual philosophical theses, and *in my opinion*, they should suspend their substantive factual philosophical beliefs, for this view is in equilibrium with my fundamental pre-philosophical convictions." This formulation, however, is not identical with the thesis of meta-skepticism—it is no more than *one equilibrium* among other (metaphilosophical) equilibria.

The meta-skeptic, then—at least in this respect—must proceed similarly to the followers of the epistemic tradition. The meta-skeptic is indeed different from the equilibrist. While, according to the equilibrist, there can be no compelling arguments in philosophy, the meta-skeptic thinks that one can argue compellingly for the philosophical thesis that philosophers cannot rationally stick to their substantive factual philosophical beliefs and so they must suspend them.

Secondly, the argument for meta-skepticism must be distinguished from the one for conciliationism. From the fact of dissensus among experts recognizing each other as epistemic peers, the conciliationists typically conclude that the rational thing to do for the participants of a debate is to suspend their beliefs or at least reassess their epistemic status. In the argument for meta-skepticism, however, the fact of dissensus *has a different role*. As the meta-skeptic sees it, philosophical disagreement (or rather, the permanent dissent in all areas of philosophy) clearly indicates that the tools of philosophy are inadequate and unsuitable for establishing truths. As Jason Brennan puts it:

> The goal of philosophy is uncover certain truths. Radical dissensus shows that philosophical methods are imprecise and inaccurate. Philosophy continually leads experts with the highest degree of epistemic virtue doing the very best they can, to accept a wide array of incompatible doctrines. Therefore, philosophy is an *unreliable* instrument for finding truth.
>
> (Brennan 2010: 3, italics mine)

To complete the argument: if the tools of philosophy are inadequate and unsuitable for establishing truths, then philosophers cannot have good epistemic reasons to stick to their substantive factual philosophical beliefs, and, willy-nilly, painfully or not, they must suspend them—except if they aren't entitled to hold them for reasons that have nothing to do with philosophy.

To sum up, the main difference between the argumentative strategies of conciliationism and meta-skepticism is that the meta-skeptic does not *directly* infer from the fact of dissensus among philosophers that philosophers cannot rationally believe in their theses. He doesn't go into the epistemology of disagreements, and his goal is not to present philosophical arguments for conciliationism and against the steadfast view. In the eyes of the meta-skeptic, the epistemology of disagreements is merely an *n+1st* philosophical problem, about which—just like in other areas of philosophy—there is disagreement among philosophers. Instead, the starting point of the meta-skeptic is that the fact of dissensus in all areas of philosophy is an *unambiguous, unassailable, and indisputable proof* that the tools of philosophy are inadequate and unsuitable for establishing truths and compellingly justifying substantive factual philosophical theses, and *from the latter*, he infers that philosophers cannot rationally believe in the truth of their substantive factual philosophical theses, and they must suspend them—except if they are entitled to believe them regardless of any philosophical consideration.

Thirdly, the meta-skeptical argument against philosophical knowledge works otherwise than standard (first-order) skeptical arguments. The latter (and here I don't mean the skeptical arguments appealing to infinite regress) are made to the following recipe. (1) Take a bizarre scenario (we are brains in a vat; we are dreaming all the time; God created the world five minutes ago, etc.), which, if true, would be indistinguishable from normal experience from a subjective perspective. (2) Show that there is no way for us to rule out the possibility that we are actually in the scenario at issue. (3) Draw the conclusion that we do not have knowledge of the external world, or of the past that is earlier than five minutes ago because all our beliefs of this type are unjustified because of (2).

Standard skeptical arguments derive their extraordinary force from the fact that although everyone is absolutely certain that the skeptical scenario does not obtain, this certainty means nothing—everyone would still be absolutely certain that it does not obtain even if it did. Everyone would still be just as certain that they are not a brain in a vat even if they happened to be just that.

The argument for meta-skepticism is made to a different recipe. (1) Take as your starting point the fact of philosophy's epistemic failure. (You can safely do that, given the permanent dissensus in all areas of philosophy.) (2) In the subsequent premises, use expressions that properly capture the nature of this failure (for example: the truth-seeking and justificatory tools of philosophy are "wrong"; "inaccurate"; "unreliable"; "inadequate for establishing truths"; "not truth-conducive"; "unsuitable for compelling justification of philosophical theses," etc.). (3) Finally, make it explicit that *based on such truth-seeking and justification*, no rational person can believe in the truth of their substantive factual philosophical theories, views, or theses—they have to suspend them.

Here's a meta-skeptical argument made to this recipe:

(1) Philosophy is a failed epistemic enterprise—the pervasive and permanent disagreement in philosophy is a clear sign that philosophers have not solved any substantive factual philosophical problems, nor have they come up with any compellingly justified substantive factual philosophical theses.

(2) The best explanation for philosophy's epistemic failure is that the truth-seeking and justificatory tools of philosophy are inadequate and unsuitable for establishing substantive factual philosophical truths and for providing compelling justification of substantive factual philosophical theses—philosophers seek truth and justify their substantive factual philosophical theses with tools that are inadequate and unsuitable for establishing truths

and for providing compelling justifications for their substantive factual philosophical theses.

(3) If philosophers seek truth and justify their substantive factual philosophical theses with tools that are inadequate and unsuitable for establishing truths and for providing compelling justifications for their substantive factual philosophical theses, then philosophers cannot rationally believe in the truth of their substantive factual philosophical theses—except those very few theses in which one, regardless of philosophical considerations, is entitled to believe.

Therefore:

(C1) Philosophers cannot rationally believe in the truth of their substantive factual philosophical theses—except those very few theses in which one, regardless of philosophical considerations, is entitled to believe.

Furthermore:

(4) If philosophers cannot rationally believe in the truth of their substantive factual philosophical theses, then they have the epistemic duty to suspend their substantive factual philosophical beliefs.

Therefore:

(C2) Philosophers have the epistemic duty to suspend their substantive factual philosophical beliefs—except those very few beliefs in which one, regardless of philosophical considerations, is entitled to believe.

1.2 The premises of the meta-skeptical argument

It is the "I'm the only one" philosophers who deny premise (1). They think it is untrue that philosophers haven't solved any philosophical problems and haven't come up with any compellingly justified substantive factual truths. For *they* have solved this or that philosophical problem and *they* do have some compelling arguments for their philosophical view. According to them, the presence of pervasive and permanent philosophical disagreement can simply be explained on the grounds that others do not recognize the compelling force of their arguments.

Like the equilibrist, the meta-skeptic doesn't believe the "I'm the only one" philosophers. In his eyes, the "I'm the only one" philosophers are unlucky, epistemically blind, fanatic, or just comic figures whose raving assertions are not to be (and must not be) taken seriously.

The meta-skeptic may admit that he cannot infallibly rule out the possibility that philosopher X has already presented some knock-down argument for some substantive factual philosophical thesis. However, according to him, it is incomparably more plausible to think that there have never been any compelling arguments in philosophy. Because if there had been any, then the community of philosophers would have recognized their compelling force—similar to the way the community of mathematicians can recognize the compelling force of a mathematical proof, however complex, ramified, and hyper-sophisticated it may be. To put it differently, in the eyes of the meta-skeptic, it would be insufficient and intellectually unscrupulous to argue against premise (1) like this: "Premise (1) is not sufficiently supported because (i) some philosophers are convinced that they have substantive factual philosophical knowledge (true belief plus corresponding compelling justification), and (ii) no one would be able to prove beyond doubt that they are mistaken."

Some may object that the whole justification of premise (1) presupposes that one should regard different philosophical positions as positions that exclude each other. That is, premise (1) of the meta-skeptical argument takes for granted that only p or not-p can be true and one of them is true. However, some, alluding to Hegel's historicism, can say that one can regard philosophical positions as complementary ones that are somehow unified by means of synthesis on a higher level, as time goes by. In other words, taken together, the seemingly contradicting philosophical positions show the *whole truth* because there is some truth in both of them and only their synthesis can present the truth in its fullness. Thus, philosophical knowledge is the knowledge of all relevant philosophical positions and their proper synthesis (for the analysis of a similar approach, see Ribeiro 2011).

The problem with this position is twofold. Firstly, it is hard to see how "p and not-p" can be true in any sense. It is one thing to claim that there is some truth in both theories that contain, among many things, p and not-p *respectively*, and another thing to argue that "p and not-p" may be true to some degree. Truth does not admit of degrees, yet the notion of synthesis would require it to be the case, since the position resulting from it must be somehow "truer" in a sense than the two pre-synthesis positions. Thus, Hegelians should not dispose so light-heartedly of the principle of non-contradiction. Secondly, this grandiose metaphilosophical vision is just one among many and is highly controversial. Are we supposed to apply the denial of this principle of logic to this metaphilosophical vision itself, which means that it does not contradict other metaphilosophical visions just because they are also part of the whole truth? Or this time, should we "freeze time" and make an exception for some reasons? To my mind, this idea is confusing and it is hard to make any sense of it.

Against premise (2), one can say that it is not true that the best explanation for philosophy's epistemic failure is that philosophy's truth-seeking and justificatory tools are inadequate and unsuitable for establishing substantive factual truths and for compellingly justifying substantive factual philosophical theses.

So far so good, but what explanation could one offer instead of it? One could say this: the reason why philosophical problems are unsolved is not that philosophy's truth-seeking and justificatory tools are inadequate and unsuitable, but *the way individual philosophers do philosophy*. The truth-seeking and justificatory tools of philosophy are *good*, it is just that philosophers use them in the wrong way—mistakes are bound to happen whenever philosophers try to use the tools of philosophy: they commit some fatal (but otherwise *avoidable*) mistake in justifying their views.

The meta-skeptic can admit that he cannot infallibly rule out the possibility that *it merely happened so* (is a *contingent* fact) that philosophers have been unable to solve philosophical problems and to come up with compellingly justified substantive factual truths; and they might as well have been successful if they appropriately used the truth-seeking and justificatory tools of philosophy—for, after all, they are adequate and suitable. However, he might add, this is a highly implausible explanation. Why?

How should I put it? *Occasional* failures can be plausibly explained with *occasional* mistakes—by contrast, a pervasive and permanent failure could *hardly* be explained this way. Let's suppose that 80 percent of customers assemble a piece of IKEA furniture by consulting its assembly instructions, and only 20 percent of them fails to assemble it. In this case, a plausible explanation is that the 20 percent of them has made some mistakes—and the assembly instructions are impeccable. But let's suppose that *nobody* is able to assemble a piece of IKEA furniture at issue by consulting its assembly instructions. In this case, it is not a plausible explanation that each and every customer has made some (otherwise *avoidable*) mistake—the plausible explanation is that the assembly instructions are unsuitable for assembling that piece of furniture while consulting them.

The situation is similar with philosophy. If it were the case that some philosophers succeed in coming up with compellingly justified substantive philosophical truths, whereas other philosophers fail to achieve that, then a plausible explanation would be that those who fail have made some mistake. But, in fact, *no* philosopher can come up with compellingly justified substantive philosophical theses. Consequently, the explanation that each philosopher makes some (otherwise *avoidable*) mistake is implausible. It is much more plausible and lifelike to suppose that the source of the trouble is that philosophy's truth-seeking and justificatory tools are inadequate and unsuitable for establishing substantive factual philosophical truths. Which is to say that *the way* (namely, using the tools of philosophy) in which philosophers seek truths and try to justify their theses is *sui generis* inappropriate for the goal.

Make no mistakes about it. When the meta-skeptic claims that the source of the trouble are philosophy's truth-seeking and justificatory tools, he doesn't mean by it that philosophy has some *special* truth-seeking and justificatory toolkit that is *different* from the toolkits of all other epistemic enterprises, and that the style of argument that uniquely characterizes philosophy is inadequate and unsuitable. Of course, he doesn't dispute that there exist general rules of arguments, nor does he dispute that philosophers know and conform to these rules. What he claims is this: the standard tools of truth-seeking and justification fail *whenever* they are applied to philosophical problems. *This is all* that the meta-skeptic means by saying that philosophy's tools are inadequate and unsuitable for establishing truths and for compellingly justifying substantive factual philosophical theses.

Here are the four most important explanations for the unresolvedness of philosophical problems in a nutshell. Firstly, problems about the world can only be solved by scientific tools but philosophy is not a science—the only reliable way to justify theoretical hypotheses is empirical, but one cannot empirically justify any philosophical hypotheses. All philosophical justifications necessarily hang in the air. Secondly, philosophical problems are extremely complex—"what makes these problems so resilient is [...] their encompassing and compounding character" (MacBride 2014: 231). For one thing, they are closely interconnected—and the conceptual clarifications of these very complex interrelations are yet to come. For another, they cannot be isolated from the results of the natural sciences—at least some philosophical problems cannot be resolved without a complete physics, which remains to be seen. Thirdly, the construction of the concepts necessary for solving philosophical problems is cognitively closed to us—the constitution of our minds is adapted to the Stone Age environment, so our cognitive equipment does not enable us to solve philosophical problems. As Colin McGinn puts it: "[o]ur mind are not cognitively tuned to [philosophical] problems" (1993: 13); "[w]e can envisage questions that require conceptual and theoretical resources that exceed the contingent limits of [ours]" (1993: 8). Fourthly, philosophers have not succeeded in solving philosophical problems because their beliefs (even those of the most excellent ones) are shaped by factors that *ought to play no role here*—factors which have *nothing to do* with the truth (see e.g., Bernáth and Tőzsér 2021). Some think that these bias factors stem from our *personal* character. For example, this is how William James sees it: "[t]emperaments with their cravings and refusals do determine men in their philosophies, and always will" (1907/1979: 39) or "[a philosopher's] temperament really gives him a stronger bias than any of his more strictly objective premises" (1907/1979: 47). Others think that the source of the trouble is that in trying to provide justification for their philosophical beliefs, philosophers inevitably appeal to their intuitions—however, people's intuitions differ significantly; what is more, they differ as a function of (cultural, geographical background, socioeconomic status, etc.) factors that have *nothing to do with* the topic under discussion and the corresponding truth (see e.g., Nichols and Knobe 2007; Nichols, Stich, and Weinberg 2003; Swan, Alexander, and Weinberg 2008; Weinberg, Nichols, and Stich 2001/2008).

It doesn't matter which explanation the meta-skeptic sympathizes with, he can consistently stick to premise (2). None of these explanations is compatible with thinking that the individual philosophers' activity is behind the unresolvedness of philosophical problems—all of them rule out the supposition that philosophers' efforts might have been crowned with success if only they had avoided some, otherwise avoidable, error in seeking to establish the truth.

Against premise (3), one can argue in this way: philosophy's tools are indeed inadequate and unsuitable for compellingly justifying philosophical theses. However, they are adequate and suitable for the task of exploring and *working out* the possible (consistent) views concerning various philosophical problems. Moreover, they *entitle* philosophers to rationally stick to that view which is in equilibrium with their fundamental pre-philosophical convictions—provided that no knock-down objections can be brought up against it.

This is the view of "human-faced" equilibrism. Thus, the equilibrist rejects premise (3) of the meta-skeptical argument. She may (and probably would) accept as true premises (1) and (2) of the meta-skeptical argument—the two reactions or attitudes to philosophy's epistemic failure come to diverge on premise (3).

The meta-skeptic may concede that philosophy's tools are indeed adequate and suitable for helping philosophers commit themselves to philosophical theories that are in equilibrium with their fundamental pre-philosophical convictions, and these tools are also adequate and suitable for helping them defend their already elaborated philosophical theories against various objections.

Nevertheless, he could go on to say that since according to equilibrism, our fundamental pre-philosophical convictions are *unjustified*, our philosophical theories that are built upon them and elaborate them are not appropriately justified for us to be able to rationally stick to them.

To put more precisely, the meta-skeptic can acknowledge that S's fundamental pre-philosophical convictions can be rational in the sense of *pragmatic* rationality (in the opposite case, it would have the untoward consequence of damaging her personal-cognitive integrity) and that S can believe in her philosophical theories in the sense of *supplemented coherentist* rationality (if they are in equilibrium with her fundamental pre-philosophical convictions *plus* there are no knock-down objections to them). However, he firmly denies that S can (in the *epistemic* sense) rationally believe in the *truth* of her substantive factual philosophical theories. This is because for it to be the case, S should have epistemically good reason to believe that the justification of her philosophical theory is accurate and truth-conducive, and it is as clear that the equilibrist (i.e., egocentric) justification is hardly enough for this.

In brief, since S cannot have good reason to believe that the egocentric justification of her substantive factual philosophical beliefs is accurate and truth-conducive (quite contrary, she has good reason to believe that the truth-seeking and justificatory tools of philosophy are inadequate and unsuitable for establishing substantive factual philosophical truths), except for some of her (inherently warranted) beliefs, *S is not epistemically entitled* to rationally stick to her substantive factual philosophical beliefs.

Finally, let's turn to premise (4). This premise draws on the concept of epistemic duty, and so the meta-skeptic strongly commits himself to a doxastic deontology. Here's a nice definition of it:

> Prior to philosophical reflection we tend to take it for granted that we are responsible for our beliefs in roughly the same way as we are responsible for our actions. Just as we have moral duties prescribing or forbidding certain types of actions in various situations, we also have epistemic duties prescribing what we should or should not believe under various conditions. Moreover, just we can be blamed for failing to fulfill our moral duties and praised for fulfilling them, we can be blamed and praised for our beliefs. *Doxastic deontology* is the view that this analogy is right: beliefs are subject to a kind of deontic evaluation which is very similar to the deontic evaluation of actions, so *there are true doxastic deontic statements*.
>
> (Forrai 2019: 688, italics mine)

What would the meta-skeptic consider as relevant and true doxastic deontic statements? The following: "As philosophers have no good epistemic reason to believe or deny that p, philosophers *must not* believe either that p or that not-p"; "As philosophers *must not* believe either that p or that not-p, they *must* suspend their beliefs in p or in not-p"; "If philosophers believe that p or that not-p, then they *deserve to be blamed for it*"; "If philosophers suspend their beliefs in p or in not-p, then they *deserve to be praised for it*."

Nevertheless, some may object that the meta-skeptic cannot commit himself to doxastic deontology—given that it is a strongly controversial philosophical theory. In his argument intended-to-be compelling, he cannot draw on a philosophical theory against which rock-hard objections can be brought (see e.g., Alston 1985, 1988).

The meta-skeptic can do the following. He may concede that we have significantly less control over our beliefs than over our actions. He may also concede that we don't have any control at all over some of our beliefs. In a word, he may concede that his commitment to doxastic deontology is not without problems.

Still, he can say two things in his defense. On the one hand, he can warn us that we must not mistake doxastic deontology for doxastic voluntarism, which says that we have power over believing whatever we want. The latter is implausible indeed—we cannot change our beliefs at will. But his commitment to doxastic deontology is a different matter, because all he demands is that we *suspend certain beliefs* of ours as soon as we realize that our epistemic justifications for them are insufficient.

On the other hand, the meta-skeptic may say that even if there are a handful of propositions in which we are entitled to believe and some other propositions in which we cannot suspend our belief due to our psychological incapability, his commitment to doxastic deontology would only be fateful to him if the set of our consciously suspendable philosophical beliefs were empty. This, however, seems to be a grossly inflated claim, what is more, an extremely insincere one at that. For why would it be psychologically impossible for a philosopher to suspend his beliefs with zero existential stake such as "Negative causation is genuine causation," "A statue and a lump of bronze which constitutes the statue are two numerically different things," or "A scar on Harry Potter's forehead in the shape of a lightning bolt is an abstract object which was created by J. K. Rowling in the 1990s"? It would be a weird claim that these propositions are those in which we are entitled to believe no matter what. In brief, according to the meta-skeptic, we cannot reject *the whole of* doxastic deontology because it *deeply pervades* our everyday practice—we unwittingly blame others for believing in crazy things, or in things which they have no grounds at all to believe in.

This is how the meta-skeptical argument looks like in outline, and I'm inclined to admit that the denial of its premises is weaker than the premises themselves are. For let's see how plausible the propositions featuring in the objections are. Please consider, for each of them, whether you can believe it seriously and sincerely!

(i) There are some "I'm the only one" philosophers (Hegelians included) who have already solved substantive factual philosophical problems and possess compellingly justified substantive philosophical truths. (ii) The best explanation for the unresolvedness of philosophical problems is that philosophers use philosophy's good truth-seeking and justificatory tools in the wrong way—and without ever noticing where and when they make (otherwise avoidable) mistakes in using them. (iii) We have good epistemic reason to believe in the truth of a substantive factual philosophical proposition p if we can show that p is in equilibrium with our epistemically unjustified but pragmatically "justified" fundamental pre-philosophical convictions and there is no knock-down objection to p. (iv) We have no epistemic duties at all because we do not have control over any of our beliefs—not even that much that would enable us to suspend them on realizing the insufficiency of our justification for them.

1.3 The conclusions of the meta-skeptical argument

1.3.1 What does the meta-skeptic mean by saying that philosophers cannot rationally believe in the truth of their substantive factual philosophical theses?

Let's assume that Katie holds the view that free will exists. And, let's also assume that she has a dispute with somebody who denies that free will exists by appealing to the thesis of psychological determinism, and she comes up with the following argument to support her view:

> You say that you think there is no free will because you think it is highly unlikely that psychological determinism is false. For this reason, you are asking me to change my belief—to give up my belief in the existence of free will and accept what you say. As if I had the duty to do that in the light of the facts you've brought up. But the reason why I cannot give up my belief in free will is exactly that because you asked me to. The way I see it is that we can only have epistemic or moral duties if we have free will, meaning we can choose how to act and what

steps to take on the road to knowledge. Animals have no moral or epistemic duties partly because they have no free will. So, I can only assume that I would have the moral or epistemic duty to give up my belief in free will only if I was also to assume that I have free will. But this would obviously be an irrational step for me to take. I only have two rational options: either I assume that we have no epistemic and moral duties, or that free will exists. However, right now when you are placing the burden of proof on me, I can see clearly that I do indeed have epistemic and moral duties. Consequently, I can also see clearly that free will must exist.

The meta-skeptic doesn't dispute that Katie is *justified* in believing in the existence of free will. *But* (and this is a very big "but"), he immediately adds that the proposition "Katie is *justified* in believing in the truth of *p*" means *nothing more* than Katie *can give reasons for why* she believes in the truth of *p*—she is able to adduce philosophical arguments for the truth of *p*. However, he continues, since the justificatory tools of philosophy are wrong, inaccurate, unreliable, and inadequate for establishing the truth of *p*, the proposition "Katie has a *philosophical justification* for the truth of *p*" is to be interpreted in the following way: "Katie has a wrong, inaccurate, unreliable, and inadequate justification for establishing the truth of *p*." Hence, *independently of* whether she can use the philosophical argument above to give a reason why she believe in the truth of *p*, she cannot (in the epistemic sense) rationally believe in the truth of *p*.

Let's assume that Tom holds the same philosophical view as Katie. He also asserts that free will exists. If someone asks him to justify his view, he can only say:

> I believe in the existence of free will because I don't experience any inner push to do this or that during my decisions and actions—the way a decision appears to me shows that (i) several possibilities are equally open to me until the moment of my decision and (ii) it solely depends on me which of these possibilities is actualized.

The meta-skeptic doesn't dispute that Katie's argument is stronger than Tom's, and so her belief is *more* justified than Tom's. *But* (and this "but" is at least as big as the previous one), he immediately adds: the proposition "Katie's belief is *more* justified than Tom's" means *nothing more* than that whereas Katie is able to give reasons, against certain objections, for why she believes in the truth of *p*, Tom's argument for the truth of *p* is merely based on the phenomenology of decisions and actions. However, he continues, since philosophy's truth-seeking and justificatory tools are inadequate and unsuitable for rationally grounding any philosopher's belief in the truth of *p*, *independently of* how "strong" philosophical arguments Katie adduces for why she believes in the truth of *p*, she cannot rationally believe in the truth of *p*. Katie does her best *in vain* to justify with philosophical arguments her belief in the existence of free will, and proceeds *in vain* as conscientiously, circumspectly, and thoroughly as possible, since the grounding of her belief is at most as "solid" as Tom's.

This is one of the hardest pills to swallow concerning the meta-skeptical view. Yet, this is exactly what the meta-skeptic claims, and he cannot claim anything else on the basis of premises (2) and (3) of the meta-skeptical argument.

To see it from another angle, let's assume that Dalma and Charlie both believe in astrology. They think that reliable horoscopes can be prepared on the basis of astrological methods. Let's also assume that Dalma is a particularly well-versed and thorough astrologist (you may even call her an expert), who prepares every horoscope with utmost circumspection and conscience. She consciously uses the Placidus house system instead of the Regiomontanus one, which she supports with different astrological arguments. As opposed to (in her opinion outdated) astrologists, she also takes into consideration the placement of the so-called "new planets" (Uranus and Neptune); she uses the sidereal zodiac instead of the less effective tropic one (due to certain astrological considerations); her humble starting point is that a horoscope is only good for personal development and personality analysis, but, as man is a free being, it is not suitable to make predictions; and she only starts preparing someone's horoscope if she knows the subject's exact time of birth. And, let's assume that Dalma puts forth the following proposition after long hours of analysis: "Someone who was born at 7.07 p.m. on June 12, 2000 much prefers security to seeking out risky adventures." Let's, however, also assume that Charlie also believes this proposition because he read in a tabloid's five-line horoscope that people born in Gemini are better off avoiding adventures due to their character traits and spending as much time as possible with friends and family, where they feel secure—and as it happened, he was born on June 12, 2000.

Although the meta-skeptic does not assert that astrology and philosophy are similar epistemic enterprises, in his eyes Katie's philosophical belief is on the same level as Dalma's astrological one, with respect to their epistemic status. Both are able to give reasons for why they believe what they believe—and *to this extent* (but *only* to this extent) their beliefs are justified. They both are top professionals who do all they can to support their beliefs with the best arguments available to them—and *to this extent* (but *only* to this extent) Katie's belief is more justified than Tom's, and Dalma's belief is more justified than Charlie's. What's more, the meta-skeptic does not dispute that, in a sense, through their unwavering efforts, both Katie and Dalma can elicit our respect—"Look how determined both Katie and Dalma are to find the truth!" *But* (and this is the biggest "but"), he adds immediately, neither of them can gain our *epistemic* respect, as their truth-seeking tools are totally inadequate for establishing truth.

Naturally, the meta-skeptic doesn't *generally* dispute that if S has justification for the truth of *p*, then S can rationally believe in the truth of *p*. He doesn't dispute that this is the case for epistemically *successful* enterprises. He doesn't dispute, either, that it is right to say about the participants of a *successful* epistemic enterprise that if they justify the truth of *p*, then they can rationally believe in the truth of *p*.

However, philosophy is a *failed* epistemic enterprise—stricken with wrong and unreliable truth-seeking and justificatory tools. The meta-skeptic may admit that it is a sad and disappointing result, but, as he may add, we are forced to realize that no matter how circumspectly, thoroughly, and conscientiously we use these tools, we cannot come to *conclusions* in which we have good epistemic reason to believe. And this is what conclusion (C1) of the meta-skeptical argument says.

1.3.2 What does the meta-skeptic mean by saying that philosophers have the epistemic duty to suspend their substantive factual philosophical beliefs?

In the introductory section of this chapter I noted that the meta-skeptic doesn't necessarily expect the philosophers to suspend all their philosophical beliefs. He doesn't necessarily expect them to suspend some of their non-substantive philosophical beliefs because he can concede that they may have good epistemic reasons for holding them true. He also doesn't necessarily expect them to suspend their beliefs on purely conceptual philosophical problems, because in their case the question of truth *simpliciter* does not arise. And he also doesn't expect them to suspend their (very few) substantive and factual beliefs to which one is entitled due to their inherent warranty, as these beliefs have nothing to do with philosophy. Apart from these, however, philosophers must suspend *all* their philosophical beliefs. More precisely, apart from these, philosophers have the epistemic duty to suspend *all* those beliefs of theirs which are based solely on philosophical considerations—*without exception*. And insofar as philosophers don't fulfil this epistemic duty of theirs, they are reproachable in the epistemic sense.

Nevertheless, in the case of some substantive factual philosophical beliefs which philosophers aren't entitled to stick to, the meta-skeptic may *exempt them* from the epistemic duty of belief suspension. According to him, *they may have excuses* (but *only* excuses) for not suspending some of their substantive factual philosophical beliefs—similarly to their having excuses (but *only* excuses) for not fulfilling some of their moral duties.

Don't get me wrong. When the meta-skeptic exempts philosophers from the epistemic duty of suspending some of their substantive factual philosophical beliefs, he does not thereby say that they can rationally believe in the truth of these theses. (Don't mistake the concept of "exempting circumstance" for the concept of "appropriate justification"!) Rather, he says:

> Although philosophers have the epistemic duty to suspend their belief in the truth of p and they are irrational if they don't do that, some non-epistemic factors like their psychological incapacity *may prevent* them from doing so. For this reason, they are exempt from suspending their p-beliefs, but they must not forget that otherwise *they would have the epistemic duty* to suspend p.

Of course, the problem is that it may differ from person to person which substantive factual philosophical beliefs they are psychologically unable to abandon despite having the epistemic duty to do so. This is to say that the set of one's *visceral beliefs* is highly personalized and depends on several contingent factors (culture, historical context, education, etc.). Now, any philosopher can say that this or that philosophical belief of theirs is a visceral one, and this being so, the meta-skeptic should exempt them from the epistemic duty to suspend this or that belief. However, the meta-skeptic cannot allow every philosopher to submit such a "petition" for their own pet philosophical beliefs—at the same time, nor can he *ex cathedra* assert that someone can viscerally believe in some substantive and factual philosophical thesis but cannot believe in some other one.

But then, how could he make a principled decision? To be sure, he cannot present us with any exact criteria. There are, however, some clear-cut cases. Among these are "All properties of physical objects (even their shape) are in fact dispositional ones" and "The causal relationship is an extrinsic relation." These are clear-cut cases because it is *highly unlifelike* to suppose that someone could have visceral beliefs in these propositions. The existential stake of these propositions is *zero*, so a philosopher who claims them to be his visceral beliefs is almost certainly insincere. Of course, appealing to unlifelikeness is not an ordinary argument, just as it is not an ordinary argument for the meta-skeptic to say that he does not believe those who claim to have among their visceral beliefs the proposition that "There are scattered objects." But he can hardly do more than appeal to the philosophers' sincerity.

One may well wonder how the meta-skeptic deals with those substantive factual philosophical beliefs that certainly have existential stake. Let's suppose that, like many others, Agnes is certain that she has had religious experiences (God appeared to her and talked to her), and based on these experiences, she comes to believe that there is a God. As God often visits her, she reaches a level where her belief in God's existence becomes a visceral belief for her. Like in the case of all visceral beliefs, the meta-skeptic can exempt Agnes from the duty to suspend belief. Of course, the meta-skeptic does not claim that Agnes can rationally believe that there is a God in the light of her religious (or allegedly religious) experiences. This would only be granted if Agnes had compelling philosophical arguments to prove that her religious experiences are veridical and not hallucinatory. It would not suffice to say that she was not on magic mushrooms or that she regularly has these religious experiences and that as far as she knows, she has never had a hallucination before. Agnes, however, can certainly not justify her belief with compelling philosophical arguments. That said, the meta-skeptic can still acknowledge (because *he can believe*) that Agnes' belief in God is a real visceral one, and thus he can exempt her from the duty to suspend belief.

Of course, most people appeal to their moral beliefs in objecting to the epistemic duty to suspend beliefs. Even those who are not averse to meta-skepticism and the suspension of beliefs often voice concerns like this:

> I'm okay with suspending my philosophical beliefs about issues such as "Are events structured particulars?"; "Are there bare dispositions?"; "Are there tropes, and if so, are they thin or thick?"—for questions like these, I don't mind, I'm willing to suspend my philosophical beliefs. In my everyday life, however, I often find myself having to decide about important moral dilemmas that affect human lives. Now, it is one of my fundamental convictions that there are objective moral facts and I'd like to make the morally right decisions in their light. So, I can't suspend my moral beliefs. What is more, it would be morally wrong for me to experiment with doing so.

According to the meta-skeptic, the situation is similar to the case of Agnes. Just as he may exempt Agnes from the duty to suspend belief because he can believe that her belief in God is a visceral one, he may exempt these philosophers from the duty to suspend their moral beliefs because he can believe that their moral beliefs are visceral. The meta-skeptic would not like these philosophers to become unable to make decisions during their lives. He *only* expects them to suspend those among their moral beliefs that they formed *on the basis of their philosophical considerations*.

Nevertheless, the meta-skeptic gives the following piece of advice for difficult decisions:

> When you are about to make an important moral decision, don't draw on ethical theories and don't start at all weighing up philosophical considerations. Avoid these, for philosophy (including moral philosophy) is an epistemic enterprise that uses inadequate and unsuitable tools to establish truths. Consequently, when you evaluate your potential decision on the basis of considerations from (moral) philosophy (whether it is morally right or wrong to make the decision at issue), then you choose an inadequate and unsuitable way to evaluate it.

But there's more to it. According to the meta-skeptic, it is definitely *worse* to use the strategy of drawing on ethical theories before making your decisions than to see these theories through meta-skeptical eyes.

Let's take the moral dilemma Sartre analyzes (see 1946/2007). A young man has to decide whether to look after his gravely ill mother or to go to war against the Nazis. The meta-skeptic thinks that it would not help him at all to turn to philosophy for advice. If he were to meet a deontologist, he would probably say:

> Stay home and look after your mother. You have special moral duties to her as your close relative. What happens in the battlefield will not be up to just you. You have no control over those events—as opposed to fulfilling your moral duties. It might even happen that you will be fatally shot in combat five seconds after going into your first action, before you could use your weapon.

And if he were to meet a consequentialist, he would probably receive the following advice:

> Go to war. This will be much more beneficial than caring for, bathing and comforting your mother and changing her chamber-pot. If you kill a lot of Nazis, you will contribute to the fall of the Nazi regime in your own way, which is incomparably a greater good than your mother's peace and comfort. Her being contented that her son is taking care of her is useless.

What the meta-skeptic tries to say is not what Sartre did (namely that everyone is condemned to be free and is responsible for everything), but that philosophical theories—including ethical theories of moral duty—are unavailing when it comes to actually making decisions. There is dissensus in philosophy about the nature of morally right actions—one ethical theory recommends a different course of action than another one does. Thus, if you do not already have any kind of (ideally visceral) willingness for the decision that is based on *non-philosophical* considerations, then you will be incapacitated in your decision-making when you turn to different ethical theories which provide mutually inconsistent pieces of advice.

In short, according to the meta-skeptic the best thing to do if you have a moral dilemma is to be a meta-skeptic and to try to make a decision on the basis of various non-philosophical considerations. If you started weighing up in a given case whether you will act morally rightly if you follow Kant's guidance or instead, if you follow Mill's, then you could put your mind to anything only after refuting one of those views by using philosophical arguments. Even tossing a coin is better than doing that—Sartre's young man could toss a coin and decide that "If it is heads, I will tend to my mother, if it is tails, I will go to war," and then, once the coin lands on the table, he could immediately introspect whether he *is happy about* the result. If so, he could accept it, if not, he could decide against it.

To sum up, the meta-skeptic cannot provide clear criteria for distinguishing the philosophical theses in which one is allowed to believe viscerally from those in which one isn't. Consequently, he has no clear criteria for distinguishing between those substantive factual philosophical beliefs from whose suspension he exempts one and those from whose suspension he doesn't. Nevertheless, one has the epistemic duty to suspend *most of* one's substantive factual philosophical beliefs. According to the meta-skeptic, there is one thing that is dishonest. It is when philosophers simply assert that they have a visceral belief in the truth of *p*, and then go on to assert that thereby they are immediately exempted from the duty to suspend their belief in *p*. In the meta-skeptic's eyes, this would be nothing else but *abusing* the epistemic requirement of suspending philosophical beliefs, which cannot be allowed under any circumstances—just as abusing our moral duties cannot be allowed either, however usual and frequent it may be.

1.4 The problem of self-defeat

Although the premises of the meta-skeptical argument presented above have great convincing power and its conclusions follow from the premises, the argument itself seems irreparably self-defeating.

Here's the thing. The first intended conclusion of the meta-skeptical argument is that philosophers cannot rationally believe in the truth of their substantive factual philosophical theses—yet the proposition that "Philosophers cannot rationally believe in the truth of their substantive factual philosophical theses" is a substantive factual philosophical thesis. Furthermore, according to premise (2) of the meta-skeptical argument, the tools of philosophy are inadequate and unsuitable for providing appropriate justifications of substantive factual philosophical theses—yet the meta-skeptic uses the tools of philosophy to justify the truth of the substantive factual philosophical thesis that "The tools of philosophy are inadequate and unsuitable for providing appropriate justifications of substantive factual philosophical theses." Moreover, the second intended conclusion of the meta-skeptical argument is that philosophers must suspend their substantive factual philosophical beliefs—consequently the meta-skeptic, too, must suspend his substantive factual philosophical belief that "Philosophers must suspend their substantive factual philosophical beliefs."

The meta-skeptical argument would not be self-defeating if the meta-skeptic could make us believe that his argument is not a philosophical one. In this case, he could say that "There is no question of self-defeat because I don't assert that non-philosophical arguments cannot be compelling." And it would not be self-defeating, either, if it were not meant to be a compelling argument, and each premise were prefixed with the expression "In my opinion." In this case, the meta-skeptic could say that "There is no question of self-defeat because all I assert is that '*In my opinion*, philosophers cannot rationally believe in the truth of any substantive factual philosophical thesis.'"

But the meta-skeptical argument is a philosophical argument, and it is intended to have compelling force. Thus, the meta-skeptic asserts that "Because my argument is a philosophical argument with compelling force, I can rationally believe in the truth of the substantive factual philosophical thesis that 'Philosophers cannot rationally believe in the truth of their substantive factual philosophical theses.'"

The meta-skeptic can give only two responses to the problem of self-defeat. Firstly, he can say that the meta-skeptical argument is not self-defeating—that of all philosophical arguments, it *alone* has compelling force; the *only* substantive factual philosophical thesis which we can rationally believe is that "we cannot rationally believe in any substantive factual philosophical theses"; and the truth-seeking and justificatory tools of philosophy fail in all cases *except* when we use them to show that "the truth-seeking and justificatory tools of philosophy fail in all cases." This is how Brennan puts it: "It may just be that all philosophy is unreliable except anti-philosophy philosophy [i.e., meta-skepticism]," and "[I]t may just be that a small set of philosophical issues is answered and that philosophical methodology works reliably on a small set of issues, i.e. just in the areas needed to make the sceptic's argument" (Brennan 2010: 8–9).

Brennan tries to show that it is mistaken to think that meta-skepticism is a *necessarily* self-defeating standpoint—after all, he says, it is *possible* that the argument for it is the only philosophical one that works for some reason. However, this kind of defense is not very convincing—it cannot be taken seriously, to say the least. For *why* on earth it would be the case that the meta-skeptical argument would be immune to premise (2), which says that philosophy's truth-seeking and justificatory tools are inadequate and unsuitable? *Why* would the epistemic status of our substantive philosophical beliefs be *that* "philosophical issue" concerning which "philosophical methodology works reliably"? Obviously, the meta-skeptic can say *something* in response—but I'm afraid that what he says could only be a contrived ad hoc "explanation."

According to the second response, the meta-skeptical argument is self-defeating but this doesn't mean that its premises undermine the truth of its conclusions. At first glance, this may seem a strange maneuver, but it is not at all unprecedented in the history of philosophy. Here's the best-known analog case.

The young Wittgenstein wrote the *Tractatus*, a work crammed with substantive factual philosophical theses. You can read in it sentences like the following: "The world is the totality of facts, not of things" (*TLP* 1.1); "The logical picture of the facts is the thought" (*TLP* 3); "The sense of a proposition is its agreement and disagreement with the possibilities of the existence and non-existence of the atomic facts" (*TLP* 4.2); "The world and life are one" (*TLP* 5.621); "There is only logical necessity" (*TLP* 6.37); "The sense of the world must lie outside the world" (*TLP* 6.41); "Scepticism is not irrefutable but palpably senseless" (*TLP* 6.51). At the end of the work, Wittgenstein asserts that "The right method of philosophy would be this: To say nothing except what can be said, i.e. the propositions of natural science, i.e. something that has *nothing to do with philosophy*" (*TLP* 6.53, italics mine). He dissolves the looming self-defeat in the following well-known way:

> My propositions are elucidatory in this way: he who understands me finally recognizes them as senseless, when he has climbed out through them, on them, over them. (He must so to speak throw away the ladder, after he has climbed up on it.) He must surmount these propositions; then he sees the world rightly.
> (*TLP* 6.54)

The meta-skeptic, too, can use a similar maneuver. For example, he may say this: "*After you have seen* the truth of the premises of the meta-skeptical argument, and *accepted* its conclusions (for the deductive steps of the argument are valid), *you don't need* the meta-skeptical argument itself any more. You can throw it away just as if it were a ladder, so you can see the epistemic status of your philosophical beliefs rightly."

I don't know how satisfying you will find maneuvers like this. If you allow Wittgenstein to make this kind of move because you don't think that what he does is cheap evasion, then you must allow the meta-skeptic to do that as well. But if you don't allow him to make it because you think that what he does is cheap evasion, then you must not allow the meta-skeptic to do that either. I agree with the latter view—in my eyes, this defense of meta-skepticism is no more convincing than the previous one.

What I think is the following. Granting that the problem of self-defeat does not deal a fatal blow to the meta-skeptical argument, and to meta-skepticism as a whole (as I'm inclined to think), neither of these responses is entirely reassuring—in fact, both of them look very much like desperate attempts to evade a quite real and intractable difficulty. At the same time, if you appeal *merely* to self-defeat in thinking that you are done with meta-skepticism once and for all and that you don't have to take the meta-skeptical argument into account any more, then you don't proceed with sufficient intellectual conscience.

Here is why. Let's suppose that you read the meta-skeptical argument *before* you face the difficulties of those metaphilosophical views which say that philosophers can rationally stick to the truth of their substantive factual philosophical beliefs. In this case, you would have every reason to think that self-defeat is such a serious problem that the meta-skeptic would have done better not to start arguing in the first place, because due to this problem he starts from a very handicapped position, so his argument stands no chance of having even the slightest convincing force.

Nevertheless, if you *have already* realized that *neither* the advocates of the "I'm the only one" view *nor* those of equilibrism give good responses to philosophy's epistemic failure, then you cannot preclude in advance that meta-skepticism could be *the best*, or at least *the sincerest* reaction to it. Thus, if you want to reject meta-skepticism, then you *cannot be content with* this much: "As there is no reassuring response to the problem of self-defeat, I don't have to take it seriously the challenge posed by meta-skepticism." It takes *more* than that. You must give reasons *why* you can rationally stick to the truth of your substantive factual philosophical beliefs, *despite* the fact that neither the "I'm the only one" view nor equilibrism seems promising—not to mention that the objections to the premises of the meta-skeptical argument seem to be built on less solid ground than the premises themselves.

To put it more sharply, if the problem of self-defeat is the *only* thing you can adduce as a reason for rejecting meta-skepticism, and if you think that this immediately lets you get rid of the challenge posed by meta-skepticism, then you don't seriously face philosophy's epistemic failure, nor the failure of the earlier reactions to philosophy's epistemic failure. Also, you don't seriously face the convincing force of the meta-skeptical argument, in that it says that if philosophy is an epistemically failed enterprise because philosophers have neither solved a single philosophical problem nor presented any compellingly justified substantive truths, then *you do have good epistemic reason* to believe that philosophy's truth-seeking and justificatory tools are inadequate and unsuitable. And, so the argument goes, if philosophers work with such truth-seeking and justificatory tools, then *you do have good epistemic reason* to believe that philosophers cannot rationally believe in the truth of their substantive factual philosophical theses. I think it would be "somewhat" displeasing and unconscientious for you to merely say that "Meta-skepticism is untenable because the meta-skeptic cannot reassuringly respond to the challenge of self-defeat"—without your being able to give *reasons why* you can rationally stick to the truth of your substantive factual philosophical beliefs.

To sum up, I don't want to say that self-defeat isn't a major problem for meta-skepticism. All I'm saying is that you need to appeal to *something other* beyond self-defeat so you can rest assured to reject meta-skepticism.

2 Dialogue with a full-fledged meta-skeptic

I hope two things from the dialogue between Sophie and the full-fledged meta-skeptic. One is that I can bring the meta-skeptic's attitude closer to you and describe it vividly—I can say what the meta-skeptic sees as the error of philosophers sticking to their philosophical beliefs and what "training" he proposes for these philosophers so they can suspend their substantive factual philosophical beliefs in conformity with the epistemic duty of belief suspension. The other is that I can show why meta-skepticism is an inappropriate reaction to philosophy's epistemic failure and why the meta-skeptic doesn't give the right answer to the question "What should we do with our philosophical beliefs in the light of philosophy's epistemic failure?" Accordingly, I will divide the dialogue into two "acts," an elaborative and a critical one.

2.1 Act One: Meta-skepticism close up

Sophie: I concede that the meta-skeptical argument is convincing and that meta-skepticism seems to be the sincerest of all reactions to philosophy's epistemic failure. That is to say, I concede that both philosophy's epistemic failure and the failure of those three previous reactions to this failure point in the direction of commitment to meta-skepticism. My first question: what is your explanation for the unpopularity of meta-skepticism as a metaphilosophical vision among philosophers?

Meta-skeptic: I explain it primarily by giving psychological reasons appealing to the frailty of human nature. I'm not naïve so I know that suspending our philosophical beliefs is not an easy thing to do. If a philosopher is in the process of developing arguments for his pet philosophical view, then it comes as no surprise that he is reluctant to suspend his philosophical beliefs.

Yet, that is what I expect him to do because it is his epistemic duty. I'm tolerant of those beliefs to which anyone is entitled to stick to (if they are *indeed* such beliefs) as well as the visceral beliefs of philosophers (if they are *indeed* such beliefs), but I'm not tolerant of their non-visceral philosophical beliefs to which they aren't entitled to stick. I think philosophers who cling to their epistemically mundane non-visceral philosophical beliefs are either throwing good money after bad because they are too cowardly to admit defeat, or they resemble the narcissistic writer who wouldn't press "Delete" to drop a sentence that they have crafted with meticulous care. Philosophers aren't courageous enough to face philosophy's epistemic failure and draw the proper conclusions about their own philosophical beliefs.

Sophie: Are cowardice and the sunk cost fallacy the only reasons for philosophers' intransigence?

Meta-skeptic: No, there's more to it. I imagine a philosopher who has put extraordinary intellectual efforts into his research, conscientiously followed the latest developments in the relevant literature for years, produced fairly complex and technically rich lines of reasoning and made subtle conceptual distinctions—and now he encounters the meta-skeptical argument. This argument is not sophisticated in the least; what's more, it doesn't contain anything that he wouldn't have known already or shouldn't have known. The philosopher feels sad. Of course, he could make some random objections, but let's assume that deep in his heart he feels that the argument is spot on.

This philosopher may feel that the whole scenario is unworthy and unfair. It is just as unworthy and unfair as those medieval knights—who trained their bodies and minds for decades and wrote romantic poems to their ladies—felt it to be unworthy and unfair to be shot by a crossbow of a simple illiterate peasant boy who only practiced for a few minutes. The triumph of this peasant boy, cut off from the world of learning and having neither knightly virtues nor outstanding skills is unworthy indeed—and perhaps the meta-skeptic scores exactly such a "triumph" over the philosopher who stubbornly sticks to his philosophical beliefs. But please don't miss the real point! It's no use for the philosopher to bring up how unworthy and unfair it is to prove the irrationality of his substantive factual philosophical beliefs with the help of the meta-skeptical argument which features the most obviously true premises. It doesn't exempt him from the duty to suspend his beliefs just because he feels it was unworthy of him, in the same way as the knight doesn't rise from the dead after the rusty and unshapely arrowhead tore up his chainmail armor and damaged his organs (liver, lungs, spleen) just because he felt it was unworthy of him and he was killed in an unfair way.

Sophie: Wow! What a graphic description!

Meta-skeptic: I'm just putting myself in the place of those who would be unwilling to abandon their philosophical beliefs even under the compelling force of the meta-skeptical argument. I understand why they think that "If someone can show us that we have to suspend our philosophical beliefs, then his argument should be aesthetically pleasing, elegant, sophisticated and witty—if we are to lose, let's lose nicely, as a hero would!" The above meta-skeptical argument (and all of its variants), however, has none of these properties. Once the self-deception of philosophers sticking to their philosophical beliefs gets unmasked, there's no elegance in it—they can only see their downfall as nasty and depressing. This circumstance may also explain why many philosophers don't accept the meta-skeptical argument as compelling and why they are unwilling to suspend their philosophical beliefs.

Sophie: It seems that you have a very low opinion of those philosophers who don't suspend their substantive factual and non-visceral philosophical beliefs.

Meta-skeptic: Are you surprised? Just try to take an impartial look at the meaning of the history of philosophy! Although they spared no time and efforts, philosophers were striving in vain to solve a single philosophical problem or to come up with a single compellingly justified substantive factual philosophical truth. They should have already realized that their truth-seeking and justificatory tools are inadequate and unsuitable, *a fortiori* they use such tools to form and justify their philosophical beliefs. And they should also have already realized that because the tools they use are inadequate and unsuitable for this purpose, they have no good epistemic reasons to stick to their philosophical beliefs—they have the duty to suspend them.

Despite that, both the members of the epistemic tradition (the "I'm the only one" philosophers) and the "human-faced" equilibrists are totally convinced that they can rationally believe in the truth of their substantive factual philosophical theses. When I hear the "I'm the only one" philosophers say that "My arguments for the truth of p are compelling"; "Without any doubt, I know that p is true"; "My counter-arguments refute, once and for all, those theories which say that p is not true," then what else should I think of them than that they are wretched people stricken with epistemic blindness? And when I hear the equilibrists say that "I can rationally believe in the truth of p because p is in equilibrium with my fundamental pre-philosophical convictions that essentially belong to my personal-cognitive integrity, and I can show that no objection against p is compelling," then I'm only waiting for the moment when it dawns on these unfortunate people that it doesn't entitle them to stick to the truth of p in the epistemic sense and they start showing the painful symptoms of epistemic schizophrenia.

Sophie: I see what you mean. Let me now ask you about the phenomenology of suspending our philosophical beliefs. It is not clear to me what it is like. If at t_1 a philosopher believes in the truth of p, then obviously, he doesn't believe at t_1 that he should suspend his belief in p. Then "something happens" and at t_2 he no longer believes that p is true nor that *not-p* is true. I cannot imagine it otherwise than, from one moment to the next, the philosopher "finds himself" thinking that "Lo, earlier I believed that p is true but now I no longer believe that p is true nor that p is false." The act of suspending our philosophical beliefs doesn't seem to be a mental event under our conscious control. As far as I'm concerned, this is what my experience is like of how certain philosophical beliefs of mine vanished into thin air as time went by.

Meta-skeptic: Indeed, we mostly "sleep through" the act of suspending our philosophical beliefs. What happens is what you say: philosophers "find themselves" no longer to believe in the truth of p nor in the falsity of p, although earlier they believed in the truth of p. However, you forget the most important thing—namely, that if a philosopher at last realizes that he has no good epistemic reason to stick to the truth of p, then from that moment on, *he has the epistemic duty to train himself* to be able to suspend his p-belief.

Thus, speaking about the epistemic duty of suspending philosophical beliefs, I don't merely expect philosophers to take notice of the following: "To be able to rationally believe in the truth of p, my justification must meet certain standards, and since the justification of my belief in the truth of p doesn't meet these standards, I irrationally believe that p is true." Likewise, I don't merely expect them to stop producing philosophical arguments for p—to restrain themselves from propagating p in any forum, resist the temptation to convince others of the truth of p in debates, and answer that "I don't know whether p is true" whenever someone asks them if they hold p true.

It isn't enough for philosophers to shut up and throw into a wastepaper basket the manuscripts of their arguments for the truth of p. I expect them to do more than not letting their philosophical beliefs "manifest themselves," because in this case they *continue* having those beliefs—it's just that they don't express them.

As a meta-skeptic, I expect philosophers to act differently. As an advocate of doxastic deontology, here is what I expect them to do: if they cannot fulfil the epistemic duty of suspending philosophical beliefs, then *they should do their best* to achieve it. The meta-skeptical argument itself is just a "springboard"—it doesn't automatically trigger the suspension of their philosophical beliefs. *They have to work hard* to achieve the suspension of their philosophical beliefs. That's why they need to do training or practicing.

Sophie: OK, but what kind of activity do you have in mind? What kind of training? Should philosophers repeat ten, twenty or a hundred times in front of their mirrors "I don't believe that p is true nor that p is false," every day in the morning, at noon, and in the evening?

Meta-skeptic: I don't take exception to that if it helps them. It's just that I don't believe it to be an efficient practice. But, speaking about training in front of the mirror, here is my proposal instead of it: whenever philosophers "find themselves" holding true a proposition as a result of a spontaneously arising train of thought, for example the proposition "H_2O is a structural universal," then *they should immediately remind themselves* that they *certainly* arrived at this philosophical thesis with the use of inadequate and unsuitable truth-seeking tools, and consequently they cannot rationally believe in its truth. The obligatory recall of the meta-skeptical argument several times a day can be an effective therapy—it can *erode* their philosophical beliefs.

Sophie: Do you expect all philosophers to start repeating the meta-skeptical argument as a mantra whenever they "find themselves" believing in the truth of some substantive factual philosophical proposition?

Meta-skeptic: That's not the whole story. Really effective meta-skeptical training consists in practicing self-reflection.

Sophie: What do you mean by self-reflection?

Meta-skeptic: Don't expect me to give a precise definition. By self-reflection I simply mean that someone sees his activity *from an outside and impartial viewpoint*. What I mean is a kind of *self-perception* which is free from distortions determining his internal cognitive perspective.

Just think about it. Most of our character flaws—vanity, envy, self-importance, cowardice, intemperance, stinginess, greed, low self-esteem, and so on—can usually be judged more accurately from the outside than from a first-person perspective. In contrast to our occurrent mental states to which we have privileged access, the situation is the opposite with our non-occurrent mental states, in particular our character traits and flaws, because others have better access to them than we do. Just as we are epistemically superior to our dentist with regard to whether it hurts when he drills our tooth, impartial outsiders are usually more reliable when it comes to judging our character traits and non-occurrent mental states.

Sophie: If I understand you right, executing self-reflection must be a difficult thing to do. It's not easy to occupy an outside viewpoint and see ourselves from "over there." We may happen to think that we see ourselves in an impartial manner, whereas in fact we fail to interiorize the undistorted, outside perspective and are still enslaved by internal distorting factors.

Meta-skeptic: It's not an easy task, indeed. We need to practice so we can reliably eliminate all internal distorting factors. We're not as lucky as Socrates was, whose daemon warned him every time he believed something for which he had no proper epistemic reason. So it's hard to do indeed, but *the only way* to the attainment of reliable self-knowledge (and, of course, reliable *philosophical* self-knowledge) is to exercise self-reflection. For us, self-reflection plays the role of Socrates' daemon.

Now let me explain the role of self-reflection—let me elucidate it with an ordinary case. Let's assume that Rachel cheats on her partner with a lot of people. She keeps lying about her nights out. She regularly mocks her partner's sagging breasts to her lovers. She slags her off, because her partner is not willing (or is hardly ever willing) to please her in bed the way she likes it. She badmouths her because her partner spoils their pets. She is often late for their dates, or simply forgets that she has an arrangement to meet her partner.

When it comes to their relationship and her acquaintances criticize her for not loving her partner, Rachel starts explaining vehemently that she does. She tells them with genuine honesty that "Whenever she is quietly snoozing next to me, I feel really touched and warm inside." Or: "When I see that she has made me my favorite meal when I get home from work, I'm overcome with waves of affection." And, if Rachel happens to be a philosopher, she might even say "When I feel this special warmth for her, this feeling has a definite phenomenal character that differs from the phenomenal character of other experiences—there is something it is like to be in love with our partner. Love is actually not a dispositional property but an occurrent mental state—it is a conscious experience with a special phenomenal character, and that is all that matters."

I'd like to emphasize three things about this not-too-uplifting story. Firstly, Rachel has formed a false belief about herself—she believes that she loves her partner, but she doesn't. Seen from an impartial outside viewpoint, Rachel's defense is unconvincing. On the contrary, it would be considered an unambiguous instance of repulsive and immoral camouflage—and of course, this undistorted, outside viewpoint is correct.

Secondly, if Rachel really believes that she loves her partner, then she gets caught in the trap of the following kind of self-deception. (1) It is an evident fact that if someone continuously does so and so (or continuously doesn't do so and so), then she has certain character flaws. (2) S knows about the truth of these conditionals. (3) Despite the fact that S, too, continuously does so and so or continuously doesn't do so and so, S fails to realize her own character flaw and uses every means to deny its existence. That is, S is not cognitively closed off from those criteria on the basis of which she *could* realize her own character flaw, yet she *still* doesn't realize it and *misjudges* herself. Rachel's self-deception is exactly like this. She knows the criteria on the basis of which she *could* realize that she misjudges herself when she believes that she loves her partner—and *yet* she doesn't realize it. Her self-deception remains hidden to her.

Thirdly, insofar as Rachel at last realizes that she really doesn't love her partner, she comes to realize it through self-reflection—she becomes able to see herself from an impartial, outside viewpoint. Her self-reflection unmasks her self-deception. Of course, it's not impossible that an $n+1st$ argument would also convince her that she deceives herself, but it is an unlifelike assumption—for (as you saw) she has always been ready to respond to various arguments with "proper" counterarguments, and very easily convinced herself of her innocence.

Now, the case of philosophers sticking to their philosophical beliefs is relevantly similar to that of Rachel. Firstly, these philosophers form false beliefs about the epistemic status of their philosophical beliefs—they believe that they can rationally stick to them, although they cannot.

Secondly, the philosophers sticking to their philosophical beliefs get caught in a similar trap of self-deception: they aren't cognitively closed off from realizing that their sticking to their philosophical beliefs has no sufficient epistemic grounds—everything is already there in the meta-skeptical argument as clearly as the sun at noon-day. Nonetheless, they don't realize it, and so their self-deception remains hidden to them.

Thirdly, when philosophers at long last realize that they have false beliefs about the epistemic status of their substantive factual philosophical beliefs—they falsely believe that they can rationally stick to them although they cannot—, they achieve it through self-reflection. Their self-reflection unmasks their self-deception. It is very unlifelike to suppose that an *n+1st* philosophical argument would convince them of their self-deception. Both the "I'm the only one" philosophers and the equilibrists are ready to respond to it with "proper" counterarguments. The former ones keep saying that "I can rationally believe in the truth of *p* because I have knock-down arguments for the truth of *p*." The latter ones keep saying that "I can rationally believe in the truth of *p* because *p* is in equilibrium with my fundamental pre-philosophical convictions, and I can show that none of the objections against *p* are compelling." Nevertheless, when they exercise self-reflection, then the "I'm the only one" philosophers at long last realize that their view is *only one among many*, and as such it has no privileged status, whereas the equilibrists at long last realize that their fundamental pre-philosophical convictions (which they de facto have) are *a matter of chance*, and so no such philosophical theory can be constructed on their basis in whose truth they could rationally believe. So, it is through their self-reflection alone that they can *rightly* "see" the epistemic status of their philosophical beliefs, and it is through their self-reflection alone that they can gain *reliable* philosophical self-knowledge.

I'm not claiming that philosophers are already successful at their very first attempt. Due to their cowardice and clinging to positions in whose defense they have invested a great deal of hard work, they tend to stubbornly stick to their philosophical beliefs, which is a serious obstacle to the detached self-reflective monitoring of these beliefs. Nevertheless, I cannot emphasize enough that the ultimate aim of doing philosophy is *to overcome this sticking point*, and the most effective way for philosophers to achieve it is to keep trying to execute self-reflection in an uncompromising manner. For if they do that, they will "get the whole picture" sooner or later, and realize that their clinging to their substantive factual philosophical beliefs is completely groundless, so they can suspend them in cognitive peace to fulfil their epistemic duty.

Sophie: I may be wrong, but I think you're over-mystifying the role of self-reflection in the story. How is it different from intellectually seeing the compelling (or at least in your opinion compelling) nature of the meta-skeptical argument?

Meta-skeptic: It is different and more than that because what the philosophers have as a result of self-reflection is not merely an intellectual grasp of the truth of a proposition (it is not mere propositional knowledge), but rather *the experience of the futility* of their sticking to their philosophical beliefs.

I'll try to explain this, too, although it's not so easy. Think about the Buddhist enlightened ones—if there are any at all. They not only intellectually see the truth of the proposition "All suffering is necessarily caused by our attachment to the objects of our desiring," but literally *let go of* their desires. I don't know how it exactly happens, but I assume it goes somehow like this: during their enlightenment, the enlightened ones *experience the complete futility* of their attachment to the objects of their desire. Their enlightenment is a conscious experience during which they come to see *face to face* the causal mechanism which connects their attachment to the objects of their desires with their suffering, and this conscious experience has such a *flash* that it *blows out* their desires once and for all and leads them to *nirvāṇa*, a state in which all suffering is extinguished.

According to the Buddhist tradition, the Buddha describes his enlightenment in the following way:

> When my concentrated mind was thus purified, bright, unblemished, rid of imperfection, malleable, wieldy, steady, and attained to imperturbability, I directed it to knowledge of the destruction of the taints. I directly knew as it actually is: "This is suffering"; [...] "This is the origin of suffering"; [...] "This is the cessation of suffering"; [...] "This is the way leading to the cessation of suffering"; [...] "These are the taints"; [...] "This is the origin of the taints"; [...] "This is the cessation of the taints"; [...] "This is the way leading to the cessation of the taints." When I [...] *saw* thus, my mind was *liberated* from the taint of sensual desire, from the taint of being, and from the taint of ignorance. When it was liberated there came the knowledge: "It is liberated."
>
> (*MN* 36, italics from the meta-skeptic)

I'd like to use this parallel to point out that it is one thing to intellectually see—thanks to the compelling nature of the meta-skeptical argument—the truth of the proposition "Philosophers cannot rationally believe in the truth of their substantive factual philosophical theses, and have the epistemic duty to suspend these beliefs." It is, however, another thing to literally *experience*, through our self-reflective monitoring, the futility of our sticking to our philosophical beliefs.

In other words, no matter how strong the meta-skeptical argument may be, philosophers can fight against it. They're smart, and are able to convince themselves of the falsity of some of its premises. By contrast, if their self-reflection reveals to them (with the experience of complete certainty whose veridicality they have no reason at all to doubt) that their p-belief is just one among many, and that their fundamental pre-philosophical convictions x, y, z (which they de facto have) are *a matter of chance*, then the self-reflective monitoring of their philosophical beliefs may be such a *flash* that "blows out" their sticking to their philosophical beliefs once and for all.

Sophie: I think I see what you mean, but the mental act of self-reflection cannot be forced.

Meta-skeptic: Indeed. There's no guarantee that philosophers will carry out a self-reflective act by which they can gain reliable self-knowledge. It's entirely up to them whether they will develop a proper perception of themselves as epistemic agents thanks to a (really executed) act of self-reflection, and experience the futility of their sticking to their philosophical beliefs. And yet, some philosophers do execute this required self-reflection.

I highly appreciate them. My appreciation is part epistemic, part moral. It is epistemic to the extent that their self-reflection puts them in a *privileged position*—they'll clearly see the epistemic status of their philosophical beliefs. And it is moral to the extent that, having overcome all psychological obstacles, they're able to *let go of* their non-visceral philosophical beliefs thanks to their experience resulting from self-reflection.

Sophie: The only thing left I'd like to know is this. Let's suppose you're right in everything you say. Self-deception is the only way for us to "wriggle out" of the compelling force of the meta-skeptical argument, and a really executed act of self-reflection (like enlightenment) is such an experience or flash that can "blow out" our sticking to our philosophical beliefs. That said, I think that the parallel with Buddhism is a bit unenlightening. While the Buddha promises great benefits (the cessation of all their sufferings) to his followers, meta-skepticism offers no prospects. What could you say to those who argue like this? "Even if I'm defenseless against the meta-skeptical argument and even if I concede that I have no good epistemic reasons to stick to my substantive factual philosophical beliefs, I don't have enough motivation to start doing the exercises proposed by the meta-skeptic. This is because the commitment to meta-skepticism has no benefits at all."

Meta-skeptic: Indeed, many think so. But they're wrong. Commitment to meta-skepticism is the *appropriate* reaction to philosophy's epistemic failure. Meta-skepticism gives the *right* answer to the question "What should we do with our philosophical beliefs in the light of philosophy's epistemic failure?" In a word, meta-skepticism is the *correct* metaphilosophical view.

But if seeing the *truth* weren't in itself enough motivation, here's a list of those further benefits that the complete identification with meta-skepticism can offer. Seeing that you cannot rationally believe in your substantive factual philosophical theses, you can get clear on your epistemic-cognitive limits. Thanks to your properly executed self-reflection, you can, in cognitive peace, let go of those of your beliefs which you now have irrationally, and so you become immune to having false beliefs. Insofar as you were an "I'm the only one" philosopher, you will be cured of your epistemic blindness. Insofar as you were an equilibrist, you won't be threatened by the disease called "epistemic schizophrenia" any more. The commitment to meta-skepticism gives you access to the Socratic wisdom "The only thing I know is that I know nothing"; "I only know that I don't know." To recap, meta-skepticism presents you with *the virtue of epistemic modesty*, which is nothing else but the main and noblest goal of doing philosophy.

2.2 Act Two: Farewell to meta-skepticism

Sophie: After thinking through what you said and how you said it, I have concluded that you don't react appropriately to philosophy's epistemic failure, and don't give the right answer to the question "What should we do with our philosophical beliefs in the light of philosophy's epistemic failure?"

Meta-skeptic: Let me hear your concerns!

Sophie: Before I start, I'd like to clarify one more thing that is important but has not been spoken of until now. My question is: why are you not a Pyrrhonian skeptic? Here's a nice and concise formulation of Pyrrhonism by Sextus:

> [W]hen the Skeptic set out to philosophize with the aim of assessing his *phantasiai* — that is, of determining which are true and which are false so as to achieve ataraxia — he landed in a controversy between positions of *equal strength*, and, being unable to resolve it, *he suspended judgment*. But while he was thus suspending judgment there followed by chance the *sought-after ataraxia* as regards belief.
>
> (*PH* I 27, italics from Sophie)

So, *like you*, a Pyrrhonian skeptic, *too*, takes the fact of pervasive and permanent philosophical dissensus as his starting point; he, *too*, suspends his substantive factual philosophical beliefs; and as a result of that, he, *too*, achieves cognitive peace.

However, *unlike you*, the Pyrrhonian skeptic is not threatened by self-defeat. This is because all he claims is this: "for every argument that I have examined and that establishes something dogmatically, there *appears to me* to be opposed another argument that establishes something dogmatically and is equal to it as regards credibility and lack of credibility" (*PH* I 203, italics from Sophie); and so, what he says is "*just* a report of a human pathos, which is apparent to the person *experiencing* it" (*PH* I 203, italics from Sophie). All he claims is this: "I am now in such a *state of mind* as neither dogmatically to affirm nor deny any of the matters in question" (*PH* I 197, italics from Sophie); "[a]nd this he says, reporting what appears to him concerning the matters at hand, not dogmatically and confidently, but just as a *description of his state of mind*, his pathos" (*PH* I 197, italics from Sophie). Slogans like "I withhold assent"; "I determine nothing"; "I suspend my beliefs," actually only "*express a personal pathos*, in accord with which the Skeptic declines for the present to take an affirmative or negative position on any of the non-evident matters of inquiry" (*PH* I 201, italics from Sophie). In brief, since a Pyrrhonian skeptic is "simply reporting, like a chronicler, what now *appears to him* to be the case" (*PH* I 4, italics from Sophie); that is, since all he does is describe his *experiences*, his position (attitude, praxis, you name it) is not self-defeating. (See e.g., Bailey 1990.)

By contrast, you do not merely want to share your experiences with us, but firmly claim that philosophers cannot rationally believe in the truth of their substantive factual philosophical theses, and for this reason they must suspend them all. And, here's the source of troubles—it seems that the content of your statement is self-defeating. Now, if your argument is self-defeating, then it would be irrational for one to accept its conclusions and commit oneself to meta-skepticism. And, whichever way I look at it, you cannot give a reassuring response to the problem of self-defeat—at least, you're most certainly unable to "whitewash" your argument.

Let me go on. Since all the Pyrrhonian skeptic does is describe his experiences, what he says does not contain any normative elements. He doesn't claim that everybody must suspend their substantive factual philosophical beliefs. Your claim, however, amounts to just that, and that is a source of troubles. This is because for you to be able to make that claim, you have to commit yourself to doxastic deontology. Without doing so, you cannot require philosophers to suspend their substantive factual philosophical beliefs. However, doxastic deontology isn't beyond dispute—there is disagreement among philosophers about whether it is a correct view or not, and there are strong arguments against it. Thus, you should show that the arguments adduced against doxastic deontology are all bad—and to achieve that, you should present philosophical arguments (what is more, knockdown philosophical arguments), although you think that all philosophical arguments are *sui generis* inadequate and unsuitable for establishing truths. It follows that either premise (4) of your argument remains unjustified, which means that it is not compelling. Or, if you attempt to justify (4), then you're bound to do that with tools that are inadequate and unsuitable according to your view, and so you end up contradicting yourself.

That is why I'm asking you again: why you are not a Pyrrhonian skeptic? In this case, too, you could achieve cognitive peace as a result of suspending your substantive factual philosophical beliefs, and you wouldn't have to excuse yourself due to self-defeat or due to committing yourself to philosophical views that you should not embrace.

Meta-skeptic: That's a good question. Look, the Pyrrhonian skeptic's proposal *cannot result in* cognitive peace. So much so, that if you think about it, this whole therapy gets stuck already *before* we suspend our beliefs. I, for one, would not suspend my philosophical beliefs just because *it appears to me* that the philosophical theories (which I more or less know and understand) concerning a given philosophical problem are of equal weight. I would be (quite) worried to find myself content with this much—after all, it may easily be the case that I'm insufficiently circumspect and thorough, and don't realize that one theory has stronger support than the other, right? The question would keep bothering me: "Theories X and Y *appear to me* to be of equal weight, but are they *really* of equal weight?" The thought would keep haunting me: "Couldn't it be the case that my impressions—on which I base the suspension of my philosophical beliefs—*deceive* me?"

What the above comes to is this: the suspension of our philosophical beliefs, the achievement of cognitive peace and its maintenance require "something" *more* than appearances. And indeed, there is "more" than that. Namely, the *insight* that the tools of philosophy are inadequate for establishing truths and for the compelling justification of substantive factual philosophical theses. For, if we gain this insight, then (but *only* then) the suspension of our philosophical beliefs will become really *reasonable*, and the suspension of our beliefs *can* really *result in* our reaching the state of undisturbed cognitive peace. In this case, X and Y do *not only* appear to us to be of equal weight, but we *also* realize that they are of equal "weight"—at least in the relevant sense that both are "products" of a wrong and unreliable truth-seeking procedure.

The main thing is that in order to achieve and maintain cognitive peace, one needs *certainty*. The Pyrrhonian, however, does not (and cannot) have certainty. He can have no experience which he could rightly judge to be veridical, as opposed to being mere appearances. Now, that is why I am not a Pyrrhonist skeptic.

Sophie: But is it not precisely the main tenet of Pyrrhonism (if I can say so) that cognitive peace can be achieved even without certainty? Here is how it all adds up, in my view. We set out to find philosophical truths. On our way, we stumble upon a number of philosophical theories which are incompatible with each other, yet appear to us to be of equal weight. At this point, we suspend our philosophical beliefs. As a result, cognitive peace becomes our companion "by chance […]" (*PH* I 29). We experience this cognitive peace to be *good*. That is when it dawns on us: "Wow! Undisturbed mental tranquillity has come to us *without* our being certain in anything—even *independently* of whether our earlier impressions of the equal weight of philosophical theories were right or not." The bottom line is that concerning the achievement of cognitive peace, *nothing depends on* whether things appear to us the way they are or the way they aren't.

Meta-skeptic: You're on the right track. Cognitive peace visits the Pyrrhonian skeptic *out of the blue*. Here's the complete passage from which you just quoted:

> What happened to the Skeptic is just like what is told of Apelles the painter. For it is said that once upon a time, when he was painting a horse and wished to depict the horse's froth, he failed so completely that he gave up and threw his sponge at the picture—the sponge which he used to wipe the paints from his brush—and that in striking the picture the sponge produced the desired effect. So, too, the Skeptics were hoping to achieve ataraxia by resolving the anomaly of phenomena and noumena, and, being unable to do this, they suspended judgment. But then, by chance as it were, when they were suspending judgment the ataraxia followed […]
> (*PH* I 29)

Now let me ask: would you embark on a path knowing in advance that by following it you will reach your goal (i.e., cognitive peace) not in the way and not at the time you expect, that is, as an outcome of your efforts, but *by chance*. Would you accept the following invitation: "If you suspend your beliefs (regardless of whether they are well-founded or not), then cognitive peace will descend upon you, not as a result of this suspension but in some other way (I don't know how), although I cannot promise this because the connection between the two is contingent?" For this is essentially what the Pyrrhonian skeptic is offering. Against this, I hold that attaining cognitive peace requires certainty (recognition of the compelling force of meta-skeptical argument plus reaching self-knowledge through practice of self-reflection)—these two ensure that you achieve cognitive peace as a result of your efforts and not as a contingent by-product.

Sophie: OK, let's leave Pyrrhonism alone—I think you've convinced me. And I've received a clear answer to my question: the reason why you're not a Pyrrhonian skeptic is that you cannot imagine undisturbed cognitive peace without certainty. At the same time … how to phrase it … speaking of your *certainty* or *certainty-awareness*, I've got to admit that its extent is scary. We've been already conversing for a good while, and as I was listening to you, I started getting the impression, and I cannot get rid of it, that you eerily resemble Philonous.

Meta-skeptic: Behold!

Sophie: Well …, it seems to me that you think yourself to be infallible like he does. You're just as much complacent and narcissistic as he is—you're an "I'm the only one" philosopher. The only difference between you guys is that whereas he's an "I'm the only one" philosopher concerning his *first-order* philosophical beliefs, the same goes for you concerning your *meta*philosophical beliefs. Moreover, your hubris is more displeasing than Philonous'. While he is unable to exercise self-reflection due to his epistemic blindness and to see his own view as *just one* among many first-order philosophical views, you keep preaching about the significance of exercising self-reflection, although you, too, are unable to see your view as *just one* among many metaphilosophical views.

Meta-skeptic: Come on, Sophie, you're just hurling insults at me. You must surely feel that what you're saying is unfair. Why shouldn't I assert—without reservation, in the possession of the meta-skeptical argument and especially in light of my veridical experiences resulting from my self-reflection—that philosophers cannot rationally believe in the truth of their substantive factual philosophical theses, and consequently they must suspend their corresponding beliefs? This is an entirely different kettle of fish than Philonous' fanaticism.

Sophie: I cannot see in what ways they differ. What I *clearly* see, however, is that while you claim that the noblest goal of doing philosophy is that it teaches epistemic modesty, you yourself seem to be the antithesis of this virtue. I clearly see that you're not epistemically more modest than the equilibrist who doesn't believe that she has compelling arguments, but—as she has a personal stake in answering certain philosophical questions and doesn't want to stand defenseless against the objections—tries to defend her beliefs with philosophical arguments.

Meta-skeptic: I'm glad that by now you've got the big picture. But apart from lashing out at me, would you please let me know at last what *objections* you have against meta-skepticism?

Sophie: Beyond standard objections, I have only another two—still, in my eyes both are stronger than any of the standard ones. Firstly, in my opinion, you give a *one-sided* description of what self-reflection reveals about our philosophical beliefs. You only emphasize that "aspect" of it which supports your view. You say that if we carry out the self-reflective monitoring of our philosophical beliefs, then *the only thing* we can realize is the futility of our sticking to our substantive factual philosophical beliefs, and this is a kind of flash which can optimally prompt us to suspend them.

Self-reflection, however, reveals more than that. It also reveals that we have a burning (or at least quite strong) *cognitive need* to take stances on substantive factual philosophical issues which affect us deeply, and which can be addressed *only* with the tools of philosophy in the first place—actually, we don't have any tools *other* than those of philosophical truth-seeking for this purpose. Now, it seems to me that you entirely overlook this indisputably existing cognitive need which is *also revealed* by self-reflection. You act as if it didn't exist.

Meta-skeptic: I know exactly what you're talking about. But, when during their self-reflection philosophers experience this "burning" cognitive need in themselves, they also experience the *hopelessness* of satisfying it. So to speak, the "aspect" of self-reflection described by me (and especially the flash which I spoke about) *overrides* the cognitive need of the philosophers you describe—by revealing the hopelessness of its satisfaction.

Sophie: I don't think it would override it. Rather, the two appear *in parallel* during the self-reflective monitoring of our philosophical beliefs, and thereby create *tension*. Let me share my own experience. *On the one hand*, my self-reflection reveals that I have the cognitive need to do something with those substantive factual philosophical questions which are important to me, and which—lacking any other truth-seeking tools—I can only address with the tools of philosophy. *On the other hand*, my self-reflection reveals your point that I don't have any good epistemic reasons to believe in the truth of propositions which I have arrived at with the use of philosophy's tools.

Meta-skeptic: Sophie, if your self-reflection really reveals this duality and the tension it generates, then it just shows that you haven't finished your job yet. I think I was speaking clearly earlier: the main goal of doing philosophy is that we *give up on* philosophical truth-seeking *once and for all* by suspending our philosophical beliefs—that the cognitive need in us to take stances on philosophical issues be *eradicated* or *blown out* due *to the recognition of its hopelessness*.

Sophie: I understand that you must make this claim, but I'm slightly revolted by this vision. Let me return to the phenomenon of epistemic schizophrenia, discussed in relation with van Inwagen's confession. On the one hand, he believes in the truth of *p*, so he believes (because he cannot do otherwise) that his belief *p* is rational. On the other hand, he also believes that his belief *p* is not rational because he cannot, with a clear conscience, ignore the whisper of Clifford's ghost, which says that there's a good chance that he has obtained his belief *p* through considerations that don't track the truth but rather the voice of the "will to believe." The lesson drawn from the story was that the only way for van Inwagen to believe in the truth of *p* in cognitive peace is *to be able to convince himself* that *beyond* his philosophical arguments, he has exclusive access to a further piece of evidence that *reliably* indicates for him the truth of *p* (more exactly, the truth of the premises of his arguments).

Let's now return to our case. On the one hand, we realize that we cannot use philosophy's tools to arrive at substantive factual philosophical theses in which we could rationally believe in the epistemic sense. On the other hand, we also realize that we have the cognitive need to take stances on substantive factual philosophical issues. I think that the *only* way for us to resolve this tension—and the *only* option for your proposed meta-skeptic "training" to bring cognitive peace—is to sink into *intellectual apathy* as a result of it.

Now, in my opinion, none of these ways of achieving cognitive peace are desirable. It is undesirable if someone convinces oneself of the truth of one's beliefs through appealing to some private evidence, and it is also undesirable if someone lets go of his philosophical beliefs once and for all in such a way that he becomes *completely insensitive* to the philosophical problems at issue.

What I want to say is that earlier you painted an implausible picture of the phenomenology of suspending our philosophical beliefs. Things are not so simple like this: S believes at t_1 that *p* is true, and no longer believes at t_2 that *p* is true, nor that *not-p* is true. Your description leaves out the most important phenomenological feature. Instead, things are like this: at t_1, S was *sincerely interested* in whether *p* is true, but at t_2, S is already *not in the least interested* in whether *p* is true. Suspending his belief *p* can only result in cognitive peace for S if the philosophical problem at issue *has already lost all its significance for S*, and so *S no longer cares* if *p* is true or false. And this *is* apathy. And in my opinion, apathy is undesirable. It is a bad thing if someone becomes indifferent and irresponsive to the philosophical questions that have so far been important (or even had existential stake) to him. In my eyes, this is nothing else but cognitive deterioration to an alarming extent.

Let me take another approach. I agree with you that the equilibrist cannot give a piece of philosophical advice with epistemic responsibility to someone who turns to him with some substantive factual philosophical problem. For if he does that, then—like we saw earlier in the case of Alex and Sammy—he will actually mislead them. But now, let me ask you a question. As a meta-skeptic, would you dare to give Alex the following piece of advice *with epistemic and at once moral responsibility*: "To hell with the mind-body problem, don't deal with it at all, eradicate all your cognitive needs, because no matter what your conclusions are, you'll bound to be irrational to believe in them, as you arrive at them using philosophy's inadequate and unsuitable truth-seeking tools!"? Or, would you dare to give Sammy this piece of advice *with epistemic and at once moral responsibility*: "Don't deal with the questions whether there is a God or there is eternal damnation, eradicate your elemental desire to know these things, because no matter how far you can go using philosophy's inadequate and unsuitable truth-seeking tools, you cannot rationally believe in them!"? Generally speaking, the question is this: "Would you dare to give *with epistemic and at once moral responsibility* to anyone the piece of advice to follow you and become a meta-skeptic, in the light of the fact that cognitive peace from suspending our philosophical beliefs can only be attained *at the cost* of sinking into total uninterestedness and apathy?"

Meta-skeptic: Take care, Sophie, because *you won't get anywhere* in the end if you choose to go down this road!

Sophie: I'm afraid you're right on that point. But now it's time I moved on to my second objection, so let's have a closer look at it.

A Pyrrhonian skeptic doesn't take a stance on the question whether any successful philosophical arguments will be formulated *in the future*— whether philosophers *will be able* to solve philosophical problems. Although he suspends his philosophical beliefs, he "continues to search" (*PH* I 3)—*just in case*. This "just in case" is in the spirit of Pyrrhonism: a Pyrrhonist doesn't take a stance on "things unclear," including "the thing unclear" concerning what the future holds—he leaves this question open. You stand on the opposite side. According to you, the right and wise thing for us to do is give up philosophical truth-seeking for good, due to its hopelessness.

Now, in view of the hopelessness of the whole enterprise, it would *only* be responsible for you to expect philosophers to suspend their philosophical beliefs and *forever* give up on seeking philosophical truths in either of the following two cases. Either you should be able to compellingly justify the thesis that philosophical problems are in principle unsolvable for beings with epistemic equipment such as ours, or you should be able to compellingly justify that we're so far away from solving philosophical problems that humanity would certainly become extinct before any of them would be solved. And, if you don't mind my saying so, I have trouble believing that you could have a compelling justifications for either of these views.

Whether we should or should not give up on philosophical truth-seeking is hardly an insignificant issue. Thus, the question arises, and it arises in a very acute form indeed: what is the basis for your belief that philosophers won't solve philosophical problems *in the future either*? What arguments do you have against the claim that philosophy (or what will be called philosophy) will acquire some new and effective truth-seeking and justificatory tools *in the future*, which will help future philosophers in finding solutions to philosophical problems?

Meta-skeptic: True, I don't have any compelling arguments, but I have quite a good inductive reason to think so.

Don't ignore the time factor! If an epistemic enterprise is young (a few years or decades old), then, indeed, the fact that it has not yet solved any problems doesn't mean that it is inadequate and unsuitable for accomplishing its mission in the first place. But philosophy isn't a freshman—it is a 2,500-year-old epistemic enterprise. Of course, this isn't decisive in and of itself, but if we add that the new philosophical problems are continuous with the old ones—that is, philosophers have been concerned for centuries with problems that are similar in relevant ways—, then our conclusion has a fairly large inductive basis. A considerable amount of time has passed since a few people first devoted themselves to solving philosophical problems, and yet the philosophers haven't managed to come up with a single solution to any of them to the present day—in addition, *there is not even the slightest indication* that a solution to any of the substantive factual philosophical problems would be in the offing.

Now, given what I just said, let me answer your question: I cannot rule out the possibility that philosophers will solve certain substantive philosophical problems in the future, just as I obviously cannot rule out the possibility that a brandy-making apparatus has been orbiting for millions of years around the planet that is farthest away from Earth. Although I cannot rule out these possibilities, I don't think I should seriously consider them, as they have *nothing* at all going for them.

I admit it would be a cute strategy if, experimenting with the "rejuvenation" of philosophy, you would say:

> Given that philosophy (and, primarily, analytic philosophy within that) has only been going on for sixty–eighty years in the way it should (that is, at an industrial level and as a quasi-normal science) and given that all the historical antecedents that had happened before those sixty–eighty years are mere footnotes, the lack of solutions to philosophical problems isn't a clear sign of philosophy's epistemic failure.

However, this attempt at rejuvenation seems to be an ad hoc maneuver—and in fact it is extremely partial and exclusive, and is based on unjustifiable ideas. The philosophy of the past sixty–eighty years (thanks to the work of thousands of philosophers) has been quite successful in formulating philosophical problems more and more precisely and developing different philosophical theories in their strongest possible form, as well as in coming up with newer and newer proposals for solutions to various philosophical problems, instead of presenting the seeds of at least a single genuine solution to any of philosophy's problems.

Sophie: There you go. My second concern is precisely related to the line of argument you've just presented. For, in fact, *you cannot know* how the solution to philosophical problems progresses; and *you're not justified to claim* that there isn't even the slightest indication that the solutions to philosophical problems would already be in the offing.

In order to appeal to induction rightly, you should be able to show that your inductive basis is *large enough indeed*. Let's take the problem of universals—one of the oldest philosophical conundrums. For this problem, the inductive basis is its unresolvedness projected on the time interval from its very first formulation to the present (spanning 2,500 years). But how large is this inductive basis? In my opinion, you cannot know how large it is. To determine that, you should know a number of factors of which you cannot have the faintest idea. It is also conceivable that (given the epistemic equipment of the human race) mankind would take 100,000 years to solve the problem of universals, and in this case, the past 2,500 years—contrary to what you say—is very little; one could say that its unresolvedness thus far is just an infantile disorder of philosophy. But it is just as easily conceivable that we're only a hundred years away from the solution.

In a word, you cannot know whether (given our epistemic equipment) philosophical problems are solvable at all, and you cannot know how much time it would take to solve them insofar as they are solvable. And, given that no substantive philosophical problems have been solved so far, you *cannot even estimate* where we are now on the road to the solution of philosophical problems—provided we are already on that road at all. Consequently, *you are not justified in believing* that your inference has an appropriately large inductive basis. I'd like to bring to your notice how Chinese Prime Minister Zhou Enlai reputedly answered a question about the influence of the French Revolution: "Too early to say."

Meta-skeptic: Let's suppose you have convinced me. But what follows from that?

Sophie: Much the same as from my previous objection, namely, that meta-skepticism is an epistemically and morally irresponsible metaphilosophical vision. For think about it sincerely. You expect philosophers to suspend their substantive factual philosophical beliefs, and give up on seeking the corresponding truths at issue; however, you *cannot even estimate* where we are now on the road to the solution of philosophical problems, hence you have no grounds to say that we're too far from it. So, your expectation about philosophers is nothing short of *irresponsible*—for if we're just (let's suppose) fifty years away from solving the problem of universals, for instance, then it is precisely your expectation that prevents them from achieving the solution.

Don't get me wrong. I'm not saying for a moment that our hope of ever solving philosophical problems is justified. Nor am I saying—as we cannot know whether we can solve them, and provided we can, we cannot know *when* we can solve them—that our epistemic duty is to hope for it; to stick to our philosophical beliefs and continue with our philosophical truth-seeking activity (see e.g., Matheson 2015). Furthermore, I strongly disagree with reasoning like the following: "Let's not suspend our truth-seeking philosophical activity because we'll be very sorry to see somebody else in our place solving this or that philosophical problem in the future," or "We mustn't suspend our philosophical beliefs because we'll be very happy if it turns out in the future that it is precisely our beliefs that have proved to be true." All I'm saying is this: you act irresponsibly when you expect philosophers to suspend their philosophical beliefs. As we know woefully little about the future, hopelessness is *just as unjustified as* hopefulness. And it's hard to see otherwise: you are *just as biased* in your gloomy pessimism as your opponents in their hopeful optimism.

With all this, I want to say that the situation is *worse* than you believe it to be: actually, our ignorance is so great that *we don't even know the extent of our ignorance*—for we cannot give a reliable estimate of *its extent*. (Here, Sophie argues similarly to Nicholas Rescher [2006: 96–107].)

Meta-skeptic: So you're saying that I would do the right thing by suspending my philosophical belief that philosophers must suspend their substantive factual philosophical beliefs? That is to say, if I were a *meta*-meta-skeptic?

Sophie: I believe so. But the reason is not that we could stick to our beliefs with epistemic responsibility. *Clearly*, it is not because that. Rather, the expression "*meta*-meta-skepticism" refers to the following. On facing the failure of the earlier three reactions (especially equilibrism) to philosophy's epistemic failure, the moment may easily come when it strongly appears to us that this accumulated (double-level) failure points in the direction of commitment to meta-skepticism. Since there is nothing else left to do, we have to give up on philosophical truth-seeking—we have to let our philosophical beliefs wither. However, while doing so, we finally realize that we *cannot even* be meta-skeptics with epistemic responsibility, and so, indirectly, that—no matter how we struggle—we have been unable to reassuringly account for the epistemic status of our substantive factual philosophical beliefs.

Part Three

7

Breakdown

It is time to take stock of my accomplishments at the end of the dialectical path which I undertook to introduce. What I'm about to say will be strongly confession-like—I'm afraid it must be this way.

1 The case of early Plato

The participants of Plato's early dialogues make attempts to define certain concepts (such as "courage," "friendship," "virtue," "justice," "wisdom," etc.), and are always forced to realize in the end that their enterprise has failed. Here are Socrates' accounts of their failures:

> If I had shown in this conversation that I had a knowledge which Nicias and Laches have not, then I admit that you would be right in inviting me to perform this duty; but as we are all in the same perplexity, why should one of us be preferred to another? I certainly think that no one should [...]
>
> (*Laches* 200e–201a)

> Then, my boys, we have again fallen into the old discarded error; [...] But that too was a position of ours which, as you will remember, has been already refuted by ourselves [...] Then what is to be done? Or rather is there anything to be done? I can only, like the wise men who argue in courts, sum up the arguments: — If neither the beloved, nor the lover, nor the like, nor the unlike, nor the good, nor the congenial, nor any other of whom we spoke — for there were such a number of them that I cannot remember all — if none of these are friends, I know not what remains to be said [...] how ridiculous that you two boys, and I, an old boy, who would fain be one of you, should imagine ourselves to be friends — this is what the by-standers will go away and say — and as yet we have not been able to discover what is a friend!
>
> (*Lysis* 222d–223b)

> But now I have been utterly defeated, and have failed to discover what that is to which the imposer of names gave this name of temperance or wisdom. And yet many more admissions were made by us than could be fairly granted; for we admitted that there was a science of science, although the argument said No, and protested against us; and we admitted further, that this science knew the works of the other sciences (although this too was denied by the argument), because we wanted to show that the wise man had knowledge of what he knew and did not know; also we nobly disregarded, and never even considered, the impossibility of a man knowing in a sort of way that which he does not know at all; for our assumption was, that he knows that which he does not know; than which nothing, as I think, can be more irrational.
>
> (*Charmides* 175b–175d)

Here is yet another example. In *Hippias Minor*, Socrates sums up the result of their joint investigation as follows: "Then, Hippias, he who voluntarily does wrong and disgraceful things, if there be such a man, will be the good man" (376b). And he goes on to add:

> Nor can I agree with myself, Hippias; and yet that seems to be the conclusion which, as far as we can see at present, must follow from our argument. As I was saying before, I am all abroad, and being in perplexity am always changing my opinion. Now, that I or any ordinary man should wander in perplexity is not surprising; but if you wise men also wander, and we cannot come to you and rest from our wandering, the matter begins to be serious both to us and to you.
>
> (376c)

The reason I'm bringing up the aporetic ending of Plato's early dialogues (see also: *Euthyphro* 15c–16a; *Hippias Major* 303d–304e; *Protagoras* 361a–361e) is that I feel as if I had been dropped into the world of these dialogues. My experience is eerily similar to Plato's at the dawn of philosophy. Just as Socrates and his interlocutors conclude that *they've come up against aporias in the end*, I also conclude *that I've come up against an aporia—my intellect has broken down*.

2 A footnote to Plato

My starting point was that the followers of philosophy's epistemic tradition made attempts to assert compellingly justified substantive philosophical truths and to solve philosophical problems, but their enterprise has failed. The community of philosophers doesn't have substantive philosophical knowledge. For this reason, all philosophers have an epistemic and moral duty to react to philosophy's epistemic failure, and insofar as they have any substantive philosophical beliefs, to try to account for their epistemic status. They have to face the disheartening thought that "If philosophy is a failed epistemic enterprise, then my philosophical beliefs are the beliefs of a member of a failed epistemic enterprise," and they must ask themselves the question: "What should I do with my philosophical beliefs in the light of philosophy's epistemic failure?"

How can they answer this question? Apart from dreaming about philosophy's future success, I think there are four possibilities that exhaust the scope of their responses. (1) "I can believe in the truth of my substantive philosophical theses—I can justify them with knock-down arguments." (2) "I can believe in the truth of my substantive philosophical theses—although I cannot justify them with knock-down arguments." (3) "I cannot believe in the truth of my substantive philosophical theses—I have to suspend my beliefs." (4) "I cannot believe in the truth of my substantive philosophical theses—they are meaningless."

I've analyzed these answers as metaphilosophical visions in detail. I think that I've successfully expounded all of them in their considered, consistent, and vivid forms. And what was the upshot of it all? It was that *I cannot identify with any of them* with a clear intellectual conscience. And this being so, it means that I cannot give a reassuring account of the epistemic status of my substantive philosophical beliefs. I cannot stick to them with epistemic responsibility, but I cannot, either, suspend them and consider them meaningless—I've run out of options. Like the participants of Plato's early dialogues, *I've come up against an aporia—my intellect has broken down.*

3 The experience of breakdown

Like the followers of the epistemic tradition, I'd like to know the right answers to certain philosophical questions. I'd like to know the corresponding substantive truths. What's more, there are some philosophical questions I'd *very much* like to know the right answers to—questions in which I have an existential stake.

I have philosophical beliefs concerning all philosophical questions that interest me. Besides, I have more or less worked out philosophical arguments for them. If you were to ask me why I believe in the truth of this or that philosophical thesis, view, or theory, I could give grounds for it by adducing philosophical considerations.

However, I don't think that my philosophical arguments have compelling force. Like the "human-faced" equilibrists, I consider my philosophical views as elaborate versions of my fundamental pre-philosophical convictions. But unlike them, I don't think that their equilibrium with my fundamental pre-philosophical convictions and my ability to show that no knock-down objections can be brought up against them would be an appropriate justification for my philosophical views. What's worse, I cannot dispel the thought that my fundamental pre-philosophical convictions are determined by factors that don't track the truth. For these reasons, I feel that the intellectual maintenance of my views isn't enough to entitle me to sustain my considered philosophical beliefs—*I cannot take epistemic responsibility* for the truth of my philosophical views. So, instead of reaching my destination and being able to seriously and sincerely believe in the truth of my philosophical views—instead of being able to seriously and sincerely believe that I've come to possess philosophical truths—I have philosophical beliefs that are pervaded with tormenting uncertainty.

But this is not the whole picture. I can only interpret the fact of permanent disagreement in all areas of philosophy in the way the meta-skeptic does. This is that philosophy's truth-seeking tools are inadequate and unsuitable for establishing truths—philosophy's justificatory tools are inadequate and unsuitable for the compelling justification of substantive factual philosophical views. Now, since (1) I'd like to avoid forming false beliefs concerning philosophical questions that are important to me *at all costs*, and since (2) I think that I have no good epistemic reasons to stick to the truth of my substantive factual philosophical beliefs, I feel that the right thing to do would be to suspend my philosophical beliefs at issue—independently of my unwillingness to consider the argument for meta-skepticism as having compelling force.

Nevertheless, in spite of there being strong epistemic reasons to suspend my philosophical beliefs, *I am unable* to do it. And in spite of thinking that I'm unable to use philosophy's truth-seeking tools to find substantive factual philosophical beliefs for whose truth I could take epistemic responsibility, *I am unable* to give up on seeking philosophical truths and to *continue* taking stands on philosophical issues that are important to me. So, instead of reaching my destination and being able to suspend my philosophical beliefs with a clear conscience, I continue to have philosophical beliefs that are—look, I've come full circle here—pervaded with tormenting uncertainty.

But this is still not the whole picture. As it seems that I have not succeeded in recovering from my chronic epistemic schizophrenia, which is undoubtedly a nasty and painful state to be in, I must confess that I long for cognitive peace. I long for the above-described and experienced tension to go away.

Let's suppose there is a time-honored drug that causes its users to change their beliefs about their philosophical beliefs. From the moment when this drug kicks in, it would gradually increase its users' *trust* in the truth of their beliefs—until it would become *complete* beyond a point. They would experience the formation of massive certainty—it would seem to them out of the question that their beliefs may turn out false. Needless to say, after taking this pill, they would forget taking it right away.

However ashamed I am to admit it, I would be *strongly tempted* to seize this opportunity. I would be insincere to myself if I denied it: since I'm longing to live in my philosophical cave knowing for sure that things are as I believe them to be, *I would be inclined* to take this drug.

Well, but …, no matter how strong my longing for cognitive peace is …, as I conjure up those philosophers who are certain of the truth of their beliefs *despite* the permanent dissensus in all fields of philosophy …, I slowly realize that *I wouldn't like to become like them.*

I don't want to become a man who's firmly convinced that his arguments for his beliefs are *compelling*—they have no weak spots, and they lead to truth with irresistible force. For it would mean that I would consider those who think differently from me my epistemic inferiors—irrational figures who don't understand my arguments and so are unable to realize that those arguments force truth into the open. Nor do I want to become a man who is firmly convinced that he has come into possession of such a special experience, *private evidence* which *shows him the truth*. For it would mean that ultimately, I *blindly trust* that the "inner voices" which "assure me" of the truth of my beliefs and/or "give me guidance" through my making philosophical arguments are perfectly *reliable* and are not bias factors; moreover, that I can judge in full confidence that the "inner voices speaking" to my interlocutors (supposing they can hear anything) are *misleading*—they lead them to falsities. And, finally, nor do I want to become a man who is firmly convinced of his own *excellence*—of his being someone who *regularly* holds true propositions to be true and *regularly* holds false ones to be false. For it would mean that my certainty stems merely from my considering myself as someone who is the *favorite* of some "higher power" (God, nature, chance, genetic lottery … I don't have the faintest idea what it could be) in the epistemic sense (*not seeing* why and how), and for whom (*not seeing* why and how) the nature of reality "gives its blessing" to every step in his philosophical arguments.

In a word, no matter how it would work, I would feel it to be *wrong* (in fact, *extremely* wrong) to take the drug. As it happens, now I think that I could resist the temptation. At the same time, I also think that later in life, there would be some moments when I would sorely regret my decision and curse myself for not having been able to overcome my qualms.

Alternatively, let's suppose there is a drug whose effect (like cases of phenomenal sorites) would be the gradual and imperceptible fading away of my philosophical beliefs and the slow disappearance of my cognitive need for taking stands in the philosophical questions which I now consider important. Needless to say, after taking this pill, I would forget taking it right away, and would wake up in the morning as a full-fledged meta-skeptic who has achieved what he aimed for.

Once again, I would lie if I said I wouldn't be tempted to seize this opportunity. I fancy that it would be an intoxicating feeling to be set free from the compulsion of philosophical truth-seeking. The reason is that—unless someone is not certain that the way things stand is the way he thinks them to be—this compulsion is primarily (or rather, exclusively) a *damnation*, because it is inevitably accompanied by constant and tormenting cognitive uncertainty.

Well, but ..., no matter how strong my longing for cognitive peace is ..., I don't want to become like the meta-skeptic who has achieved what he aimed for through suspending his philosophical beliefs. He's a man whose need for philosophical truth-seeking has been eradicated once and for all, who has become indifferent to all philosophical problems (especially those in which he had an existential stake), and who is unimpressed by those philosophical questions the answers to which he had earlier longed to know. In short, he's a man who has sunk into intellectual apathy. As it happens, now I think I could resist the temptation to take the pill. At the same time, I'm certain that in the future I would often feel that this was a grave mistake and that—motivated by my qualms—I made a silly and self-destructive decision.

So what is the phenomenology of my breakdown experience like? "At first go," I can describe it like this: *on the one hand*, I'm inexorably motivated to give answers to philosophical questions that are important to me. *On the other hand*, however circumspect I am in doing my best to appropriately justify my philosophical beliefs, I cannot seriously and sincerely commit myself to the truth of propositions that I obtained using philosophy's truth-seeking tools. "At second go," it would look like this: *on the one hand*, I would do almost anything to get rid of my epistemic schizophrenia and achieve the desired state of cognitive peace. *On the other hand*, I think that my epistemic schizophrenia could only go away and I could only achieve the desired cognitive peace if I became a kind of man that I don't feel it is right to become.

4 No belief, no cry

According to some philosophers, there is a way out. Here's their proposal:

> The situation doesn't look so rosy indeed—still, the confession you've just made is a "little bit" melodramatic. Instead of monitoring your own soul and troubling yourself about the tensions you claim to feel, and instead of posing as someone cast into the depths of the hopelessness of making the right choice (as sung by Kierkegaard), don't be lazy and make a quick cost-benefit calculation.

> We understand that you cannot give a reassuring account of your philosophical beliefs in light of philosophy's epistemic failure. Your misgivings seem well-founded indeed—we cannot put a finger on any point in your phenomenological account of the experience of breakdown which we could consider as unreasoned, ungrounded, or exaggerative. At the same time, we suppose that you love philosophy. You like thinking about philosophical problems, construct arguments for and against philosophical views, and debate over philosophical issues with others. That is, you would prefer to continue doing philosophy if there is a way.

> Now, you should see that the *only* way out for you is what the "no belief, no cry" version of equilibrism offers. In the spirit of this vision, you may continue to participate in the work of the community of philosophers, which is exciting and rich in intellectual challenges. And the only price you must pay in exchange for this benefit is that you set aside your philosophical beliefs while doing philosophy.

> You have a choice: either you get bogged down in the experience of breakdown, or you move forward and commit yourself to the "no belief, no cry" version of equilibrism.

I'm not saying that it would be easy to make this decision, but I think I cannot and would not like to pay the cost of commitment to the "no belief, no cry" version of equilibrism. My first reason is that I, for the life of me, cannot abstract from the circumstance that I *believe* in the truth of such and such philosophical propositions, and that I have a personal stake in such and such beliefs of mine. My second reason is that in my eyes, there is no special value in our getting an ever-clearer picture of how we can consistently think about various philosophical problems in an increasingly sophisticated way, thanks to doing philosophy, *if we actually don't and wouldn't like to believe* in the truth of any philosophical thesis, view, or theory. My third reason is that I can hardly consider doing philosophy with a complete neglect of philosophical beliefs other than *a mere intellectual game*—a game which doesn't have any value except for the participants' pleasure caused by intellectual challenges.

I may see it wrongly, and actually, there's more to it. It may be that my reluctance is idiosyncratic and I feel this vision to be a superficial and unprincipled opportunism because of my personal or epistemic character. It may be that what others see as "epistemic Eden" is a horrible dystopia for me. And it is not impossible either (what's more, even probable) that the ethos of philosophy, as it is done in the contemporary academic ghetto, precisely supports the metaphilosophical vision of the "no belief, no cry" equilibrism—and it is just that I'm a stubbornly untimely man.

If that's the case, although it is bad for me to think about it and even worse to imagine it, after my death, I should be placed in the murky basement of a building to be demolished, inside a translucent formaline vat, having a small copper plate at the bottom of it with the indistinct inscription: "*Ecce hominem* who frustrated himself with his inability to account for the epistemic status of his philosophical beliefs, but to his own detriment, he did not realize that his qualms and doubts were behind the times."

5 Beyond the breakdown

What is *beyond* the experience of breakdown? Obviously, *nothing*. The experience of breakdown is just the experience of "This ends here."

Nevertheless, you may think that an important part is still missing from my confession. You may argue like this:

> I understand that the experience of breakdown is the experience of "This ends here." But, the experience of breakdown *doesn't last forever*—like every experience, it has a temporal beginning and an end. So, after experiencing breakdown, *you must react* to the experience of breakdown itself. You cannot avoid *repeatedly* asking and answering the question: "What should I do with my

philosophical beliefs?" There is a *future* past the breakdown—and you must say something about this future as well.

You've earlier said that you're unable to give up on philosophical truth-seeking. You've admitted that you're driven and animated by the *unconditioned* motivation (may I say, the Kantian *das Unbedingte*) to take sides on those philosophical issues that are important to you. True enough, you'd *take a risk* in doing so, but even this risk would be better than to *resign yourself* to having come up against an *aporia* and *not doing anything* after the breakdown of your reason.

Indeed, life will go on after the experience of breakdown. At the same time, I think, the experience of breakdown or of "This ends here" isn't something that one could well react to. Thus, whatever I can say about the future has no special significance. For *after* the experience of breakdown, the repeated questions "Should I now take a risk or not?"; "What should I do with my substantive philosophical beliefs?"; and "How should I handle the unconditioned motivation that still animates me?" seem *inconsequential and insubstantial* to me.

Let me explain why. Although this kind of breakdown of the intellect—so to speak—is a conscious experience with "discomforting" phenomenological features, it is a rather *clear* moment at that. During the experience of breakdown, I realize *why I cannot* identify in good intellectual conscience with any of the reactions given to philosophy's epistemic failure. This is when it dawns on me *why I'm unable* to commit myself to any metaphilosophical vision. During the experience of breakdown, I see, *more clearly* than ever, the nature of my inability to answer the main question of my essay "What should I do with my philosophical beliefs in the light of philosophy's epistemic failure?" And, provided that my qualms about various metaphilosophical visions don't stem from self-deception, perhaps I understand it *in its entirety*.

All this means that no matter how I answer *your* questions, all the considerations I could bring up in support of my answers would be *cancelled out* by other considerations that are just as strong as the ones adduced by me, as I have already realized it during the experience of breakdown. No matter how I "choose," *the epistemic position* with which I could take sides *would inevitably be worse* than the one I was in during the experience of breakdown. And since everything relevant has already been said *including* the experience of breakdown, I would simply come full circle *again and again*. That's why I feel that the questions you put to me after the experience of "This ends here" are all inconsequential and insubstantial.

Let me approach it differently. In my essay, Sophie has impersonated my daemon. She wasn't constructive, and never gave positive advice. Her activity was confined to warning me about *what I must not* believe and *why I must not* believe it. So, I cast her as somebody in a rhetorical-dialectical role similar to the one Socrates attributed to his daemon: "It is a voice, and whenever it speaks it turns me away from something I am about to do, but never encourages me to do anything" (Plato *Apology* 31d).

Now imagine that Sophie sees the following. There's an essay on the ethics of philosophical beliefs whose author encounters the "moment of truth" when he experiences the breakdown of his intellect; when it becomes clear to him why he is unable to reassuringly account for the epistemic status of his philosophical beliefs. Then, Sophie sees that after the experience of "This ends here," absorbedly and in the deepest of his thoughts, the author of this essay mulls over the question: "All right, but in what spirit should I do philosophy *in the future*?"

Do you think that Sophie could see the newly arisen zeal of the author of this essay with anything but *irony*? What I have in mind is not necessarily incisive, raw, passionless, and distancing irony, but—if there's such a thing—irony with *a tinge of pity and compassion*, which is, at bottom, still irony.

To conclude my essay a bit pathetically but perhaps without a kind of encroaching pathos, I would like to say that I could see myself *only* with irony if I forgot the painful inconsequentiality and insubstantiality of the future-directed questions and caught myself thinking about "survival strategies" after the experience of "This ends here."

Bibliography

Allaire, E. B. (1963/1998), "Bare Particulars," in S. Laurence and C. Macdonald (eds.), *Contemporary Reading in the Foundations of Metaphysics*, 259–63, Oxford: Blackwell.
Almeida, M. J. (2008), *The Metaphysics of Perfect Beings*, New York: Routledge.
Alston, W. P. (1976), "Self-Warrant: A Neglected Form of Privileged Access," *American Philosophical Quarterly*, 13: 257–72.
Alston, W. P. (1985), "Concepts of Epistemic Justification," *The Monist*, 68 (1): 57–89.
Alston, W. P. (1988), "The Deontological Conception of Epistemic Justification," *Philosophical Perspectives*, (2): 257–99.
Aristotle (1924), *Metaphysics*, trans. W. D. Ross, Oxford: Clarendon Press.
Armstrong, D. M. (1968), *A Materialist Theory of the Mind*, London: Routledge.
Armstrong, D. M. (1978), *Universals and Scientific Realism*, vol. 2: *A Theory of Universals*, Cambridge: Cambridge University Press.
Armstrong, D. M. (1997), *A World of States of Affairs*, Cambridge: Cambridge University Press.
Ayer, A. J. (1954/1972), "Freedom and Necessity," in A. J. Ayer, *Philosophical Essays*, 271–84, London: Palgrave Macmillan.
Bailey, A. (1990), "Pyrrhonean Scepticism and the Self-Refutation Argument," *The Philosophical Quarterly*, 40 (158): 27–44.
Balaguer, M. (2004), "Coherent, Naturalistic, and Plausible Formulation of Libertarian Free Will," *Noûs*, 38 (3): 379–406.
Ballantyne, N. (2014), "Knockdown Arguments," *Erkenntnis*, 79 (3): 525–43.
Ballantyne, N. and Coffman, E. J. (2011), "Uniqueness, Evidence and Rationality," *Philosophers Imprint*, 11 (18): 1–13.
Barnett, Z. (2019), "Philosophy without Belief," *Mind*, 128 (509): 109–38.
Beebee, H. (2018), "Philosophical Scepticism and the Aims of Philosophy," *Proceedings of the Aristotelian Society*, 118 (1): 4–24.
Bell, D. (1991), *Husserl*, London: Routledge.
Berkeley, G. (1713/1998), "Three Dialogues Between Hylas and Philonous," in G. Berkeley *Philosophical Works* (ed. Michael R. Ayers), 129–399, London: Everyman.
Bernáth, L. and Tőzsér, J. (2020), "Epistemic Self-Esteem of Philosophers in the Face of Philosophical Disagreement," *Human Affairs*, 30 (3): 328–42.
Bernáth, L. and Tőzsér, J. (2021), "The Biased Nature of Philosophical Beliefs in the Light of Peer Disagreement," *Metaphilosophy*, 52 (3–4): 363–78.
Bourget, D. and Chalmers, D. (2014), "What Do Philosophers Believe?," *Philosophical Studies*, 170 (3): 465–500.

Bourget, D. and Chalmers, D. (2021), "Philosophers on Philosophy: The 2020 PhilPapers Survey." Available online: https://philpapers.org/archive/BOUPOP-3.pdf.

Brennan, J. (2010), "Scepticism about Philosophy," *Ratio*, 23 (1): 1–16.

Bruce, M. and Barbone, S. (eds.) (2011), *Just the Arguments: 100 of the Most Important Arguments in Western Philosophy*, Oxford: Wiley-Blackwell.

Chalmers, D. (2002), "Does Conceivability Entail Possibility?," in T. Gendler and J. Hawthorne (eds.), *Conceivability and Possibility*, 145–200, Oxford: Oxford University Press.

Chalmers, D. (2004), "Epistemic Two-Dimensional Semantics," *Philosophical Studies*, 118 (1–2): 153–226.

Chalmers, D. (2015), "Why Isn't There More Progress in Philosophy?," *Philosophy*, 90 (1): 3–31.

Chisholm, R. M. (1966), "Freedom and Action," in Keith Lehrer (ed.), *Freedom and Determinism*, 11–44, New York: Random House.

Christensen, D. (2007), "Epistemology of Disagreement: The Good News," *Philosophical Review*, 116 (2): 187–218.

Clarke, R. (2003), *Libertarian Accounts of Free Will*, New York: Oxford University Press.

Cohen, J. L. (1989), "Belief and Acceptance," *Mind*, 98 (391): 367–89.

Cohen, J. L. (1992), *An Essay on Belief and Acceptance*, Oxford: Clarendon Press.

Crane, T. (1995), "The Mental Causation Debate," *Proceedings of the Aristotelian Society*, Supplementary Volume 69: 211–36.

Crane, T. (1998), "Intentionality as the Mark of the Mental," in A. O'Hear (ed.), *Current Issues in Philosophy of Mind*, 229–51, Cambridge: Cambridge University Press.

Crisp, T. M. (2003), "Presentism," in M. J. Loux and D. W. Zimmerman (eds.), *The Oxford Handbook of Metaphysics*, 246–80, Oxford: Oxford University Press.

Descartes, R. (1637/2000), "Discourse on the Method," trans. D. Cress, in R. Ariew (ed.), *René Descartes. Philosophical Essays and Correspondence*, Indianapolis/Cambridge: Hackett Publishing Company.

Descartes, R. (1641/1991), "Meditations on First Philosophy," trans. J. Cottingham, in J. Cottingham, Robert Stoothoff, and Dugald Murdoch (eds.), *The Philosophical Writings of Descartes*, vol. 2, Cambridge: Cambridge University Press.

Dietrich, E. (2011), "There is No Progress in Philosophy," *Essays in Philosophy*, 12 (2): 329–44.

Dummett, M. (1981), *Frege: Philosophy of Language* (2nd edn.), Cambridge, MA: Harvard University Press.

Elga, A. (2007), "Reflection and Disagreement," *Noûs*, 41 (3): 478–502.

Elgin, C. (2007), "Understanding and the Facts," *Philosophical Studies*, 132 (1): 33–42.

Engel, P. (1998), "Believing, Holding True and Accepting," *Philosophical Explorations*, 1 (2): 140–51.

Feldman, R. (2006), "Epistemological Puzzles about Disagreement," in S. Hetherington (ed.), *Epistemology Futures*, 206–36, New York: Oxford University Press.

Fichte, J. G. (1806/1999), "The Characteristics of the Present Age," trans. W. Smith, in D. Breazeale (ed.), *The Popular Works of Johann Gottlieb Fichte*, 302–675, Bristol: Thoemes Press.

Fischer, E. (2011), "How to Practise Philosophy as Therapy: Philosophical Therapy and Therapeutic Philosophy," *Metaphilosophy*, 42 (1–2): 49–82.

Fischer, J. M. (2007), "Compatibilism," in J. M. Fischer, R. Kane, D. Pereboom, and M. Vargas (eds.), *Four Views on Free Will*, 44–84, Oxford: Blackwell.

Fischer, J. M. and Ravizza, M. (1998), *Responsibility and Control: An Essay on Moral Responsibility*, Cambridge: Cambridge University Press.

Forrai, G. (2019), "Doxastic Deontology and Cognitive Competence," *Erkenntnis*, 86 (3): 687–714.

Frances, B. (2014), *Disagreement*, Cambridge: Polity Press.

Frankfurt, H. G. (1971), "Freedom of the Will and the Concept of a Person," *Journal of Philosophy*, 68 (1): 5–20.

Franklin, C. E. (2018), *A Minimal Libertarianism: Free Will and the Promise of Reduction*, Oxford: Oxford University Press.

Frege, G. (1918/1956), "The Thought: A Logical Inquiry," trans. P. T. Geach, *Mind*, 65 (259): 289–311.

Gallois, A. (1998), *Occasions of Identity: The Metaphysics of Persistence, Change and Sameness*, New York: Oxford University Press.

Ginet, C. (1990), *On Action*, Cambridge: Cambridge University Press.

Goldhill, O. (2016), "One of the Most Famous Living Philosophers Says Much of Philosophy Today is 'Self-Indulgent,'" *Quartz*, August 28. Available online: https://qz.com/768450/one-of-the-most-famous-living-philosophers-says-much-of-philosophy-today-is-self-indulgent/.

Goldman, A. (1967), "A Causal Theory of Knowing," *Journal of Philosophy*, 64 (12): 357–72.

Goldstein, R. (2014), *Plato at the Googleplex: Why Philosophy Won't Go Away*, New York: Pantheon Books.

Goodman, N. (1984), *Of Mind and Other Matters*, Cambridge, MA: Harvard University Press.

Greco, D. and Hedden, B. (2016), "Uniqueness and Metaepistemology," *Journal of Philosophy*, 113 (8): 365–95.

Gutting, G. (2009), *What Philosophers Know: Case Studies in Recent Analytic Philosophy*, Cambridge: Cambridge University Press.

Gutting, G. (2015), *What Philosophy Can Do*, New York and London: W. W. Norton and Company.

Hacker, P. M. S. (1993), *Wittgenstein: Meaning and Mind. An Analytical Commentary on the* Philosophical Investigations, vol. 3, Oxford: Blackwell.

Hadot, P. (1987/1999), *Philosophy as Way of Life, Spiritual Exercises from Socrates to Foucault*, trans. Michael Chase, Oxford: Blackwell.

Hawking, S. and Mlodinov, L. (2010), *The Grand Design*, New York: Bantam Books.

Heidegger, M. (1927/1962), *Being and Time*, trans. J. Macquarrie and E. Robinson, Oxford: Blackwell.

Heidegger, M. (1929/1993), "What is Metaphysics?," trans. D. F. Krell, in D. F. Krell (ed.), *Martin Heidegger: Basic Writings* (Revised and Expanded edn.), 89–110, San Francisco, CA: Harper Perennial Modern Classics.

Honderich, T. (1988), *A Theory of Determinism*, Oxford: Oxford University Press.

Horgan, T. and Tienson, J. (2002), "The Intentionality of Phenomenology and the Phenomenology of Intentionality," in D. Chalmers (ed.), *Philosophy of Mind: Classical and Contemporary Readings*, 520–33, Oxford: Oxford University Press.

Horwich, P. (2012), *Wittgenstein's Metaphilosophy*, Oxford: Oxford University Press.

Huemer, M. (2011), "Epistemological Egoism and Agent-Centered Norms," in T. Dougherty (ed.), *Evidentialism and Its Discontents*, 17–33, Oxford: Oxford University Press.

Hume, D. (1739/2000), *A Treatise of Human Nature*, ed. D. F. Norton and M. J. Norton, Oxford: Oxford University Press.

Huoranszki, F. (2011), *Freedom of the Will: A Conditional Analysis*, New York: Routledge.

Husserl, E. (1907/1990), *The Idea of Phenomenology*, trans. W. P. Alston and G. Nakhnikian, Dordrecht: Kluwer Academic Publishers.

Husserl, E. (1910–11/2002), "Philosophy as Rigorous Science," trans. Q. Lauer, in B. Hopkins and S. Crowell (eds.), *The New Yearbook for Phenomenology and Phenomenological Philosophy*, 249–95, London and New York: Routledge.

Husserl, E. (1927/1971), "Phenomenology," trans. R. E. Palmer, *Journal of the British Society for Phenomenology*, 2 (2): 77–90.

Husserl, E. (1929/1998), *The Paris Lectures*, trans. P. Koestenbaum, Dordrecht: Kluwer Academic Publishers.

Husserl, E. (1936/1970), *The Crisis of European Sciences and Transcendental Phenomenology*, trans. D. Marr, Evanston, IL: Northwestern University Press.

Jackson, F. (1982), "Epiphenomenal Qualia," *The Philosophical Quarterly*, 32 (127): 127–36.

Jackson, F. (1986), "What Mary Didn't Know," *The Journal of Philosophy*, 83 (5): 291–95.

Jackson, F. (2017), "Only Connect," in R. Blackford and D. Broderick (eds.), *Philosophy's Future: The Problem of Philosophical Progress*, 51–9, Hoboken, NJ: John Wiley & Sons, Inc.

James, W. (1907/1979), *Pragmatism*, Cambridge, MA: Harvard University Press.

Jonge, C. D. and Whiteman, G. (2014), "Arnie Neass (1912–2009)," in J. Helin, T. Hernes, D. Hjort, and Robin Holt (eds.), *The Oxford Handbook of Process Philosophy and Organization Studies*, 432–51, Oxford: Oxford University Press.

Kahane, G. (2017), "If Nothing Matters," *Noûs*, 51 (2): 327–53.

Kane, R. H. (1996), *The Significance of Free Will*, New York: Oxford University Press.

Kant, I. (1781/1998), *Critique of Pure Reason*, trans. P. Guyer and A. W. Wood, Cambridge: Cambridge University Press.

Kant, I. (1783/2004), *Prolegomena to Any Future Metaphysics*, trans. G. Hatfield, Cambridge: Cambridge University Press.

Kelly, T. (2010), "Peer Disagreement and Higher Order Evidence," in R. Feldman and T. A. Warfield (eds.), *Disagreement*, 111–74, Oxford: Oxford University Press.

Kenny, A. (1984), *The Legacy of Wittgenstein*, Oxford: Blackwell.

King, N. L. (2012), "Disagreement: What's the Problem? Or a Good Peer is Hard to Find," *Philosophy and Phenomenological Research*, 85 (2): 249–72.

Kripke, S. A. (1982), *Wittgenstein on Rules and Private Language*, Cambridge, MA: Harvard University Press.

Kvanvig, J. (2013), "Curiosity and a Response-Dependent Account of the Value of Understanding," in T. Henning and D. Schweikard (eds.), *Knowledge, Virtue and Action*, 151–75, Boston, MA: Routledge.

Kvanvig, J. (2018), "Knowledge, Understanding, and Reasons for Belief," in D. Starr (ed.), *The Oxford Handbook of Reasons and Normativity*, 685–705, New York: Oxford University Press.

Lewis, D. (1966), "An Argument for the Identity Theory," *Journal of Philosophy*, 63 (1): 17–25.

Lewis, D. (1973), *Counterfactuals*, Oxford: Blackwell.

Lewis, D. (1983), *Philosophical Papers*, vol. 1, New York: Oxford University Press.

Lewis, D. (1984), "Putnam's Paradox," *Australasian Journal of Philosophy*, 62 (3): 221–36.

Lewis, D. (1986), *On the Plurality of Worlds*, Oxford: Blackwell.

Loar, B. (1990), "Phenomenal States," *Philosophical Perspectives*, 4: 81–108.

Locke, J. (1689/1996), *An Essay Concerning Human Understanding*, ed. Kenneth P. Winkler, Indianapolis, IN: Hackett Publishing Company.

Lockie, R. (2018), *Free Will and Epistemology: A Defence of the Transcendental Argument of Freedom*, London: Bloomsbury Publishing.

Lowe, J. E. (2008), *Personal Agency: The Metaphysics of Mind and Action*, Oxford: Oxford University Press.

Lynch, M. P. (2009), *Truth and One and Many*, Oxford: Clarendon Press.

MacBride, F. (2014), "Analytic Philosophy and its Synoptic Commission: Toward the Epistemic End of Days," *Royal Institute of Philosophy*, 74: 221–36.

Matheson, J. (2011), "The Case for Rational Uniqueness," *Logos & Episteme*, 2 (3): 359–73.

Matheson, J. (2015), "Disagreement and the Ethics of Belief," in J. Collier (ed.), *The Future of Social Epistemology: A Collective Vision*, 139–48, London and New York: Rowman & Littlefield.

McGinn, C. (1991), *The Problem of Consciousness*, Oxford: Blackwell.

McGinn, C. (1993), *The Limits of Inquiry*, Oxford: Blackwell.

Mele, A. R. (1995), *Autonomous Agents*, New York: Oxford University Press.

Mele, A. R. (2006), *Free Will and Luck*, New York: Oxford University Press.

Melnyk, A. (2003), *A Physicalist Manifesto: Thoroughly Modern Materialism*, Cambridge: Cambridge University Press.

MN Ñāṇamoli, B., and Bodhi, B. (trans.), *The Middle Length Discourses of the Buddha: A Translation of the Majjhima Nikāya*. Somerville, MA: Wisdom Publications, 2009.

Moore, G. E. (1912), *Ethics*, New York: Henry Holt.

Nichols, S. and Knobe, J. (2007), "Moral Responsibility and Determinism. The Cognitive Science of Folk Psychology," *Noûs*, 41 (4): 663–85.

Nichols, S., Stich, S., and Weinberg, J. (2003), "Meta-skepticism: Meditation in Ethno-Epistemology," in S. Puper (ed.), *The Skeptics*, 227–47, Aldershot: Ashgate.

Nozick, R. (1981), *Philosophical Explanations*, Cambridge, MA: Belknap Press.

O'Connor, T. (2000), *Persons and Causes: The Metaphysics of Free Will*, New York: Oxford University Press.

Papineau, D. (2002), *Thinking about Consciousness*, Oxford: Oxford University Press.

Pereboom, D. (2014), *Free Will, Agency and Meaning in Life*, Oxford: Oxford University Press.

PH Sextus Empiricus, *Outlines of Pyrrhonism*, trans. B. Mates, New York: Oxford University Press, 1996.

Pink, T. (2017), *Self-Determination: The Ethics of Action*, vol. 1, Oxford: Oxford University Press.

Pitt, D. (2004), "The Phenomenology of Cognition or *What Is It Like to Think That p?*," *Philosophy and Phenomenological Research*, 69 (1): 1–36.

Plato, *Complete Works*, ed., with introduction and notes, by John M. Cooper, Indianapolis/Cambridge: Hackett Publishing Company, 1997.

Priest, G., Beall, J. C., and Armour-Garb, B. (eds.) (2004), *The Law of Non-Contradiction*, Oxford: Oxford Clarendon Press.

Pritchard, D. (2009), "Knowledge, Understanding and Epistemic Value," in A. O'Hear (ed.), *Royal Institute of Philosophy Supplements*, 64: 19–43, New York: Cambridge University Press.

Pritchard, D. (2010), "The Value of Knowledge: Understanding," in A. Haddock, A. Millar, and D. Pritchard (eds.), *The Nature of Value of Knowledge: Three Investigations*, 1–88, Oxford: Oxford University Press.

Putnam, H. (1987), *The Many Faces of Realism*, LaSalle, IL: Open Court.

Rea, M. C. (2003), "Four-Dimensionalism," in Michael J. Loux and Dean W. Zimmerman (eds.), *The Oxford Handbook of Metaphysics*, 246–80, Oxford: Oxford University Press.

Rescher, N. (2006), *Philosophical Dialectics: An Essay on Metaphilosophy*, New York: State University of New York Press.

Ribeiro, B. (2011), "Philosophy and Disagreement," *Critica*, 43 (127): 3–25.

Rorty, R. (1979), *Philosophy and the Mirror of Nature*, Princeton, NJ: Princeton University Press.

Sainsbury, R. M. (2009), *Paradoxes* (3rd edn.), Cambridge: Cambridge University Press.

Sartre, J. P. (1946/2007), *Existentialism is a Humanism*, trans. C. Macomber, ed. John Kulka, New Haven, CT and London: Yale University Press.

Scanlon, T. M. (1998), *What We Owe to Each Other*, Cambridge, MA: Harvard University Press.

Scanlon, T. M. (2008), *Moral Dimensions*, Cambridge, MA: Harvard University Press.

Schafer, K. (2015), "How Common is Peer Disagreement? On Self-Trust and Rational Symmetry," *Philosophy and Phenomenological Research*, 91 (1): 25–46.

Schlick, M. (1930–31/1959), "The Turning Point of Philosophy," trans. D. Rynin, in A. J. Ayer (ed.), *Logical Positivism*, 53–60, New York: The Free Press.

Schopenhauer, A. (1818/2010), *The World as Will and Representation*, trans. and ed. J. Norman, A. Welchman, and C. Janaway, with an introduction by C. Janaway, Cambridge: Cambridge University Press.

Searle, J. R. (1983), *Intentionality: An Essay in the Philosophy of Mind*, Cambridge: Cambridge University Press.

Sider, T. (2011), *Writing the Book of the World*, Oxford: Oxford University Press.

Smith, A. M. (2005), "Responsibility for Attitudes: Activity and Passivity in Mental Life," *Ethics*, 115 (2): 236–71.

Stoljar, D. (2017a), *Philosophical Progress: In Defence of a Reasonable Optimism*, Oxford: Oxford University Press.

Stoljar, D. (2017b), "How Philosophy Makes Progress: On the Identity of Philosophical Problems over Time," *DailyNous*, November 7. Available online: https://dailynous.com/2017/11/07/philosophy-makes-progress-guest-post-daniel-stoljar/.

Stoljar, D. (2017c), "Is There Progress in Philosophy? A Brief Case for Optimism," in R. Blackford and D. Broderick (eds.), *Philosophy's Future: The Problem of Philosophical Progress*, 107–17, New York: John Wiley & Sons, Inc.

Swan, S., Joshua, A., and Weinberg, J. (2008), "The Instability of Philosophical Intuitions: Running Hot and Cold in Truetemp," *Philosophy and Phenomenological Research*, 76 (1): 138–55.

Swinburne, R. (1990), *The Existence of God* (Revisited edn.), Oxford: Clarendon Press.

Timpe, K. and Jacobs, J. D. (2016), "Free Will and Naturalism: How to be a Libertarian, and a Naturalist Too," in K. J. Clarke (ed.), *The Blackwell Companion to Naturalism*, 319–35, Oxford: Wiley-Blackwell.

van Fraassen, B. (1980), *The Scientific Image*, New York: Oxford University Press.

van Inwagen, P. (1975), "The Incompatibility of Free Will and Determinism," *Philosophical Studies*, 27 (3): 185–99.

van Inwagen, P. (1990), *Material Beings*, Ithaca, NY: Cornell University Press.

van Inwagen, P. (1996), "It Is Wrong, Everywhere, Always and for Anyone, to Believe Anything upon Insufficient Evidence?," in J. Jordan and D. Howard-Snyder (eds.), *Faith, Freedom and Rationality*, 137–54, Savage, MD: Rowman & Littlefield.

van Inwagen, P. (2004), "Freedom to Break the Laws," *Midwest Studies in Philosophy*, 28: 334–50.

van Inwagen, P. (2006), *The Problem of Evil*, Oxford: Oxford University Press.

van Inwagen, P. (2009), *Metaphysics* (3rd edn.), Boulder, CO: Westview Press.

van Inwagen, P. (2010), "We're Right, They're Wrong," in R. Feldman and T. A. Warfield (eds.), *Disagreement*, 10–28, Oxford: Oxford University Press.

van Inwagen, P. (2020), "The Neo-Carnapians," *Synthese*, 197 (1): 7–32.

Vargas, M. (2013), *Building Better Beings: A Theory of Moral Responsibility*, Oxford: Oxford University Press.

Wedgwood, R. (2010), "The Moral Evil Demons," in R. Feldman and T. A. Warfield (eds.), *Disagreement*, 216–45, Oxford: Oxford University Press.

Wegner, D. M. (2002), *The Illusion of the Conscious Will*, Cambridge, MA: MIT Press.

Weinberg, J., Nichols, S., and Stich, S. (2001/2008), "Normativity and Epistemic Intuitions," in J. Knobe and S. Nichols (eds.), *Experimental Philosophy*, 47–58, Oxford: Oxford University Press.

White, R. (2013), "Evidence Cannot Be Permissive," in M. Steup, J. Turri, and E. Sosa (eds.), *Contemporary Debates in Epistemology* (2nd edn.), 312–22, Oxford: Blackwell.

Wiggins, D. (2001), *Sameness and Substance Renewed*, Cambridge: Cambridge University Press.

Wittgenstein, L., *Philosophical Investigations* (*PI*), trans. G. E. M. Anscombe, Oxford: Blackwell, 2001.

Wittgenstein, L., *The Blue and Brown Books* (*BB*), New York: Harper, 1958.

Wittgenstein, L., *Tractatus Logico-Philosophicus* (*TLP*), trans. D. F. Pears and B. F. McGuinness, with introduction by B. Russell, London: Routledge, 1961.

Wittgenstein, L., *Zettel* (*Z*), ed. G. E. M. Anscombe and G. H. von Wright, Oxford: Basil Blackwell, 1967.

Wittgenstein, L., *On Certainty* (*OC*), trans. D. Paul and G. E. M. Anscombe, ed. G. E. M. Anscombe and G. H. von Wright, New York: Harper, 1969.

Wittgenstein, L., *Philosophical Grammar* (*PG*), trans. A. Kenny, ed. R. Rhees, Berkeley: University of California Press, 1974.

Wittgenstein, L., *The Big Typescript: TS 231* (*BT*), Oxford: Basil Blackwell, 2012.

Wright, C. (1998), "Truth: A Traditional Debate Reviewed," *Canadian Journal of Philosophy*, Supplementary Volume 24: 31–74.

Zagzebski, L. (2001), "Recovering Understanding" in M. Steup (ed.), *Knowledge, Truth, and Duty: Essays on Epistemic Justification, Responsibility, and Virtue*, 235–52, Oxford: Oxford University Press.

Index

Allaire, E.B. 62
Almeida, M.J. 123
Alston, W.P. 162, 173
Anselm of Canterbury 39
apathy 4, 201–2, 214
aporia 6, 210–11, 217
Aristotle 12–3, 56, 61
Armour-Garb, B. 14
Armstrong, D.M. 61, 65
Ayer, A.J. 60

Balaguer, M. 59
Ballantyne, N. 25–6, 54
Barbone, S. 17
Barnett, Z. 149, 156
Beebee, H. 121, 149–50
beliefs vs. acceptances 149–51
Bell, D. 31
Berkeley, G. 12, 15, 51, 62
Bernáth, L. 115, 171
bias (or bias factors) 7, 139–41, 145, 148, 171, 205, 213
Bourget, D. 55
breakdown 8, 209–18
Brennan, J. 110, 165, 182–83
Bruce, M. 17
Buddha 193–94

certainty 106–7, 109, 111, 113, 166, 194, 198–99, 213
Chalmers, D. 20–1, 55, 64
charlatanism 96–7
Chisholm, R.M. 60
Christensen, D. 54
Clarke, R. 60
Clifford's ghost 143, 145–46, 201
cognitive need 96, 126, 200–2, 214
cognitive peace (or peace of mind) 5, 81, 89–90, 96, 148, 152, 154, 192, 195–99, 201–2, 213–15
Cohen, J.L. 150
conceptual engineering 5, 69, 72

conceptual vs. factual philosophical problems 130–34
conciliationism 54, 165
cost-benefit equations 2, 37, 60, 127, 215
Crane, T. 51–2, 61
Crisp, T.M. 62

Dennett, D. 128
Derrida, J. 12
Descartes, R. 12, 19–20, 34–5, 40, 47, 65–9, 72–4, 100–1, 117–18
Dietrich, E. 56–7, 60–3, 75
disagreement/dissensus in philosophy 1–3, 43–55, 64, 75–6, 97, 111–12, 117, 161, 165–67, 181, 196–97, 212–13
doxastic deontology 172–74, 189, 196–97
Dummett, M. 16
duty (*epistemic*) 7, 22–3, 75–6, 113, 125, 129, 135–37, 154, 159, 162, 164, 167, 172, 174–75, 177–79, 181, 185–86, 188–89, 192–93, 205, 211

Elga, A. 54
Elgin, C. 38
emotional problems 82, 89
Engel, P. 150
entitlement to believe 4, 142, 149, 162–63, 165–67, 171–73, 177–78, 186, 188, 212
Epictetus 81
Epicurus 22
epistemic attractiveness 58, 73–4, 114
epistemic blindness 112, 114–17, 127, 188, 195, 199
epistemic inferiors 3, 108, 110, 112–14, 116, 127, 143, 213
epistemic modesty 195, 199
epistemic narcissism 115, 186, 199
epistemic peers 6–7, 54, 108, 110, 112, 165
epistemic schizophrenia 142–45, 148, 152–53, 188, 195, 201–12, 214–15
epistemic self-confidence 113, 115–17, 141

epistemic status of beliefs 2–3, 5–6, 8, 54, 75–6, 97, 104, 106, 111, 143, 165, 176, 183–84, 191–92, 194, 206, 211, 216, 218
epistemic superiors 3, 115–16, 141, 190
epistemic values 12, 36, 38–9
epistemically privileged position/status 3, 107–9, 112–15, 146, 192, 194
epistemology of disagreement 53–5, 165
equilibrium/equilibria 4, 76, 119–25, 127–28, 134–39, 141–42, 146, 150–53, 155–56, 164, 171–72, 174, 188, 192, 212
equilibrism 119–58, 164, 171–72, 184, 206, 215–16
excellence 97, 213

fanaticism 97, 115–16, 167, 199
Feldman, R. 54
Fichte, J.G. 12, 123
Fischer, E. 81
Fischer, J.M. 58
flash 141, 193–94, 200
Forrai, G. 172
Frances, B. 54
Frankfurt, H.G. 59
Franklin, C.E. 59
free will 1, 49, 57–60, 72, 123, 143, 150–51, 174–76
Frege, G. 14

Gallois, A. 153
Ginet, C. 59
God 1, 15, 18, 28, 30, 39, 123, 130–31, 133–34, 138, 140, 147, 151, 157, 166, 179, 202, 213
Goldhill, O. 128
Goldman, A. 29
Goldstein, R. 63
Goodman, N. 16
Greco, D. 54
Gutting, G. 120, 122, 127–28, 156

Hacker, P.M.S. 88
Hadot, P. 12, 82
Hawking, S. 127
Hedden, B. 54
Hegel, G.W.F. 12, 168, 174
Heidegger, M. 12, 37, 51–2
Honderich, T. 58

Horgan, T. 53
Horwich, P. 92
Huemer, M. 54, 147
Hume, D. 12, 19, 101
Huoranszki, F. 60
Husserl, E. 12, 32–6, 86, 102–5

"I'm the only one" philosophers/view 99–100, 104–6, 111–12, 114, 116–18, 127, 143, 167, 174, 184, 188, 192, 195, 199
insincerity 112, 134, 139, 141, 156–57, 173, 178, 213
introspection 18–9, 32, 89, 181
intuitions 110–11, 113–14, 116, 119, 144, 151, 153, 171
irony 89, 115, 148, 218

Jackson, F. 62, 65–6, 72–4
Jacobs, J.D. 124
Jonge, C.D. 82
justification ("*egocentric*") 125, 135, 137, 142, 149, 164, 172
justification (*externalist*) 29–31, 44, 48, 160
justification (*internalist*) 28–9, 31, 36, 48
justification (*phenomenological*) 31–6

Kahane, G. 24
Kane, R.H. 59
Kant, I. 12, 19, 101–2, 104–5, 181, 217
Kelly, T. 54
Kenny, A. 86
Kierkegaard, S. 12, 215
King, N.L. 55
knock-down argument (*def.*) 17
Kripke, S. 91
Kvanvig, J. 37–8

Leibniz, G.W. 2, 12, 63, 66, 69, 72, 128
Lewis, D. 15, 47, 61–2, 66, 110, 119–21, 123, 125, 127, 143–46, 148–49, 152–53
Loar, B. 73
Locke, J. 12, 61–2
Lockie, R. 22
logical space 5, 37, 64–5, 120, 126, 128, 152, 155
Lowe, J.E. 59
Lynch, M.P. 13

MacBride, F. 156, 170
Malebranche, N. 12, 66
Marcus Aurelius 81
Marx, K. 12
Matheson, J. 54, 205
matter of chance 145, 192, 194
McGinn, C. 49, 170
Mele, A.R. 58–9
Melnyk, A. 73
meta-meta-skepticism 8, 206
metaphilosophical vision 6, 65, 121–22, 126, 129, 152, 154, 168, 186, 205, 216–17
meta-skepticism 8, 76–7, 119, 129, 159–206
Mill, S.T. 181
mind-body problem 60–1, 63, 65, 67–9, 72–4, 83, 138–41, 155–56, 158, 202
Mlodinov, L. 127
Moore, G.E. 60

"no belief, no cry" equilibrism 152–56, 215–16
Nozick, R. 17, 59

O'Connor, T. 60

Papineau, D. 73
Parmenides 12
Pereboom, D. 58
permissivism 54, 112, 128
philosophical arguments (*infallible*) 19–21
philosophical arguments (*modest transcendental*) 21–4
philosophical arguments (*with empirically justified premises*) 25–7
philosophical knowledge 12, 30, 38, 44, 56, 71, 75–6, 119, 121, 127, 142, 166, 168, 211
philosophical understanding 36–9
philosophy (*epistemic tradition*) 11–2, 14–6, 18–9, 21, 26–7, 29–31, 36–9, 41, 43, 46, 55, 64–5, 75–6, 82, 100, 104–6, 108, 119, 121, 125–27, 129, 141–42, 164, 188, 210–11
Pink, T. 59
Pitt, D. 52
Plato 12, 15, 40–1, 65, 140, 209–11, 218
pre-philosophical convictions 4, 8, 76, 110, 114, 122–26, 134–42, 144, 146, 148, 153, 157–58, 164, 171–72, 174, 188, 192, 194, 212

Priest, G. 14
private evidence 146–48, 201, 213
Pritchard, D. 37–8
progress in philosophy 46, 55–75, 95, 126
Putnam, H. 16, 40, 66
Pyrrhonian skepticism 195–99, 202

Quine, W.v.O. 68, 70–1

rational beliefs (*definition and types*) 159–61
Rea, M.C. 62
reliability or truth-conduciveness 29–30, 44, 136, 144, 148, 160–61, 166, 172, 190, 192, 194
Rescher, N. 206
responsibility (*epistemic*) 4–8, 130, 137–42, 148, 202, 206, 211–12
responsibility (*moral*) 1, 49, 57–60, 124, 202
Ribeiro, B. 168
Rorty, R. 12, 89

Sainsbury, R.M. 15
Sartre, J.P. 180–81
Scanlon, T.M. 59
Schafer, K. 54
Schelling, F.W.J. 12
Schlick, M. 103–4, 106
Schopenhauer, A. 116
Searle, J.R. 51–52
self-deception 5, 187, 191–92, 194, 217
self-defeat 4, 90–1, 95–7, 163–64, 181–85, 196–97
self-reflection 77, 109–11, 113–16, 140, 143, 189–95, 199–201
seriously and sincerely believing 4, 6–7, 130, 137, 139, 141–42, 147, 149, 151, 174, 212, 214
Sextus Empiricus 81, 195
Sider, T. 15
Seneca 81
skepticism (*see* meta-skepticism)
Smith, A.M. 59
Socrates 41, 190, 195, 209–10, 218
Spinoza, B. 12, 25, 66, 105
steadfast view 54, 112, 128, 165
sticking to beliefs 142, 185, 187, 191–94, 200

Stoljar, D. 65–75
suspension of beliefs 3–4, 8, 54, 76–7, 96, 119, 121, 129, 141–42, 145–46, 159, 161–67, 173–74, 177–82, 185–89, 192–93, 195–203, 205–6, 211–12, 214
Swinburne, R. 39

therapy 4, 77, 81–82, 89–93, 189, 197
Thomas Aquinas 12, 39
Tienson, J. 53
Timpe, K. 124
Tőzsér, J. 115, 171
trust in the truth of *p* 7, 137, 139, 141, 147–48, 213
truth (*truisms about truth*) 13–6
truth (*non-substantive philosophical truths*) 1, 37, 57, 64, 71, 75, 127, 161, 177

truth-seeking and justificatory tools of philosophy 3, 7, 76, 160, 166, 169–70, 174, 177, 182–83, 185, 203

uncertainty 5, 141, 152, 212, 214

van Fraassen, B. 149–50
van Inwagen, P. 25, 45, 61–3, 143–46, 201
Vargas, M. 59

Wedgwood, R. 54
Wegner, D.M. 58
White, R. 54
Whiteman, G. 82
Wiggins, D. 65
Wittgenstein, L. 82–97, 118, 134, 183–84
Wright, C. 13

Zagzebski, L. 38

www.ingramcontent.com/pod-product-compliance
Lightning Source LLC
Chambersburg PA
CBHW071833300426
44116CB00009B/1530